Katherine Mansfield – The Early Years

Frontispiece. Katherine Mansfield in Brussels, 1906.

Katherine Mansfield –
The Early Years

Gerri Kimber

EDINBURGH
University Press

Edinburgh University Press is one of the leading university presses in the UK. We publish academic books and journals in our selected subject areas across the humanities and social sciences, combining cutting-edge scholarship with high editorial and production values to produce academic works of lasting importance. For more information visit our website: edinburghuniversitypress.com

Edinburgh University Press Ltd
The Tun – Holyrood Road
12(2f) Jackson's Entry
Edinburgh EH8 8PJ

Typeset in 11/13pt Adobe Garamond Pro by
Servis Filmsetting Ltd, Stockport, Cheshire
and printed and bound in Great Britain by
CPI Group (UK) Ltd, Croydon CR0 4YY

A CIP record for this book is available from the British Library

ISBN 978 0 7486 8145 7 (hardback)
ISBN 978 0 7486 8146 4 (webready PDF)
ISBN 978 0 7486 8147 1 (epub)

Published with the support of the Edinburgh University Scholarly Publishing Initiatives Fund.

Contents

List of Illustrations

Acknowledgements

All biographers of Katherine Mansfield, New Zealand's most celebrated author, must, at some point, make at least one trip to that most holy of all Mansfield manuscript repositories: the Alexander Turnbull Library at the National Library of New Zealand, Te Puna Mātauranga o Aotearoa, in Wellington. I was fortunate to make a number of visits during the writing of this biography, thanks to the generous support of several organisations. My grateful thanks go to the Friends of the Turnbull Library (FoTL), who awarded me a research grant in 2015, which enabled me to spend a whole precious month absorbed in the KM archives (and especially to Rachel Underwood and Kate Fortune of the FoTL, who were so generous with their time). Many thanks also go to the following organisations, who generously provided grants to support the research for this biography in New Zealand, for which I am immensely grateful: the University of Northampton (in particular, Professor Janet Wilson and Professor Richard Canning); the New Zealand Society of Great Britain (in particular, Tania Bearsley and Robyn Allardyce-Bourne); and the Society of Authors' K. Blundell Trust.

The biography draws in part on the research Ruth Elvish Mantz undertook during a trip to New Zealand in 1931, when she was able to interview the family, friends and acquaintances of Mansfield, whose memories were still sharp enough to provide the young American biographer with rich source material, all of which is now held at the Harry Ransom Center at the University of Texas at Austin. I was lucky enough to be able to make two trips to Austin during the writing of this biography: the first thanks to a research grant provided by the University of Northampton in 2013, and the second as the recipient of a Harry Ransom Research Fellowship in 2014, which enabled me to spend several glorious weeks immersed in the rich archives at Austin. In addition, a

Mansfield conference in May 2015, organised by Professor W. Todd Martin at the Newberry Library in Chicago, enabled me to spend time viewing their substantial Mansfield archives, again with a generous grant from the University of Northampton.

The librarians at all the above institutions were, without exception, outstandingly helpful and friendly. Thanks in particular go to: in Wellington, Chris Szekely, Fiona Oliver, Jocelyn Chalmers, Linda McGregor, Jenni Christoffels, Gillian Headifen, Amy Hackett (and particularly Fiona Oliver, who spent several hours hunting out an edition of Hans Christian Andersen's fairy tales that KM could have read as a girl in NZ, and the indefatigable Jocelyn Chalmers, whose patience with my interminable queries is boundless); in Austin, Rick Watson – whose patience and diligence are exemplary – Jack Blanton, Pat Fox, Michael Gilmore, Bridget Gayle Ground, Jean Cannon, Jill Morena, Melanie Alberts, Betsy Gushee and Chelsea Weathers; in the Newberry, Martha Briggs, Alex Teller and John Powell. The Alexander Turnbull Library, in particular, was very generous in allowing the use of so many of their images at a reduced rate, for which I remain extremely grateful. In addition, thanks go to the very helpful staff at King's College London Archives, and especially Lianne Smith.

Enormous thanks are due to Jackie Jones, my publisher at Edinburgh University Press, who believed in this volume from the start, who read and commented on the final manuscript, and whose many kindnesses kept me on track. She is a publisher in a million. Special thanks also go to the team at EUP, James Dale, Adela Rauchova, Carla Hepburn, Rebecca McKenzie, and my meticulous copy-editor, Wendy Lee. My grateful thanks also go to the Society of Authors, who represent the literary estates of Katherine Mansfield and John Middleton Murry, for permission to quote from their work, and in particular, Sarah Burton, for her extraordinary diligence. I am also truly indebted to C. K. Stead, an outstanding Mansfield scholar in his own right, who generously agreed to provide a Foreword to the volume.

My most heartfelt thanks go to my friends Susan Price and Beverley Randell, who made a flat in Wellington available to me whenever I wanted it. Their combined knowledge of Wellington and its history is unrivalled and their generosity boundless. I know I drove them insane with my questioning. Only they know how much I owe them. My dear friend, Janine Renshaw-Beauchamp, Mansfield's sister Jeanne's granddaughter, generously allowed reproduction of some rare family photos. Stephanie Hancox and her mother, Conor Williamson, descendants of KM's cousin, Eric Waters, also generously allowed me to use family photographs and supplied some valuable research material. Very special thanks go to the daughter of Edith Robison (née Bendall), Barbara Webber, and granddaughter, Lindy Erskine, for permission to use two of Edith's drawings and to reproduce a photograph of Edith at art school, and to Moira Taylor and Elizabeth Nathaniels for introducing me to Lindy.

Two very special friends and colleagues, Professor Claire Davison and Professor Janet Wilson, also read and commented on the manuscript. Their combined wisdom and knowledge of KM have undoubtedly enhanced this biography, especially the footnotes for Volume 4 of the *Edinburgh Edition of the Collected Works of Katherine Mansfield*, in large part the work of Claire Davison, whose erudition has considerably enhanced my understanding of KM's early diary entries. The staff at the Katherine Mansfield Birthplace in Wellington were also unfailingly helpful; special thanks go to the Chair of the Board, Nicola Saker, who invited me to her sumptuous home on Hobson Street and offered me a glimpse of how the Beauchamps might have lived, and the ever-helpful Director, Emma Anderson. I also thank Jennifer Walker, whose knowledge of the Beauchamp family (especially Mansfield's great-uncle, Henry Herron Beauchamp, and his descendants) is second to none, and who answered several questions for me and generously made available her own research. Henry Herron Beauchamp's papers are held at the Huntington Library, San Marino, California; my thanks to them for permission to reproduce some quotations, and to the librarian, Gayle Richardson, who answered several questions for me. Chris Naylor kindly gave permission for me to quote from his mother Elizabeth's wonderfully detailed memoirs of the Beauchamp clan. Dr John Martin, Parliamentary Historian at the New Zealand Parliament, was very generous with his time, answered numerous questions, and showed me the original ledgers where KM and her sister Vera had signed for books borrowed from the General Assembly Library in 1907–8. At the Marylebone Cricket Club (MCC), Neil Robinson, the library and research manager, answered my questions on the MCC cricket team that went to New Zealand in 1906 on board the S. S. *Corinthic* with great patience, and offered some invaluable information and photographs.

Other friends and colleagues to thank include: Mary McKay Duncan, who became a wonderful friend in Austin when I arrived knowing virtually no one; the great American Mansfield scholar Larry Mitchell, who provided valuable assistance when needed, and who drove across Texas to take me for dinner; Judy Siers, one of the loveliest people I met in Wellington, who took me to see the Royal New Zealand Ballet perform *A Midsummer Night's Dream*; Liz Clark, who located some wonderful material about Karori for me; Kevin Ireland, for answering questions with unfailing charm and perspicacity; Michael Forrest, whose knowledge of KM and Marie Bashkirtseff is quite astonishing; Moira Taylor, who suggested some fascinating material; Martin Griffiths, who kindly shared his in-depth knowledge of the Trowell brothers; Joe Williams, who undertook some research for me; Julie Kennedy, who answered queries about Picton and sent me a very useful image; Kevin Boon, who kindly drove me to Day's Bay and elsewhere; Clare O'Leary and Cathy Ellis, for a delightful afternoon by the sea at Breaker Bay; the wonderful New Zealand publisher Roger Steele, who took me for lunch; and Sarah Dennis and her husband Dominique Santini, who revealed all the delights of Cuba Street in Wellington to me.

Finally, and most importantly, I would like to thank my family: Ralph and Bella Kimber, whose love and patience know no bounds; my parents, Grace and John Cibulskas; and my sister, Bernadette Cibulskas, for her constant generosity.

Every effort has been made to trace the copyright holders of the estates of Ruth Elvish Mantz, Ian A. Gordon, Walter Rippmann, M. Huguenet, Miss Barbara Harper and the Reverend Charles Prodgers. The author and publisher would be glad to make suitable acknowledgements in future editions of the book.

Textual Note

Probably the most pressing question, as I set out to write this biography of Katherine Mansfield, was what, in fact, to call her. Mansfield? Not really. This is a book about a young girl called Kathleen Mansfield Beauchamp. That academic shortening to the rather blunt Mansfield reflects neither the young protagonist portrayed here, nor any name that she was using for the greater part of this biography. Well, Katherine, then? Again, hardly anyone in the pages of this childhood record called her 'Katherine'. She was Kass to her family and schoolfriends, Kathleen to her teachers and Katie to a few others. After much deliberation – and with apologies in advance to those readers who dislike acronyms – I settled for KM. The initials KM could stand for Kathleen Mansfield or Kass Mansfield or Katie Mansfield or Katherine Mansfield. They are purposefully ambiguous and therefore suit my multi-named protagonist admirably.

N.B. All ellipses are KM's unless placed in brackets thus [. . .], when they represent my own textual omissions.

Foreword

C. K. Stead

The temperament of the young Katherine Mansfield, especially during the teenage years, had all the inconvenient turbulence of genius in a middle-class setting. It was an environment which provided rare opportunities – travel, education abroad, libraries, musical training, comfortable social interactions and affluence. Even the father, whom the young Kathleen (soon to be Katherine) complained about so bitterly, fostered her advance as a writer, gave her access to interesting people in high places, exercised influence to ensure she could use what was probably the best library in New Zealand, paid for her musical education, established the cottage at Day's Bay that was the setting for some of her finest stories, and in the end sent her back to London with an income of £100 per annum, enough for a young literary aspirant to live on and make a start. Harold Beauchamp, with the hairy hands that so disgusted his teenage daughter, was in reality as much the beneficent provider as the philistine obstructer she complained about; and she was to do him something nearer to justice when she portrayed him in her mature stories as the bumbling and boastful but none the less competent, affectionate and well-intentioned Stanley Burnell.

All of this emerges in Dr Gerri Kimber's close study of Mansfield's early years, from childhood, through the four years in London at Queen's College, Harley Street, where she met her life-long friend-and-willing-slave, Ida Baker; and then the return to New Zealand and a period lived richly but always in hope of, and anxiety about, getting back to London. Sexuality during these years was, as one might expect, intense, but unusual in that it was put on written record; and rarer still because so much literary fashion coloured the record and even gave it much of its unconventional direction. The influence of Oscar Wilde rendered it both ambiguous and fashionably decadent, giving it a flavour that combined *fin de siècle* with *épater le bourgeois*. She was in and out of love, with Edie, with Tom, with Maata, with Tom again, each passion expunging the last, and all recorded as if the latest was the serious one and would endure.

The young Mansfield was a shameless *poseur*; but with so much talent one admires rather than deplores the poses. To a possible editor she wrote, 'I am poor – obscure – just eighteen years of age – with a rapacious appetite for everything and principles as light as my purse.' This was partly true – the age at least was accurate; and the rapacity, though not as unprincipled as she was pretending, was certainly an aspect of her teenage character. But this was a statement written for effect. So much she did was for effect, and one needs to see her in the light of her true talent and of her future, to appreciate her battles with herself and with her family and the colonial society.

Her contempt for New Zealand and impatience with its limitations were at times strident; and her prescription for its cure was a highly sophisticated reading list of 'advanced' authors. 'These people', she said of New Zealanders, as if she were not one of them, 'have not learned their alphabet' – a sturdy put-down! To her family she was, more often than not, a pain in the neck; and reactions to her from the wider Wellington social circle were often mixed or negative. As a child, compared to her sisters, she was said to be 'a thundercloud', the 'outlaw' in a very conventional and proper family. An acquaintance is recorded as saying, 'To see Vera was to love her [. . .] to see Kathleen was to remember her.' This was a time when the child, tending to tubbiness and with steel-rimmed spectacles, would have responded to maternal warmth. She received it from her grandmother, but from her mother, it seems, very little, and it is not surprising she was famous for tantrums.

Yet she was capable, even in those early years, of great eagerness and charm. And after her schooling in London it was impatience that made her appear at her worst – the determination to fulfil her destiny as a writer / musician / artist, and the feeling of being blocked at every turn. Quite simply she wanted to get on with the job, and 'these people' who 'didn't know their alphabet' were standing in her way.

But it would be 'these people' who would ultimately form the individuals and the society of her most successful stories; and she would not be ready to comprehend and fully represent them until she had experienced extreme personal suffering. Finally, she would be shocked back into full consciousness of them, their reality (which was also hers), their pains and pleasures, their failures and achievements, by the death of her beloved brother in World War One.

One feels admiration for the vigour of the young Mansfield mind as represented in this book, an exquisite sensibility, a precocious intellect, ahead of itself in age, in reading, in linguistic competence, and yet still with so much to learn.

Mansfield scholars have had most of the elements of the story told here, but always in fragments and disparately located. Dr Kimber has brought the fragments together, and added new material, so what we have now is a much more complete account of the young writer's childhood and youth and the forces that shaped her development.

For Bella

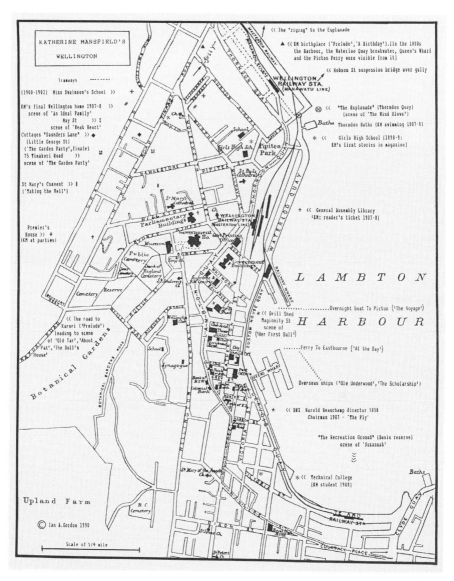

Katherine Mansfield's Wellington.

Introduction

It is always well, says Nietzsche, to divorce an artist from his work, and to take him less seriously than it. This is no doubt good advice if one is interested in the work rather than the life of an artist, but it presupposes that a divorce can be made, something which is not always easy, as the case of Katherine Mansfield may serve to illustrate.[1]

All previous major biographies of KM, except the one written in 1933 by Ruth Elvish Mantz and John Middleton Murry (who was KM's lover, then husband and eventual posthumous editor of her works), devote relatively little space – or no space at all – to KM's life up to 1908;[2] as a result, a tangible biographical imbalance has led to a distorted view of the unimportance of KM's early life. In *The Life of Katherine Mansfield*, Mantz, young and inexperienced, found herself at the mercy of Murry's editorial power, when it was suggested by the publisher, Constable, that he rewrite parts of it. Thus, Mantz's original intention of writing – on her own – a full biography of KM's life eventually became a rather fanciful, romantic – and, in places, inaccurate – distortion of her early life, which Murry made the decision to end in 1912 and the beginning of KM's relationship with him. In fact, it should more accurately have been called *The Early Life of Katherine Mansfield*. For Mantz, the collaboration with Murry was a frustrating and unhappy experience, and the rest of her life, until her death in 1979, was, to a large extent, taken up with the writing of numerous versions of the biography as *she* would have written it, though sadly she was never able to find a publisher for any of her manuscripts. Fortunately, all of Mantz's KM manuscripts and research materials are now in the Harry Ransom Center at the University of Texas at Austin, and for KM scholars are an invaluable resource, barely touched by previous biographers.

This biography, wherever possible, allows KM to speak for herself. From her early teens onwards, KM made a conscious effort to record what was happening to her, whether in a diary entry, in a letter, in her fiction or even in her poetry. As Ian Gordon notes:

> Katherine Mansfield to a degree almost unparalleled in English fiction put her own experiences into her stories. She wrote of nothing that did not directly happen to her, even when she appeared to be at her most imaginative and fanciful. Her stories, read in their order of composition, gain force and significance, and are illuminated at all points by the events of her own history. Her whole work read in this manner emerges as a kind of *recherche du temps perdu*, a remembrance of things past [. . .][3]

Of course, allowance must be made for artistic licence. No claim is being made that everything KM wrote in her fiction – or indeed in her diary entries – actually happened. But if the reader wants to understand KM, the small child growing up in Karori, for example, no amount of biographical research can compete with KM's own portrait of Kezia in the Burnell stories. If you want to understand the essence of her much-loved uncle, Val Waters, his spirit is to be found in Jonathan Trout. All the characters from her childhood – even walk-on parts for outsiders, such as 'Old Tar' – are present in her fiction, and it would be a foolish biographer who chose to take the high road and ignore the wealth of biographical material waiting to be unlocked in her fiction. For Gordon,

> Katherine Mansfield in these sensitively felt stories is not merely recording experience. She is expressing a view of life on a basis of recorded memories. [. . .] Her accurate rendering of background is only part of her larger accuracy in the rendering of life.[4]

A fellow pupil at Karori school once wrote to Mantz: 'the Beauchamp family are identical with the Burnells in the story ['The Doll's House']. It gives the atmosphere of the school much more accurately than I could write of it.'[5]

This biography therefore makes no apology for placing KM's fiction, poetry and personal writing centre-stage, wherever possible, and especially in the years 1907–8 when she systematically started to record details of her life for the first time. Sadly, as an adult, KM decided that her youthful diaries, together with the hundreds of letters sent to friends such as Ida Baker during this period, were an embarrassment. Many were destroyed. The burning of the letters KM sent to Ida during the final months spent in New Zealand in 1907–8 robs us of much of the evidence of her state of mind at this time. Thankfully, other sources remain.

Not all the diaries from this time were destroyed, and a good deal of extant fiction, together with normal biographical material such as letters, newspapers and conversations with individuals, allow us to create a vivid picture of KM and her family during this period.

Moreover, from the very beginning, KM's range of subject matter in her stories was not broad; for Gordon, it was even more restricted than that of Jane Austen's 'few families in a country village. For [KM], one family and a few relationships she had known were enough to express a universality of experience.'[6] Her stories may be placed in England, in Wellington, in continental Europe, but the stress is always on character and relationships, not time and place. She would eventually be celebrated for her rejection of conventional plot structure and dramatic action in favour of the presentation of character through narrative voice. KM was present at the beginning of the modernist movement in Europe and became one of its most exciting and cutting-edge protagonists. For this biography in particular, which concentrates solely on her childhood and adolescence, the delineation in her fiction of children and young adults reveals a remarkable ability to enter into the mind of her subject, where the smallest details illuminate the bigger picture, as here in 'Prelude' (1917):

Kezia liked to stand so before the window. She liked the feeling of the cold shining glass against her hot palms, and she liked to watch the funny white tops that came on her fingers when she pressed them hard against the pane. As she stood there, the day flickered out and dark came. With the dark crept the wind snuffling and howling. The windows of the empty house shook, a creaking came from the walls and floors, a piece of loose iron on the roof banged forlornly. Kezia was suddenly quite, quite still, with wide open eyes and knees pressed together. She was frightened.[7]

A universal childhood experience – staring through a window, hands pressed against the glass – is turned into a particularly New Zealand one, where the passage from day to night is a far swifter process than in the northern hemisphere. An empty room, an empty house and darkness become the symbols of the Beauchamps' move from 11 Tinakori Road to Chesney Wold, Karori, as described through the eyes, and in the unique language, of Kezia, a family name which she would have heard on numerous occasions as a child.

In KM's fiction, there is a focus on small, seemingly insignificant details at the expense of comprehensive description, an early preference for the vignette, which provides the reader with only fleeting glimpses of people and places, and a preoccupation with colour and an emphasis on surfaces and reflections. Her employment of multiple, shifting perspectives which are both subjective and fractured also displays an affinity with impressionism, as does the attention she pays to the ephemeral effects of artificial and natural light, weather effects and seasonal changes. These impressions can add more colour to an understanding of KM than a myriad dull biographical facts, as this biography hopes to demonstrate.

Chapter 1   Ancestors

Kathleen Mansfield Beauchamp (1888–1923), only later to become known as Katherine Mansfield, was born into a formidable colonial clan of high-spirited adventurers,[1] for whom adversity was a welcome challenge, and who were determined to make good. Indeed, Harold Beauchamp had once written to his cosmopolitan, literary daughter, KM, who had made a life for herself in Europe, affirming his belief that all anyone really needed for a good start in life was a parcel of land and a couple of cows. The lives of the various Beauchamp 'Pa-men' ancestors, celebrated for their larger-than-life personalities and pioneering spirit, would captivate KM's imagination as both a child and an adult.

The family can be traced all the way back to the conquering Normans in 1066 and one Hugh de Beauchamp, but this noble line soon gave way to more modest family circumstances. By the eighteenth century, a certain Robert Beauchamp was, in 1717, to be found in Cheapside, London, in a modest cottage (rent £4 p.a.), and recorded as a pawnbroker and member of the Broderers Company. His son Edward, born in 1751, was also a pawnbroker and salesman, working out of 147 High Holborn. Edward was, in fact, a silversmith, but 'the reason for the absence of the Beauchamps from standard works on London goldsmiths and silversmiths is because Edward was basically a pawnbroker first and a silversmith second,'[2] a common feature of many silversmiths at this time. His son, John Beauchamp (1781–1852), was trained as a silversmith, with his own distinctive hallmark – the letters JB surrounded by a square. He lived in Hornsey Lane, Highgate, and would go on to become the first 'Pa-man'.

John had inherited a prosperous business from his father, Edward, but his fortunes took a downturn. According to his grandson, Harold Beauchamp (KM's father), 'John did certainly invent a new imitation silverware which he called "British Plate". But he did not patent it and did not manufacture it on a large

Figure 1.1 Mrs Mary Stone by C. R. Leslie, R.A. 1794–1859 [c. 1830], great-great-grandmother of Katherine Mansfield and mother of Anne Stone.

scale. Perhaps he had not the necessary capital.'[3] (The process was eventually taken up by German manufacturers, who made a good deal of money from it.) John's business did not thrive, and in 1833 he was declared bankrupt.

John's wife, Anne Stone, came from an artistic family. Her brother was the well-known Victorian artist, Charles Robert Leslie, who, together with John Constable, formed part of an artistic and intellectual circle within which John moved freely; Harold Beauchamp notes how he 'was very fond of poetry, especially his contemporaries Byron and Coleridge, whom he could recite by heart'.[4] Indeed, John also penned his own poetry and became known as the 'poet of Hornsey Lane', thanks to the publication in the local press of one of his poems, 'The Rook', composed of ten verses and ending thus:

Fate meets us when we least expect
As covered much, as bone he pecked,
The cat was prowling by.
He fought with desperate courage true
Lost! What could maimed valour do?
But nobly striving, die.[5]

Harold Beauchamp's children loved to recite the following lines, bringing to life both their great-grandfather John, and their grandfather Arthur:

I'm the last of the old Hornsey Laners
The last of the Beauchamp campaigners
The last of the eight it's sad to relate,
I'm the last of the old Hornsey Laners![6]

John and Anne had seven surviving sons, brought up at 'Clayhill', a house in North London. They all attended Highgate Boys' Grammar School, obtaining a solid, classical education. In this family, with its roots in commerce, a university education was not deemed as important as obtaining an apprenticeship (many years later, even Harold's son, Leslie Heron, would not take up a university place but instead would become a clerk at the National Insurance Company in Wellington, with aspirations to rise swiftly through the ranks). However, none of the sons seemed remotely interested in the family trade of silversmithing. John, the eldest son, died young. Horatio and Arthur followed a cousin, Walter, by emigrating to Melbourne, Australia, and were followed a few years later by their brother Cradock, who, together with Arthur, would then move to New Zealand.

Two other brothers made the journey to Melbourne: Samuel, who, suffering from tuberculosis, was forced to return to England in 1856, dying en route, and Ralph, who found work there as a cleric. Another brother, Frederick, stayed at home in England for some time in order to manage the family affairs, finally also making the journey to Melbourne with his wife and children. It was Frederick's son, George Beauchamp, who travelled to the Urewera, a remote part of the North Island of New Zealand, where he married a girl from the Tuhoe tribe and produced five sons, all with solid Beauchamp names: George, Sam, John, Henry and Arthur. When KM made her own trip to the Urewera in 1907, she might so easily have met up with her own relations.

Henry Herron Beauchamp (1824–1907, after whom KM's brother, Leslie Heron, was named, the clerk having misspelt the baptismal name as 'Heron'), was the fourth son, who had left school at thirteen, having been apprenticed to a firm of merchants with shipping interests. By the age of twenty-four he was in Mauritius, trading in sugar, ending up in Sydney in 1848. In 1855 Henry married Louise Weiss Lassetter (known to the family as 'Louey'). In 1850, Louey had travelled with her sister Annie to Sydney, where they stayed with their aunt, Kezia Iredale. Henry would eventually, in 1870, return to London, where he kept meticulous diaries noting every aspect of his daily life. It was to Henry and Louey, at their home, 'The Retreat', in Bexley, Kent, that Harold Beauchamp's three young daughters would go for Christmas holidays whilst being educated at Queen's College in Harley Street from 1903 to 1906. Great-Uncle Henry was known to Harold and the Beauchamp siblings as 'Great-Uncle Dee-pa', a term of considerable affection. His daughter, Mary Annette, always known in the family as May, would restyle herself 'Elizabeth', becoming the best-selling author Elizabeth von Arnim and, late in KM's life, a trusted confidante and friend. Another of Harold's children – Charlotte Mary – always known to the family as Chaddie (pronounced 'Shaddy') – was also named after Henry's eldest daughter (also known as Chaddie), who married George Waterlow; their son, Sydney Waterlow, would become an author and literary critic in his own right (well known to KM, Murry and their literary circle), and later a respected diplomat. He was, in fact, an early suitor of Virginia Woolf, who turned down his offer of marriage in November 1911.

All of John's sons left England to make their fortune abroad, with varying degrees of success. The Napoleonic wars had left Britain suffering economic depression, and as a result employment was scarce. The brothers' maiden aunt Jane, John's sister, in the meantime had become a companion to Lady Laura Tollemache, who left Jane £2,000 on her death. With her new-found wealth, Jane would eventually go on to purchase several parcels of land in 1839, in Wellington, New Zealand, then one of Britain's newest colonies. As she noted:

> I had for several years admired the national character of the aborigines; their desire of civilisation and religious truth; to this was added the growing miseries in England occasioned by its dense and unemployed population. As an object of general benefit, therefore, I thought it an interesting enterprise, fully aware a profitable return of the money expended must be distant, if ever obtainable in my lifetime.[7]

Jane indicated how she hoped one or more of her seven nephews might eventually travel to New Zealand in order to benefit from her portions of land following her death in the early 1850s; both Cradock and Arthur would do just that.[8]

Cradock arrived in Picton, New Zealand, in 1862, following his brother Arthur, who had established himself in this tiny corner of the north of New Zealand's South Island. Both brothers sold their Aunt Jane's land sections in Wellington in favour of this quiet backwater, considering that Wellington was too much of a risk, it having been largely demolished by three recent major earthquakes in 1840, 1848 and 1855. Cradock set up home on 200 acres of bush at Anakiwa, in Queen Charlotte Sound, with his wife Harriet, whose aunt had been principal of Cheltenham Ladies' College, and who had brought her niece to New Zealand in the early 1860s. Harold Beauchamp was

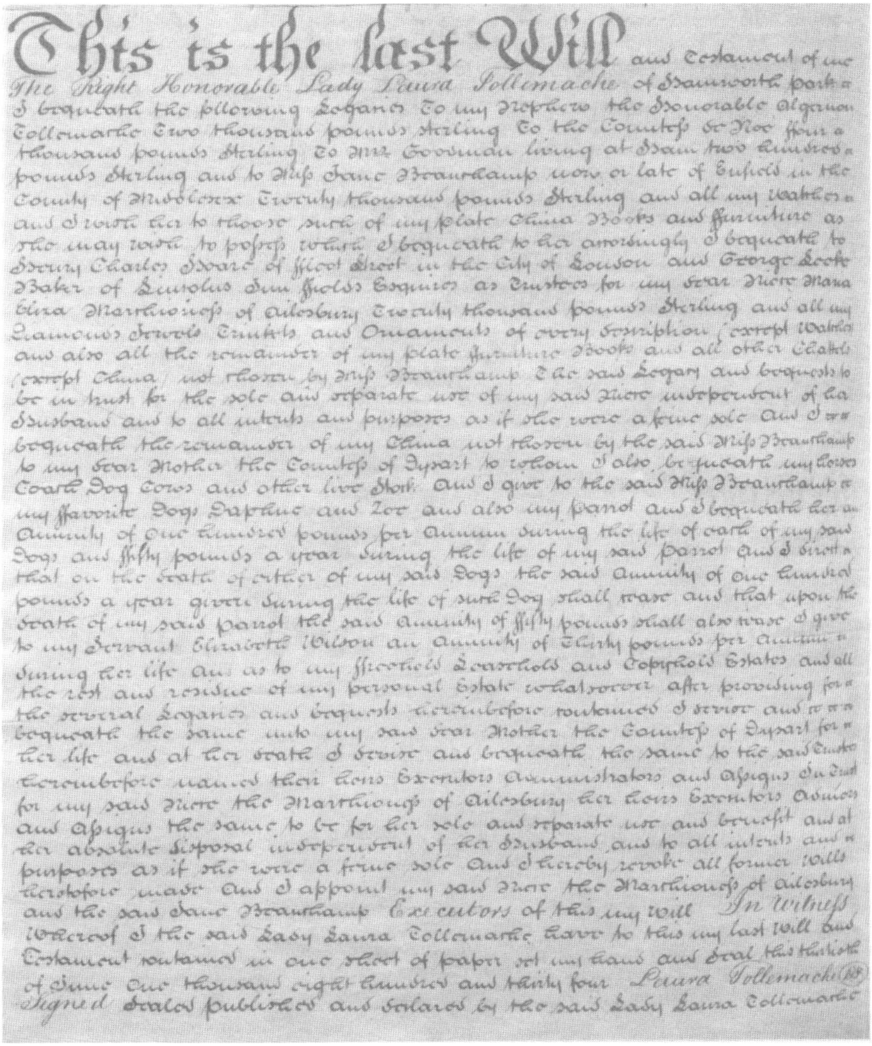
This is the last Will and Testament of me
The Right Honorable Lady Laura Tollemache of Hamworth Park
I bequeath the following Legacies To my Nephew the Honorable Algernon
Tollemache Two thousand pounds sterling To the Countess De Noe four
thousand pounds Sterling To Mr Goodman living at Ham two hundred
pounds Sterling and to Miss Jane Beauchamp now or late of Enfield in the
County of Middlesex Twenty thousand pounds Sterling and all my Watches
and I wish her to choose such of my plate China Books and furniture as
she may wish to possess which I bequeath to her accordingly I bequeath to
Henry Charles Hoare of Fleet Street in the City of London and George Scott
Baker of Lincolns Inn Fields Esquires as Trustees for my dear Niece Maria
Eliza Marchioness of Ailesbury Twenty thousand pounds Sterling and all my
Diamonds Jewels Trinkets and Ornaments of every description (except Watches
and also all the remainder of my plate furniture Books and all other Chattels
(except China not chosen by Miss Beauchamp The said Legacy and bequests to
be in trust for the sole and separate use of my said Niece independent of her
Husband and to all intents and purposes as if she were a feme sole And I give
bequeath the remainder of my China not chosen by the said Miss Beauchamp
to my dear Mother the Countess of Dysart to whom I also bequeath my Horses
Coach Dog Cows and other live Stock And I give to the said Miss Beauchamp
my favorite Dogs Daphne and Zoe and also my parrot and I bequeath her an
Annuity of One hundred pounds per Annum during the life of each of my said
Dogs and fifty pounds a year during the life of my said parrot And I direct
that on the death of either of my said Dogs the said Annuity of one hundred
pounds a year given during the life of such Dog shall cease and that upon the
death of my said parrot the said Annuity of fifty pounds shall also cease I give
to my Servant Elizabeth Wilson an Annuity of Thirty pounds per Annum
during her life And as to my Freehold Leasehold and Copyhold Estates and all
the rest and residue of my personal Estate whatsoever after providing for
the several Legacies and bequests hereinbefore contained I devise and
bequeath the same unto my said dear Mother the Countess of Dysart for
her life and at her death I devise and bequeath the same to the said Trustees
hereinbefore named their heirs Executors Administrators and Assigns In trust
for my said Niece the Marchioness of Ailesbury her heirs Executors Admors
and Assigns the same to be for her sole and separate use and benefit and at
her absolute disposal independent of her Husband and to all intents and
purposes as if she were a feme sole And I hereby revoke all former Wills
heretofore made And I appoint my said Niece the Marchioness of Ailesbury
and the said Jane Beauchamp Executors of this my Will In Witness
whereof I the said Lady Laura Tollemache have to this my last Will and
Testament contained in one sheet of paper set my hand and seal this thirtieth
of June One thousand eight hundred and thirty four Laura Tollemache (LS)
Signed sealed published and declared by the said Lady Laura Tollemache

Figure 1.2 Front page of the will of Lady Tollemache.

Cradock's godchild and, when young, frequently spent holidays with them on the Anakiwa homestead. Vera and Chaddie, KM's two eldest sisters, were sent there whilst Annie Beauchamp, Harold's wife, was giving birth to their fourth child, Gwendoline. A young KM would also visit her great-aunt and uncle several times. Their son Herbert's daughter, Ethel, also developed a talent for writing, but this was soon suppressed as the family feared she would go the way of Harold's third daughter, KM, who by then had already become something of a black sheep among her Beauchamp relatives. Ethel recorded her early

Figure 1.3 Anakiwa.

success getting stories published: 'I think the family was slightly impressed, but Kathleen's shadow darkened their orthodox lives.'[9] Nevertheless, Harold would remain close to his cousin Ethel well into adulthood. A prolific letter writer, she kept him in touch with the goings-on of his various Beauchamp relations.

Arthur Beauchamp, John's sixth son and KM's grandfather, was the most celebrated of all the 'Pa-men'. His restless nature and inability to settle anywhere for too long prompted many family stories, some apocryphal. It was said that his chickens were so used to being transported to new locations that, at the merest sight of a move, they would lie on their backs with their feet in the air, ready to be trussed up. He married his young bride, Mary Elizabeth Stanley, in 1854, whilst still in Australia. Harold was their first child to survive, the previous two having died soon after birth, and he would become the eldest of eight siblings. The family moved to New Zealand in 1861, and, just like his brother, Arthur swapped his Aunt Jane sections in Wellington for some land in Picton, on the South Island, near to his brother Cradock.

By all accounts, Arthur was a witty and engaging individual. He set himself up as a general merchant and auctioneer, and soon prospered. One 'Pa-man' story concerned his opposition to the Marlborough Provincial Council being moved to Blenheim:

In a filibustering attempt to block this move, he made a ten hour and forty minute speech which he finished by saying – 'Mr Speaker, having made these few preliminary remarks, I will now proceed to speak on the subject under discussion' – unfortunately he then collapsed and had to be carried out.[10]

News of this speech was even reported in the local newspaper, the *Marlborough Express*, where it was recorded that 'Mr Arthur Beauchamp was allowed by Captain Baillie to insult the members and disgrace himself by vomiting forth ten hours and a half of nonsense, ribaldry and Billingsgate.'[11] Condemnations of his actions notwithstanding, he eventually became the MP for Picton and attended parliament in Wellington, advocating liberal policies that included a more just land policy for the Maori. Like all his siblings, he had received a good classical education in England, and wrote verse himself, even including poetry

Figure 1.4 Group photograph of the Beauchamp family outside the Beauchamp house at Anakiwa, c. 1892. Back row from left: Claude, Ethel (Mrs Grimsdale Anderson), Nettie (Mrs John Duncan), Stanley, Arthur (father of Harold and brother of Cradock). Middle row from left: Reg, Mrs Cradock Beauchamp (née Harriet Broughton), Cradock Beauchamp. In front from left: Helen (Mrs Stuart Greensill), a Broughton cousin, Laura (Mrs Barclay), Clem.

in some of his political speeches.[12] His restlessness, however, soon got the better of him and he and his long-suffering wife and family endured numerous moves around New Zealand, finally returning once more to Picton in 1907, where he died in 1910 at the age of 82. (This restlessness would be inherited by his grand-daughter, KM, who resembled him far more than she ever did her own father.) Arthur's wife, Mary, lived another seven years, dying in 1917. Harold revered his mother and understood that his father's restlessness had given her a difficult life. He therefore determined that the women in his family would be offered every security and advantage that money could provide and KM was certainly a beneficiary of this approach. In addition, Harold's enjoyment of music and poetry, inherited from his Beauchamp ancestors (he was a proficient singer and pianist), would also run in the blood of his children, and especially his third daughter, KM.

Chapter 2　Harold and Annie Beauchamp

Harold Beauchamp was the antithesis of his itinerant father Arthur and yet, in his own way, he was no less colourful a character. Solid, dependable but with a strong ambitious streak, at the height of his career he was one of the richest businessmen in New Zealand, Chairman of the Bank of New Zealand, and knighted for his services to New Zealand commerce in 1923. However, if Harold could have actually chosen one of John Beauchamp's sons as a father, it would undoubtedly have been Henry Herron (after whom he named his precious only son). Henry's work ethic and success in Australia meant that within twenty years he was able to return to England a wealthy man. Harold only met his uncle for the first time in 1875, when he was aged seventeen, Henry having travelled to New Zealand to visit his brothers, Cradock and Arthur. Uncle and nephew immediately hit it off, engendering a warm relationship that lasted until Henry's death in 1907.

There are several mentions of Harold in Henry Herron's unpublished diaries. It was Harold who wrote to his uncle about the death of his brother, Walter: 'Monday [28 May 1888] Recd Harold B's letter of 20th April advising death at Christchurch N/Z on 2d Apl of his brother Walter very suddenly from brain disease. He had nearly completed his 21st year. Poor Arthur and Mary!'[1] For Harold, no visit to England was complete without several visits to Uncle Henry. On two occasions at least, Henry and Harold visited the old ancestral Beauchamp home: 'In great heat and dust went with Harold Beauchamp on a pious pilgrimage to the old home in Hornsey Lane and adjacent parts.'[2] And again in 1903, this time with the whole family: 'Accompanied Harold B and his 5 children on a pilgrimage to the old house in Hornsey Lane which being in the hands of workmen we roamed through at pleasure.'[3] KM, therefore, within a few days of arriving in England for the first time, was taken to see the place

Figure 2.1 Picton, 1890.

from where her Beauchamp forebears had set off to the Antipodes to make their fortunes, instilling in her, at an early age, the importance of family ties.

Harold's early life was based in Picton, where his father Arthur had settled in 1861. He left school at fourteen, and immediately started working for his father in his auctioneering business. In his memoirs, Harold recalled one particular family move, instigated by Arthur, to Beatrix Bay, near Pelorus Sound, where Arthur had purchased some land. At the time it was hard to imagine a more remote place:

> We lived chiefly on fish, mutton, wild pork and birds such as pigeons, *kakas*[4] and – I blush to say – *tuis*.[5] [. . .] As a lad I assisted in the felling of bush, milking, and other outside jobs; and as there was no domestic help I often assisted my mother in the house and gained some proficiency in cooking, scrubbing, washing, and some other things.[6]

Harold's own children never knew such privations; he was proud to bring them up with servants to do chores. One of the party on KM's trip to the Urewera in

Figure 2.2 Queen Charlotte Sound.

Figure 2.3 Premises of Arthur Beauchamp, stock salesman and auctioneer, Wanganui,
        1869–76.

Figure 2.4 Arthur Beauchamp's son, aged 2, by rocking horse, c. 1870s.

1907 would recall that when KM was presented with a potato to cook, she had no idea how to peel it: 'the same way as you peel an apple', she was told.[7]

In 1876, Arthur eventually moved his family to Wellington, where he set up yet another auctioneering business: Beauchamp, Campbell & Company. For a time, Harold worked for his father but left on 7 May 1877, to join W. W. Bannatyne & Company, an established firm of Wellington importers. Arthur meanwhile resigned from this latest auctioneering business and took off once more in a series of moves that must have been the despair of his long-suffering wife and family. Harold later wrote of his mother:

> She had a serene character and even temperament that enabled her to meet any trouble with perfect equanimity. As a pioneer she encountered difficulties and hard work of every description [. . .] It must have been trying in the extreme to break up her home so often to follow my father in his wanderings from place to place; but she never questioned the wisdom of that. I can only describe her as an earthly saint.[8]

Many years later, in 1902, Arthur decided to return to England for a visit, staying with his brother Henry Herron. KM recalled this apocryphal visit in

Figure 2.5 Harold Beauchamp's mother, Mary Beauchamp.

a letter written in 1921, demonstrating both affection and a certain degree of pride in her grandfather's eccentricities:

> My grandpa said a man could travel all over the world with a clean pair of socks and a rook rifle. At the age of 70 he started for England thus equipped but Mother took fright & added a handkerchief or two. When he returned he was shorn of everything but a large watering can which he'd bought in London for his young marrows.[9]

Finally, in 1907, Arthur and Mary returned to Picton, the place where they had first set up home in New Zealand fifty years earlier. Arthur died there on 28 April 1910, at the age of eighty-two. In his obituary, the *Marlborough Press* wrote: 'He fought for that which he considered right with might and main, and his public services in Marlborough, his loyalty to Picton and his fine qualities as a citizen earned for him the esteem and gratitude of the people.'[10] There is no record of KM noting the death of her grandfather (most of her personal papers from that time having been systematically destroyed), but following the death of his wife Mary in Picton on 24 November 1917, KM wrote in a letter to Murry: 'My grandma is dead. She had a stroke & died.'[11]

Harold meanwhile was forging ahead with his career at Bannatyne's. He would work his way up to become a partner and ultimately a director. On his

Figure 2.6 Grandma Dyer with her husband, Joseph Dyer.

joining the firm in 1877, Wellington had been the capital of New Zealand for a mere twelve years. With a rapidly developing economic climate, the rather run-down Bannatyne's soon started to thrive, and Harold became indispensible. In discussing his decision to make a life in Wellington with Bannatyne's, rather than follow in his father's footsteps, he later remarked:

> Remaining in Wellington thus enabled me not only to make a fine business out of this long-established firm, but also to become associated as a director with some of the leading public companies of New Zealand. No other city could have opened up such opportunities to a young man.[12]

Early on at Bannatyne's, Harold had met – and become infatuated with – the fourteen-year-old Annie, sister of Joseph Dyer, a clerk at the company. His mind firmly set, he waited patiently for six years, before marrying her on 18 February 1884 at St Paul's Cathedral in Wellington. Annie, always frail following childhood illness, also came from a close family. Her mother, Margaret Isabella Dyer – KM's beloved 'Grandma', would take over the running of Harold's household for thirteen years. Having brought up nine children of her own, yet still only in her late forties, she was instrumental in the care of Harold's own brood.

Margaret's father was Samuel Worthington Mansfield (after whom KM was

Figure 2.7 Harold Beauchamp.

Figure 2.8 Annie Beauchamp.

Figure 2.9 St Paul's Pro-Cathedral, Wellington.

named), a Sydney publican. He had married Margaret Barnes, an émigrée to Australia from Bath in England, in 1834. Their daughter, Margaret Isabella Mansfield, was born on 21 January 1839. In 1855, she married Joseph Dyer, then a thirty-six-year-old insurance clerk; she was just sixteen. Of their nine children, Annie was the fourth. The family moved to Wellington in 1864, Joseph having been appointed manager of the New Zealand branch of the Australian Mutual Provident Society. In poor health, Joseph struggled to make ends meet and he eventually died in 1877. Annie's younger sister, Isabella Dyer, known to the Beauchamps as Aunt Belle, would also move in with Harold and Annie after their marriage, alongside her mother, as would another sister, Edith (known as Kitty), for a short time. It was Belle who accompanied the family to London and looked after the three girls during their stay at Queen's College in Harley Street. Belle brought vitality and a liveliness to the household which Annie could not, due to her delicate health. In Annie's place she partnered Harold at tennis and cards, sang while Harold played the piano, and generally helped to entertain guests. Annie and Belle's older sister, Agnes, married Frederick Valentine Waters, known as Uncle Val. Together with their two sons, Barrie and Eric, they were frequent visitors to the Beauchamp household, along with their spaniel. When Harold moved his family to Karori in 1893, the Waters family moved as well, renting a small house nearby. The childhood of the Beauchamp and Waters children would be a closely-knit one, as KM would later depict in her Burnell stories. In 1897, Annie's brother Frank would marry the daughter of then New Zealand Prime Minister, Richard Seddon, thus firmly allying Harold and his family to New Zealand's great and powerful.

In her story, 'A Birthday' (1911), KM gives a clear-sighted portrayal of Harold's courtship of her mother, indicating the story had been told many times to their children:

> She certainly was a little thing. He remembered once saying when they were engaged, 'Just as high as my heart,' and she had jumped on to a stool and pulled his head down, laughing. A kid in those days, younger than her children in nature, brighter, more 'go' and 'spirit' in her. The way she'd run down the road to meet him after business! And the way she laughed when they were looking for a house. By Jove! that laugh of hers! At the memory he grinned, then grew suddenly grave. Marriage certainly changed a woman far more than it did a man. Talk about sobering down. She had lost all her go in two months![13]

Annie's delicate health had been brought on by a severe bout of rheumatic fever in her youth, which had weakened her heart. Yet having been married to Harold in February 1884, she was pregnant within a year, and by the time her last child, Leslie Heron, was born ten years later in February 1894, she had undergone six difficult births. It is no wonder that she developed a horror of childbirth and was always a reluctant mother, as KM describes so poignantly in 'Prelude' (1917):

> Yes, that was her real grudge against life; that was what she could not understand. That was the question she asked and asked, and listened in vain for the answer. It was all very well to say it was the common lot of women to bear children. It wasn't true. She, for one, could prove that wrong. She was broken, made weak, her courage was gone, through child-bearing. And what made it doubly hard to bear was, she did not love her children. It was useless pretending. Even if she had had the strength she never would have nursed and played with the little girls. No, it was as though a cold breath had chilled her through and through on each of those awful journeys; she had no warmth left to give them. As to the boy – well, thank Heaven, mother had taken him; he was mother's, or Beryl's, or anybody's who wanted him.[14]

According to family sources, after the birth of Leslie, the longed-for son, Annie Beauchamp would undergo several abortions. Her health was probably too delicate to give birth again, and the virile Harold Beauchamp would not give up his conjugal rights:

> Contraceptive methods were limited and ineffective in the 19th century [. . .] Pills that promised to 'restore regularity' were easily available for women to take if their period was late (though they may not have been very effective). [. . .] Couples decided that they couldn't cope with another baby, and the woman went to a local abortionist.[15]

In the case of Annie, her children in adulthood recalled how on numerous occasions the 'doctor' would be sent for and a covert abortion would be carried out.

Chapter 3   11 Tinakori Road: 1888–1893

On 31 December 1888, the population of the whole of New Zealand was recorded as 649,349, of which 41,969 were Maori. Wellington at the time of KM's birth was a small town by today's standards, with a population of around 28,000 people, marked by a massive disparity in the lives of the rich

Figure 3.1 Looking over Thorndon, Wellington, showing no. 11 Tinakori Road.

and poor. In 1865, when the town had become the capital of New Zealand, there had been a huge shortage of housing, since all the government departments moved from Auckland to Wellington, and many civil servants had suddenly flooded the sleepy little town. This situation would not change for many years.

Ironically, given that many people immigrated to New Zealand in the hope of a better life, unemployment was a serious problem until the end of the nineteenth century, even though the government policy was still *funding* such immigration and thereby increasing the population. There was almost no state aid and the new immigrants (known as 'new chums') arrived to find that there was no work for them and precious little housing, for all the reasons indicated above. Returning to their country of origin was, for most, economically impossible, and so they had to tough it out as best they could, in the hope of better times ahead. Wages for those in work were low and, for the most part, the quality of housing for rental was pitifully inadequate:

> At its fiercest, the depression straddling the late 1870s and early 1880s led to such appalling conditions as overcrowding (one family per room not being unusual), the spread of infectious diseases, and the building of hovels along narrow private streets ungoverned by health, fire or building inspection, but reaping plump profits for their developers.[1]

Some parts of the town were like medieval London in that there was no drainage or sewers, slops were thrown outside, and some streets 'resembled a charnel house with masses of bones and animal matter lying around'.[2] Even worse, some tenants took in hospital laundry in order to make a living, including used poultices and dressings that were simply left lying in the streets. Whatever the immigrants had brought with them by way of household goods, clothes and so on were all sold to pay steep rents and buy food, and when these were gone, homelessness was a real and ever-present occurrence. Indeed, homelessness reached its peak ten years after KM's birth in the late 1890s, when the Harbour Board 'fitted up one of its sheds as a night shelter to prevent the homeless from being thrown into prison for vagrancy'.[3] There were soup kitchens in the centre of town, and in 1899 the Salvation Army opened New Zealand's first working-man's hostel. Inevitably, as a result of poverty, levels of crime were comparatively high for such a small population, as was the number of suicides.

Prostitution was an inevitable sideline for a number of poverty-stricken young women – some girls as young as eleven – for many of whom it was their sole means of earning money. In 1887, just a year before KM's birth, a police raid in Ghuznee Street depicted a collection of six hovels, each only a metre and a half high, their floors swilling in human filth and the occupants sleeping in sacks. It was run by a man who depended on his daughters' prostitution for an income, and whose two sons (aged ten and twelve) were charged with being children living with prostitutes, that is, with their sisters. The man was sent to prison for three months while the children were sent away to industrial schools in the South Island until they turned fifteen.[4]

In 1885, police records showed that Wellington had twenty brothels containing around sixty prostitutes, most of them in Thorndon, the part of Wellington where several of Harold's homes would be situated. Thus the poor slums in Thorndon were to be found just a stone's throw away from the substantial houses of the well-to-do, as KM's story 'The Garden-Party' (1921) would reveal so starkly.

One major feature of the town's poverty was, of course, disease, and particularly epidemics, due to the cramped slum conditions of the poor and the accompanying lack of sanitation. Outbreaks of typhoid (a real and ongoing concern, killing seventy-seven people in 1891), cholera, scarlet fever, dysentery and diphtheria were common. At its worst, the infant mortality rate in the slum areas was as high as eighty per cent. Even outbreaks of bubonic plague were not uncommon, though eventually the authorities took severe measures in order to reduce the possibility of rats coming ashore from berthed ships. However, disease did not affect just the poor. Cholera would kill KM's sister, Gwendoline, born at 11 Tinakori Road on 9 October 1890; she would not live to see her first birthday. Harold's brother Charles died of typhoid in Wellington in 1892 and just a year later his sister Florence aged 31, would die of the same disease. These deaths of close family would have been at the forefront of Harold's mind when he decided to move the family completely away from Wellington in 1894, to the then rural community of Karori, some three miles distant. As he noted in his *Reminiscences*, the move was 'for the benefit, not only of the children's health but also of my own'.[5]

Infectious diseases aside, however, the upwardly mobile Harold Beauchamp and his family would know a different and more prosperous life to his own childhood. Following their marriage, Harold and Annie, together with her mother and two sisters, rented various properties in Thorndon, and then moved to a house Harold had had built in the Wellington suburb of Wadestown. Their first child, Vera Margaret, was born there on 22 October 1885 and Charlotte Mary (Chaddie) on 9 July 1887. But, as Harold recorded, 'finding the wind at Wadestown intolerable, I acquired the lease of a section, No. 11 Tinakori Road, and erected a house on it.'[6]

Tinakori Road, in Thorndon, was an excellent location in several respects

Figure 3.2   11 Tinakori Road, birthplace of Katherine Mansfield.

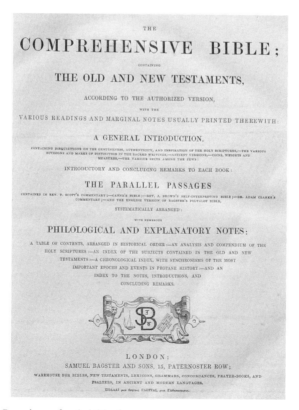

Figure 3.3   The Beauchamp family bible: front page.

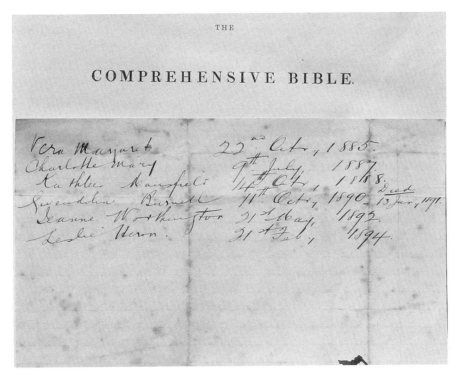

Figure 3.4 The Beauchamp family bible: list of births.

for both Harold and his growing young family, and they took up residence at no. 11 at the beginning of 1888. It was near to the harbour and his work at Bannatyne's, and St Paul's was a short walk away for Sunday services, as were the burgeoning Botanic Gardens further up the Tinakori Road. The land upon which no. 11 was built had been leased for £25 per annum; that lease was not relinquished until 1925, though the family vacated the now cramped house in 1894. The square, two-storey home, though modest and rather plain in its exterior appearance with its painted corrugated iron roof (the long economic depression was also having its effect on the building trade), was nevertheless of sound construction, built from native New Zealand timbers, rimu, totara and matai, was deceptively large inside and even boasted a flushing toilet:

> Interior trims such as cornices and architraves were comparatively restrained. However, the balusters of the Victorian staircase [. . . showed] the fashionable Chinese influence but in a design extremely rare in New Zealand. Wallpapers were limited to a dado and frieze with plain painted paper above.[7]

Figure 3.5 Katherine Mansfield in 1889.

The gardens at the front and back were not large, given the relatively small size of the plot: 'At the front was a square lawn, with arum lilies growing rank as weeds, and the back fence stood on the brink of a bushy gully running down to the sea.'[8] Just down the road was the 'zig-zag', a steep path that went down to the Thorndon Esplanade and the harbour. Thorndon was a 'mixed' area of the well-to-do and the very poor. A pedestrian suspension bridge crossed a steep gully leading to the large and gracious houses on Hobson Street, whilst below, in narrow lanes such as Little George Street, were the hovels of the poor.

Here it was, then, in Thorndon, that KM spent the first five years of her life, born upstairs in the back bedroom on the right, at no. 11 Tinakori Road, on 14 October 1888, a Sunday morning. Today, New Zealand recognises KM as one of its greatest literary icons and her birthplace is one of the country's most visited tourist attractions, where schoolchildren especially love to see where Kezia had her origins, the little fictional girl in whom KM imbued so much of herself in her New Zealand 'Burnell' cycle of stories. Indeed, Kezia was an old family name, and several generations of Beauchamp women could lay claim to it, a fact well known to KM. It was a name she underlined in her schoolgirl bible: 'And he called the name of the first, Jemima; and the name of the second, Kezia; and the name of the third, Kerenhappuch';[9] from all we know of the young KM, she would undoubtedly have taken far more interest in stories of her ancestors than her scripture lessons.

In 'The Aloe' (1915), KM fictionalises the moment of her own birth in that upstairs back bedroom (having always believed that the moment of her birth was marked by a fierce storm in Wellington, though meteorological records disprove such a theory).[10] The passage is not reproduced in 'Prelude' (1917), her polished version of the original story:

> From the window you saw beyond the yard a deep gully filled with tree ferns and a thick tangle of wild green, and beyond that there stretched the esplanade bounded by a broad stone wall against which the sea chafed and thundered. (Kezia had been born in that room. She had come forth squealing out of a reluctant mother in the teeth of a 'Southerly Buster.' The Grandmother, shaking her before the window, had seen the sea rise in green mountains and sweep the esplanade – The little house was like a shell to its loud booming. Down in the gully the wild trees lashed together and big gulls wheeling and crying skimmed past the misty window.)[11]

Kezia's wandering through the empty house before being taken to Karori offers us KM's memories of her first childhood home:

> Slowly she walked up the back steps and through the scullery into the kitchen. Nothing was left in it except a lump of gritty yellow soap in one corner of the window-sill and a piece of flannel stained with a blue bag in another. The fireplace was choked with a litter of rubbish. She poked among it for treasure, but found nothing except a hair-tidy with a heart painted on it that had belonged to the servant girl. Even that she left lying, and she slipped through the narrow passage into the drawing room. The venetian blind was pulled down but not drawn close. Sunlight, piercing the green chinks, shone once again upon the purple urns brimming over with yellow chrysanthemums that patterned the walls – The hideous box was quite bare, so was the dining room except for the sideboard that stood in the middle, forlorn, its shelves edged with a scallop of black leather. But this room had a 'funny' smell. Kezia lifted her head and sniffed again, to remember. Silent as a kitten she crept up the ladderlike stairs. In Mr. and Mrs. Burnell's room she found a pill box, black and shiny outside and red in, holding a blob of cotton wool. 'I could keep a bird's egg in that,' she decided.[12]

Another of KM's stories, 'A Birthday', depicts life at no. 11 and the birth of a child. Although the story uses German names in order to make it seemingly consistent with the other stories set in Germany, first published in the London weekly paper, the *New Age*, and later collected in the volume *In a German Pension* (1911), 'A Birthday' is very much located in Wellington. There is even mention of the small suspension bridge spanning the gully behind Tinakori Road. Andreas and Anna Binzer are early depictions of her parents, with her father's bluff self-centredness and her mother's delicate health. In the story, the mother gives birth to the much-longed-for son, although in reality Leslie was born only after the family had moved to Karori (Annie returning to the safety of town and the proximity of doctors for her confinement). Tinakori Road was up and coming but bordered by the 'lower classes'. Andreas Binzer

> looked down at the row of garden strips and backyards. The fence of these gardens was built along the edge of a gully, spanned by an iron suspension bridge, and the people had a wretched habit of throwing their empty tins over the fence into the gully.[13]

There follows a wholly life-like description of Thorndon on a Sunday morning at the beginning of the 1890s:

> He walked down the street – there was nobody about at all – dead and alive this place on a Sunday morning. As he crossed the suspension bridge a strong stench of fennel and decayed refuse streamed from the gully [. . .] He turned into the main road. The shutters were still up before the shops. Scraps of newspaper, hay, and fruit skins strewed the pavement; the gutters were choked with the leavings of Saturday night. Two dogs sprawled in the middle of the road, scuffling and biting. Only the public-house at the corner was open; a young barman slopped water over the doorstep.
>   Fastidiously, his lips curling, Andreas picked his way through the water. [. . .] 'Everything here's filthy, the whole place might be down with the plague, and will be, too, if this street's not swept away. I'd like to have a hand on the government ropes.'

The story's detail demonstrates how, years later, KM was aware of the unsanitary conditions of parts of Wellington during her childhood; perhaps Harold, too, had noted the appalling conditions to his family, wishing he had the political power to enact change.

In November 1889, a month after KM's first birthday, Harold and Annie decided to make the first of their numerous trips 'home' to England, on this first occasion following the advice of doctors; Annie, by the time KM was born, 'was delicate and inert, an invalid from child-bearing'.[14] Her three little daughters

Figure 3.6 Grandma Dyer.

were left in the capable hands of her mother, Grandma Dyer, with her sisters Belle and Kitty assisting. Nevertheless, this rupture from their parents at such a young age must have been keenly felt by the siblings; KM would forever after have a deep-seated affection for her beloved Grandma, whose unwavering affection for this awkward child remained steadfast. At probably the most traumatic moment of her life, in June 1909, alone in Bavaria awaiting the birth of her child (which would be still-born), KM would write a diary entry addressed to Garnet Trowell, the baby's father:

> The only adorable thing I can imagine is for my Grandmother to put me to bed – & bring me a bowl of hot bread & milk & standing, her hands folded – the left thumb over the right – and say in her adorable voice:– 'There darling – isn't that nice'. Oh, what a miracle of happiness that would be. To wake later to find her turning down the bedclothes to see if your feet were cold – & wrapping them up in a little pink singlet softer than a cat's fur . . . Alas![15]

And as late as 1922, in a diary entry on 1 January, she would write: 'I dreamed I sailed to Egypt with Grandma, a very white boat,' and three weeks later on 21 January:

Grandma's birthday.

Where is that photograph of my dear Love leaning against her husband's shoulder, with her hair parted so meekly and her eyes raised. I love it. I long to have it. For one thing Mother gave it to me at a time when she loved me. But for another – so much more important – it is she, my own grandma, young and lovely. That arm, that baby sleeve with the velvet ribbon – I must see them again. And one day I must write about Grandma at length, especially of her beauty in her bath – when she was about sixty. Wiping herself with the towel. I remember now how lovely she seemed to me. And her fine linen, her throat, her scent. I have never really described her yet.[16]

Though we are only able to trace a few of the family's movements at this time, we know that KM was just six months old when, having developed jaundice, she was taken to Anakiwa by her Grandma, together with her two older sisters, Vera and Chaddie, to stay with Uncle Cradock and his wife Harriet. Mantz records how, in later life, her cousins remembered her as a '"yellow, ill-looking baby", who took an inexplicable fancy to a certain stone in the garden, and refused to be quiet unless they sat on the uncomfortable seat and nursed her'.[17]

As a two-year-old child, still the baby of the family, KM 'turned to her own duality for companionship – as Katherine turned, later, to Kezia'.[18] KM would

Figure 3.7 The Beauchamp sisters, c. 1890.

Figure 3.8 Family group of the Nathans, who lived next door to the Beauchamps at 11 Tinakori Rd (the 'Samuel Josephs').

develop a sense of solitariness and isolation that would stay with her all her life, and which, early on, mutated into irrational fears – mainly of the dark and of the wind – turning to nightmares that also haunted her as an adult. In 'The Aloe', Kezia is depicted as having similar fears, as the daylight fades and she finds herself alone in 11 Tinakori Road:

> As she stood the day flickered out and sombre dusk entered the empty house, thievish dusk stealing the shapes of things, sly dusk painting the shadows. At her heels crept the wind, snuffling and howling. The windows shook, a creaking came from the walls and floors, a piece of loose iron on the roof banged forlornly – Kezia did not notice these things severally, but she was suddenly quite, quite still with wide open eyes and knees pressed together – terribly frightened. Her old bogey, the dark, had overtaken her, and now there was no lighted room to make a despairing dash for. Useless to call 'Grandma' – useless to wait for the servant girl's cheerful stumping up the stairs to pull down the blinds and light the bracket lamp . . . There was only Lottie in the garden. If she began to call Lottie *now* and went on

calling her loudly all the while she flew down the stairs and out of the house she might escape from *It* in time. It was round like the sun. It had a face. *It* smiled, but *It* had no eyes. *It* was yellow. When she was put to bed with two drops of aconite in a medicine glass *It* breathed very loudly and firmly and *It* had been known on certain particularly fearful occasions to turn round and round. *It* hung in the air. That was all she knew and even that much had been very difficult to explain to the Grandmother. Nearer came the terror and more plain to feel the 'silly' smile. She snatched her hands from the window pane, opened her mouth to call Lottie, and fancied that she did call loudly, though she made no sound . . . *It* was at the top of the stairs; *It* was at the bottom of the stairs, waiting in the little dark passage, guarding the back door —[19]

These irrational fears never left KM, and nightmares, especially later, when seriously ill with tuberculosis, would haunt many night-time hours. She also developed a violent temper from a young age, something else which stayed with her all her life, and which, even as an adult, she occasionally found hard to curb.

Another child was born in the house on 11 October 1890, almost exactly two years after KM's own birth: Gwendoline Burnell Beauchamp. KM now had yet another sister to compete with for her precious Grandma's affections. In a long diary entry of May 1917, KM recalls Gwen's birth and death, and her very earliest memories of childhood:

Things happened so simply then, without preparation and without any shock. They let me go into my mother's room (I remember standing on tiptoe using both hands to turn the big white china doorhandle) & there lay my mother in bed with her arms along the sheet and there sat my grandmother before the fire with a baby in a flannel across her knees. My mother paid no attention to me at all – perhaps she was asleep for my Grandmother nodded & said in a voice scarcely above a whisper 'Come & see your new little sister'. I tiptoed to her voice across the room & she parted the flannel and I saw a little round head with a tuft of goldy hair on it and a tiny face with eyes shut – white as snow. 'Is it alive' I asked. 'Of course' said Grandmother – 'look at her holding my finger'. And yes a hand scarcely bigger than my doll's in a frilled sleeve was wound round her finger. Do you like her, said the grandmother. Yes. Is she going to play with the doll's house? By & bye said the grandmother – & I felt very pleased. Mrs Heywood had just given us the doll's house. It was a beautiful one with a verandah & balcony & a door that opened and shut and two chimneys. I wanted badly to show it to somebody else. Her name is Gwen, said the grandmother. Kiss her. I bent down & kissed the little goldy tuft– but she took no notice. She lay quite quite still with her eyes shut. Now go & kiss Mother said the grandmother. But Mother did not want to kiss me. Very languid, leaning against the pillows she was eating some sago. The sun shone through the windows & winked on the brass knobs of the big bed. After that Grandmother came into the nursery with Gwen and sat in front of the nursery fire in the rocking chair with her. Meg & Tadpole were away staying with Aunt Harriet Beauchamp, and they had gone before the new doll's house arrived so that was why I so longed to have somebody to show it to. I had gone all through it myself from the kitchen to the dining room up into the bedrooms into the drawing room with the doll's lamp on the table heaps & heaps of times. When will she play with it? I asked Grandmother. By & bye darling. It was spring – our garden was full of big white lilies. I used to run out & sniff them & come in again with my nose all yellow. Can't she go out. At last one very fine day she was wrapped in the new shawl & Grandmother carried her into the cherry orchard & walked up and down under the falling cherry flowers. Grandmother wore a grey dress with white pansies on it. The doctor's carriage was waiting at the door & the doctor's little dog Jackie rushed at me & snapped at my bare legs. When we went back to the nursery & the new shawl was taken away little white petals like feathers fell out of the folds – but Gwen did not look at them. She lay in Grandmother's arms, her eyes just open to show a line of blue, her face very white &the one tuft of goldy hair standing up on her head. All day & all night grandmother's arms were full. I had no lap to climb into, no pillow to rest against – they belonged to Gwen. But Gwen did not notice this. She never put up her hand to play with the silver brooch that was a moon with five little owls sitting on it. She never pulled Grandmother's watch out of her bodice & opened the back by herself to see Grandfather's hair. She never buried her head close to smell the lavender water or took up Grandmother's spectacle case & wondered at it being really silver. She just lay still & let herself be rocked. Down in the kitchen one day old Mrs McElvie came to the door & asked Bridget about the poor little mite. Bridget said 'Kept alive on bullock's blood hotted in a saucer over a candle.' After that I felt frightened of Gwen. I decided that even when she did play with the dolls house I would not let her go upstairs into the bedrooms – only downstairs & then only when I saw she could look. Late one evening I sat by the fire on my little carpet hassock & Grandmother rocked, singing the song she used to sing me, but more gently. Suddenly she stopped & I looked up. Gwen opened her eyes & turned her little round head to the fire & looked & looked at it & then – turned her eyes up to the face bending over her. I saw her tiny body stretch out & her hands flew up. Ah! Ah! Ah! called the grandmother. Bridget

dressed her [i.e. me] next morning. When I went into the nursery I sniffed.
A big vase of the white lilies was standing on the table. Grandmother sat
in her chair to one side with Gwen in her lap, & a funny little man with
his head in a black bag was standing behind a box of china eggs. 'Now' he
said and I saw my grandmother's face change as she bent over little Gwen.
Thank you said the man coming out of the bag. The picture was hung over
the nursery fire. I thought it looked very nice. The doll's house was in it
too – verandah & balcony and all. Gran held me up to kiss my little sister.[20]

In light of the above, KM's most famous story, 'The Doll's House' (1921), can
clearly be considered a homage to her dead baby sister (the celebrated Burnell
New Zealand cycle of stories being named after her dead sibling's – and her
mother's – middle name), since this diary entry, written four years before the
story, presages leading characters, including Mrs Kelvey.[21]

There is a poignant photograph of Grandma Dyer holding the dead baby
Gwendoline (a mawkish Victorian custom), with the windows of a large doll's

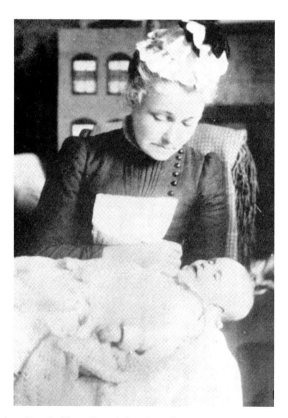

Figure 3.9 Grandma Dyer holding Gwendoline Beauchamp.

Figure 3.10 Gwendoline Beauchamp's grave, Bolton Street Cemetery, Wellington.

house visible in the top left-hand corner, just as described in the above recollection. Curiously, both sisters would die on the same day – 9 January – Gwendoline of infantile cholera in 1891, aged just three months, and KM in 1923 of tuberculosis, aged thirty-four. Gwendoline was also the only one of Harold's and Annie's six children to be buried in New Zealand. Her small grave can still be seen in its original location in Wellington's Bolton Street cemetery (numerous other graves having been controversially moved – or destroyed – to make way for a motorway).[22] Vera and Chaddie ('Meg and Tadpole') had been sent away to the Anakiwa homestead of Harold's Uncle Cradock and his wife Harriet, due to the burden of the new baby, leaving just KM at home in the care of her grandmother.

Poor Annie could scarcely have recovered from the death of Gwendoline when she fell pregnant again just a few months later; Jeanne Worthington Beauchamp was born on 20 May 1892, also at no. 11 Tinakori Road. From this time onwards, however, family sources revealed that Annie's famous aloofness (exemplified by Linda Burnell in 'Prelude' and 'At the Bay') really came to the fore. She was worn-out from child-bearing and the loss of a baby:

Her husband, with his continual need of her support, took what time and life she had to spare. The children flitted about her in the little box-like house. She would go out among the flowers, for which she had a passion: arum lilies and pincushions around the little square mat of lawn in the front garden; and to the wild gully, at the back – filled with green and tree ferns; beyond that, the world appeared unreal.[23]

And so the role of mother was handed over to the grandmother, as was the housekeeping and the cooking.

Chapter 4   Chesney Wold, Karori: 1893–1898

Following the death of his daughter Gwendoline – as well as his brother and sister – from infectious disease, Harold Beauchamp took the bold step of moving his young family away from Wellington, hoping thus to prevent any further deaths. He took a five-year lease on a large house with a fourteen-acre garden (more of a 'farmlet', as he himself noted) called Chesney Wold, named after the estate of Sir Leicester Dedlock and Honoria, Lady Dedlock, in Charles Dickens's novel, *Bleak House*. The house, at no. 372 Karori Road, was three miles from Wellington, in a small settlement called Karori, surrounded by what was then mainly open country. Stephen Lancaster, who had emigrated from Blackburn in Lancashire to New Zealand in 1857, had built the house in 1866. He farmed a large area in Karori, and was one of the main suppliers of milk to the small colonial capital. He was also responsible for building an assortment of houses in Karori, three of which, including Chesney Wold, were lived in by his family. The settlement was remote at that time, the very name Karori, which in Maori means 'devious', reflecting the journey undertaken by travellers from Wellington for three miles along a difficult, twisting little road.

In the large gardens of Chesney Wold were trees and flowerbeds, surrounded by paddocks, an orchard, and various stables and farm buildings. The house had been built at right angles to the road, facing east. In front of it, a circular drive, which tried to look grand, swept around a shrubbery and a lawn, in the middle of which grew a solitary aloe. Harold would walk the three miles – downhill – into town most mornings (taking about an hour), and Pat Sheehan, the Beauchamp's newly acquired Irish handyman, would collect him from town in a horse and cart. As Harold noted in his *Reminiscences,*

Figure 4.1 View from the Karori tram, showing Old Karori Road.

Figure 4.2 Chesney Wold, Karori, Wellington.

Figure 4.3 Chesney Wold, Karori, 1880s.

Figure 4.4 Chesney Wold, Karori, 1893.

I have always been a great walker, and I found that though we kept two horses at Karori I was able, by walking into town or out, to get more regular exercise there than would have been the case had we been living in town.[1]

Harold threw himself into life in the small rural community, becoming a vestry-man at St Mary's Church, a benefactor, and Chairman of the local branch of the Liberal and Labour Federation.

Epidemics might have been left behind in Wellington, but illness – influenza in particular – was to be found everywhere, and Karori was no exception. A letter written by a resident in 1895 makes this point clear, with even a reference to Annie:

> So many are ill here; Mrs Callanan, influenza, mending. Mrs Davies, very ill, Mrs Beauchamp, ill, Mrs McKenzie [. . .] made a curry, crushed some bones [. . .] A sharp piece of bone stuck in her throat and she can't swallow anything and is getting very weak. She has a 4 months baby too. The Doctor can't find the bone. [. . .] Then Mrs Bulkeley has pleurisy. And Judge Richmond died of flu on Saturday. It went to his lungs – he was 74 and greatly beloved.[2]

Yet, influenza and crushed bones aside, it was hard to imagine a more perfect setting for raising children, and KM spent five of the most formative years of her childhood in Karori, until the age of ten. Years later, as a professional writer, she would draw on her rich memories of her Karori childhood to fashion some of the most memorable stories ever written by a New Zealand author, using innovative, experimental techniques that we now associate with literary modernism. Stories based on life in Karori include 'About Pat' (1905), 'Autumns: I' (1915), 'Prelude' (1917) and 'The Doll's House' (1921).

'About Pat', written when KM was seventeen and still at school in London, is a clear recollection of the family's life at Chesney Wold (published in the *Queen's College Magazine* in December 1905), which begins:

> In the days of our childhood we lived in a great old rambling house planted lonesomely in the midst of huge gardens, orchards and paddocks. We had few toys, but – far better – plenty of good, strong mud and a flight of concrete steps that grew hot in the heat of the sun and became dreams of ovens.[3]

KM's recollections in this youthful piece bring to life the Karori garden and the lives of the three eldest siblings. Helping Pat in the garden was Mr McKelvey, father of the two little girls later immortalised in 'The Doll's House', who 'in his soberer moments was a wizard with the garden beds'.[4] A little man, with a bushy face, he made the most extraordinary sounds. One day, he told the children

Figure 4.5 The Karori Hills and McKelveys' house, 1890s.

"'I tried to marry once before". We said, "Why didn't you, Mr. McKelvey?" "She said 'No', not 'Yes'.""[5] His wife, Mrs McKelvey, was the local washer-woman, employed by many families in Karori.

In a diary entry from 1915, KM, in her Kezia persona, recalled a conversation overheard between various adult members of the family at Chesney Wold:

> Sitting astride the bow window ledge, smelling the heliotrope – or was it the sea? – half of Kezia was in the garden and half of her in the room.
> [. . .]
> 'How marvellously that ribbon has lasted, Harrie! Marvellously!'
> That was Aunt Beryl's voice. She, Aunt Harrie and Mother sat at the round table with big shallow teacups in front of them.
> In the dusky light, in their white puffed-up muslin blouses with wing sleeves, they were three birds at the edge of a lily pond. Beyond them the shadowy room melted into the shadow; the gold picture frames were traced upon the air; the cut-glass doorknob glittered; a song – a white butterfly with wings outspread – clung to the ebony piano.[6]

Details of the room at Chesney Wold come to life: gold picture frames, crystal doorknobs and an ebony piano. In an unpublished story from 1906 called 'My Potplants', more glimpses of Karori are to be found:

Down at the bottom of our garden ran a little stream, and here I spent many happy hours. With my shoes and socks off, and my frock tucked high all round me, I used to wade, and attempt to catch certain very tiny fish that swam and played in its depths – or rather, its shallownesses. If I ever did catch one I always put it in a glass jam jar filled with water and carried it home to keep till it should grow into a whale. Alas, it never did grow at all though it was not for lack of care and attention.[7]

In a later story called 'Autumns: I' (1915), KM's memory vividly recaptures the Karori homestead:

There were two orchards belonging to the old house. One, that we called the 'wild' orchard lay beyond the vegetable garden; it was planted with bitter cherries and damsons and transparent yellow plums. For some reason it lay under a cloud; we never played there, we did not even trouble to pick up the fallen fruit; and there, every Monday morning, to the round open space in the middle, the servant girl and the washerwoman carried the wet linen; grandmother's nightdresses, father's striped shirts, the hired man's cotton trousers and the servant girl's 'dreadfully vulgar' salmon pink flannelette drawers jigged and slapped in horrid familiarity.

But the other orchard, far away and hidden from the house, lay at the foot of a little hill and stretched right over to the edge of the paddocks – to the clumps of wattles bobbing yellow in the bright and the blue gums with their streaming sickle-shaped leaves. There, under the fruit trees the grass grew so thick and coarse that it tangled and knotted in your shoes as you walked and even on the hottest day it was damp to touch when you stopped and parted it this way and that looking for windfalls – the apples marked with a bird's beak, the big bruised pears, the quinces, so good to eat with a pinch of salt, but so delicious to smell that you could not bite for sniffing . . .[8]

In all these accounts, KM often spent time alone. As the middle of five children, she neither 'belonged' to the older set of Vera and Chaddie, nor was old enough to play with the 'babies', Jeanne and the new-born son, Leslie Heron (known to the family as Chummie or 'Boy'), born on 21 February 1894 in the civilised surroundings of Nurse Patrick's private hospital in Upper Featherston Terrace in Thorndon, less than a year after the family's move to Karori. He was baptised at St Mary's Church, Karori, on 9 December 1894, as, strangely enough, were Annie Beauchamp and her sister, Belle.

In the late 1920s, the Anakiwa Beauchamps related how "'To see Vera was to love her [. . .] to see Kathleen was to remember her.'"[9] Vera was the perfect eldest child, obedient, responsible, always more of an adult than a child. Chaddie was pretty and affectionate, and charmed everyone who met her. KM, prone to chubbiness (the Nathan boys who had lived next door to no. 11 Tinakori Road used to shout 'fatty' at her over the fence), developed a fearsome temper as well as an idiosyncratic sense of humour, both traits inherited from her father. One acquaintance of KM's remembered being told 'that though she loved flowers, she hated to see them picked, and that in her childhood she saw somebody throw withered flowers from a vase into the fire, and had cried hysterically [. . .] to think of burning such exquisite personalities'.[10] It did not help matters that, in 1896, KM had started wearing steel-rimmed spectacles. Here was yet another reason for her to be singled out – to be different. No biographer has ever been able to ascertain why they were deemed necessary at this time; her capacity to note the smallest details of everyone and everything are not the normal traits of a myopic child. Nevertheless, she soon outgrew them and did not wear glasses as an adult.

When Harold was in the mood to be jolly, he would play with the children, and sing songs to them at bedtime, such as:

On the banks of the Wamangaroa
They discovered the bones of a moa,
The largest I ween that e'er was seen
On the banks of the Wamangaroa.
Its back measured two feet by the tape, Sir,
And it was a most elegant shape, Sir –
And he dug his own grave by the bright rippling wave
On the banks of the Wamangaroa.[11]

He would also teach them phrases that his father Arthur had learnt from the Maori: 'Kanui taku aroka atu kia oke (Great is my love to you) . . . Kia whiti tonu te ra kirunga kiaoke (May the sunshine of happiness ever rest upon you).'[12] Very occasionally, the children would be given a rare treat and allowed to go to Harold's place of work, as KM recalled much later in a diary entry for 21 May 1918, where an empty building brought back recollections of her father's office: 'I smell it as that. I see the cage of the clumsy wooden goods lift & the tarred ropes hanging.'[13] Another talisman of her childhood was her father's brass pig pen-wipe, which always sat on his desk. With her love of the miniature, it captivated her from an early age. Harold would give it to her when she finally departed for England in 1908, and it remained one of her most treasured possessions. In her final will, dated 14 August 1921 (having originally asked Murry to leave it to Vera),[14] she poignantly requested that it be returned to her father, along with her bible.

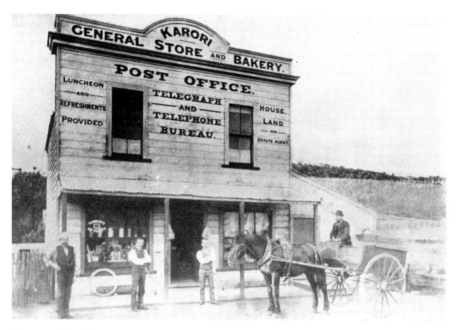

Figure 4.6 The Karori store.

Interviews with friends and family of the Beauchamps offer an overall negative impression of KM at this time:

> In fact, those who were grown-ups then – teachers, aunts, friends – say that Kass Beauchamp was 'the last child in the world they ever expected to become a writer.' To them, she was 'careless,' 'lazy,' 'impatient,' 'indifferent,' 'dull,' 'slow and fat.' They felt she needed prodding to quicken her perception and to make her more alert, and sweeter – 'like her sisters.' That she should be hypersensitive enough to remember for years a chance look between the grown-ups – passed over her head – would certainly have seemed to them incredible. As it would have seemed had they been told she bore it hard that her sisters seemed preferred before her, since everyone responded to their soft sweetness.[15]

Years later, Jane Donald, a teacher at the school, remembered how 'every morning for several years I used to meet Kathleen Beauchamp, a fat little girl, trailing along, well behind her sisters' on the walk to school.[16] A fellow pupil noted that she was also prone to severe colds and was frequently absent from school as a result.[17] KM was certainly a difficult child but she could be soft-hearted, as the story 'Mary' (1910) demonstrates, the plot centring on an actual event which happened between herself and Chaddie (here called 'Mary', her

Figure 4.7 The Beauchamp family.

Figure 4.8 Katherine Mansfield with her brother and sisters at Karori school, 1898.

true middle name), one day at school in Karori. Here again, KM reworks actual events into autobiographical fiction, bringing her home life at Chesney Wold into sharp relief:

> On poetry afternoons grandmother let Mary and me wear Mrs. Gardner's white hemstitched pinafores because we had nothing to do with ink or pencil.
>
> Triumphant and feeling unspeakably beautiful, we would fly along the road, swinging our kits and half chanting, half singing our new piece. I always knew my poetry, but Mary, who was a year and a half older, never knew hers. In fact, lessons of any sort worried her soul and body. [. . .]
>
> I was a strong, fat little child who burst my buttons and shot out of my skirts to grandmother's entire satisfaction, but Mary was a 'weed'.[18]

On this particular day, the children had been told to learn Thomas Hood's poem 'I remember, I remember' by heart, with prizes to be awarded for the best recitation on each side of the little classroom. On KM's side, the prize was a 'green-plush bracket with a yellow china frog stuck on it'. KM, whose forte was reciting (a gift that would stay with her into adulthood), was the frontrunner for the prize, as 'Mary' well knew: "'Kass", she said, "think what a s'prise if I got it after all; I believe mother would go mad with joy. I know I should. But then . . . I'm so stupid, I know."' From this point in the story, Kass is determined that her sister will win the prize. She wills Mary to give a good recital, but Mary breaks down and her performance is dire. Kass, whose performance is as brilliant as everyone knew it would be, goes up to the teacher and says: "'If I've got it, put Mary's name. Don't tell anybody, and don't let the others tell her – oh, please."' The teacher announces that Mary indeed has won the prize.

> On the way home we passed the Karori bus going home from town full of business men. The driver gave us a lift, and we bundled in. We knew all the people.
>
> 'I've won a prize for po'try!' cried Mary, in a high, excited voice.
>
> 'Good old Mary!' they chorused.
>
> Again she was the center of admiring popularity.
>
> 'Well, Kass, you needn't look so doleful,' said Mr. England, laughing at me; 'you aren't clever enough to win everything.'
>
> 'I know,' I answered, wishing I were dead and buried.
>
> I did not go into the house when we reached home, but wandered down to the loft and watched Pat mixing the chicken food.
>
> But the bell rang at last, and with slow steps I crept up to the nursery.
>
> Mother and grandmother were there with two callers. Alice had come up from the kitchen; Vera was sitting with her arm round Mary's neck.

'Well, that's wonderful, Mary,' mother was saying. 'Such a lovely prize, too. Now, you see what you really can do, darling.'

'That will be nice for you to show your little girls when you grow up,' said grandmother.

Slowly I slipped into my chair.

'Well, Kass, you don't look very pleased,' cried one of the tactful callers. Mother looked at me severely.

'Don't say you are going to be a sulky child about your sister,' she said.

Even Mary's bright little face clouded.

'You are glad, aren't you, dear?' she questioned.

'I'm frightfully glad,' I said, holding on to the handle of my mug, and seeing all too plainly the glance of understanding that passed between the grown-ups.[19]

Bitterly regretting her actions, Kass determines to tell Mary the truth. That night, after crying into her pillow, she walks across the bedroom to Mary's bed, but Mary looks so innocent that she cannot go through with it. Her heart melts, and so instead, 'I stooped and kissed her.'[20]

What does this episode tell us about the young KM? That her mother tended to think the worst of her; that other people tended to think the worst of her; that it was usual for her to spend time in the garden with Pat the handyman (as we might deduce from other stories); and that she herself felt very misunderstood, although she believed herself to have a wicked streak, for, after crying into her pillow, Kass states, 'the Devil entered into my soul.' Compared to Vera and Chaddie, she certainly must have come across as challenging, and adults are always quick to assign character traits to children, which are then seemingly set in stone for life. KM seems always to have been the odd one out. In fact, in 1897, KM did win the school composition prize, for a short story called 'A Sea Voyage', now lost, but presumably based on a trip the Beauchamps had made in December 1894 (summertime in New Zealand) to Picton, the little harbour on the tip of the South Island, where her paternal grandparents Arthur and Mary had their home, and of course to visit the Anakiwa homestead nearby, where Great-Uncle Cradock and his wife Harriet lived. As an adult, KM would later remember with great fondness these regular childhood trips to the South Island, most memorably depicted in her story 'The Voyage' (1921):

The sun was not up yet, but the stars were dim, and the cold pale sky was the same colour as the cold pale sea. On the land a white mist rose and fell. Now they could see quite plainly dark bush. Even the shapes of the umbrella ferns showed, and those strange silvery withered trees that are like skeletons. . . . Now they could see the landing-stage and some little houses, pale too, clustered together, like shells on the lid of a box. The other passengers tramped up and down, but more slowly than they had the night before, and they looked gloomy.

And now the landing-stage came out to meet them. Slowly it swam towards the Picton boat, and a man holding a coil of rope, and a cart with a small drooping horse and another man sitting on the step, came too.[21]

Harold's cousin Ethel, the daughter of Cradock and Harriet, remembered KM clearly in later life, noting:

[Kass] used to irritate her father, and he didn't pay much attention to her. He showed marked preference for Vera. Kass used to sit about in all sorts of positions, dreaming, and he kept at her, trying to make her sit up straight. [. . .] She was different from the rest of the family and looked different – fat and sallow. [. . .] She loved to hear about Maori legends, told by Cradock Beauchamp's old maid Armena, who apparently had five husbands buried in the old Maori burial ground on the hill near the homestead. [. . . O]nce KM left her old leather rag doll, Hinemoa, hanging from a tree in a ravine where the children had been playing. She was inconsolable, so in heavy rain, one of the boys was sent to fetch it and returned carrying the wet leather doll by the arm, and with such a red face.[22]

Closer to KM in age – and convivial playmates – were her cousins Eric and Barrie (Barrington) Waters, the children of Uncle Val Waters and his wife, Annie's sister Agnes. When the Beauchamps moved to Karori, so did the Waters family, about a mile further along the Karori Road from Chesney Wold, to a little house known as 'the monkey tree cottage'.[23] Eric was a small, painfully thin, effeminate little boy, in complete contrast to his mischievous older brother Barrie and his faithful spaniel. KM was always fond of her Uncle Val, recreated as the sympathetic character Jonathan Trout in the Burnell stories. In a letter written to Dorothy Brett in 1921, she would remember him: 'One of [Cézanne's] men gave me quite a shock. He is the spit of a man I've just written about – one Jonathan Trout. To the life. I wish I could cut him out & put him in my book.'[24]

Valentine Waters was a kind, self-effacing man, who had a certain innocent outlook on life, which cost him promotion at work:

He was a man of charm and kindness, yet he never got ahead. For years he was Assistant Secretary to the Post and Telegraphs, when he should have been head of a Government department. Opportunities came for him to advance; his charm advanced him, but his kindness held him back. There

Figure 4.9 Agnes Mansfield Dyer, Katherine Mansfield's aunt.

Figure 4.10 Frederick Valentine Waters (known as Val), Katherine Mansfield's uncle.

Figure 4.11 Barrie and Eric Waters.

was always someone who, he thought, was entitled to promotion before him, or someone who, he thought, needed it more. So his real life was lived in his hobbies. He had two. One was music. He was baritone soloist with the Wellington Musical Union (under Mr. Parker); and organist at St. Mark's Church; and he led the choir at Karori. His other hobby was gardening – or perhaps it was his excuse for playing with the children – for his results were as varied and unexpected as his changes in appearance. He tied a handkerchief over his head, donned dungarees for his work, and was always wheeling something in a barrow; but the children never knew what face he would be wearing.[25]

He also used to enjoy organizing theatrical events for the children at the parochial hall and there exists a charming photograph of the four Beauchamp girls dressed up as characters from Tom Thumb, for a children's fancy-dress party he had arranged. He was choirmaster at St Mary's church in Karori from 1894 to 1912 and renowned for his fine baritone voice. Val's wife Agnes was an entirely different creature, similar in her delicate health to her younger sister, Annie Beauchamp. Agnes's headaches were legendary in the family, and

Figure 4.12 Four of the Beauchamp children dressed up, 1896.

the children would tiptoe around her, whilst the young maid/housekeeper, Rose Ridler, an orphan who had been taken in by the family at the age of twelve, saw to the day-to-day running of the house.[26]

Rose also taught Sunday school in the afternoons at the Karori Parochial Hall, which the Beauchamp girls attended in stiffly starched aprons. For the main church service in the morning, they were accompanied by their grandmother; if they went in the evening, then Harold would take them. In the absence of any streetlights, a lantern similar to the one described in 'Prelude' would see them home. During the family's stay in Karori, Harold was on the vestry and gave some money to fund three prizes for essays on the children's monthly sermon. Lily McKelvey, whom KM depicted together with her sister so poignantly in 'The Doll's House', won the third prize. Harold and Uncle Val also helped to clear the debt owed by the parish of Karori to the diocese: 'F. V. Waters, the choirmaster, arranged a series of concerts and socials, circulars were sent out by Harold Beauchamp, and a ladies' committee was formed to do the collecting.'[27] KM and her two older sisters were also bridesmaids at St Mary's for the wedding of another of Annie's sisters, Edith Amy Dyer.

There is a poignant postscript to the intertwined lives of the Beauchamps and Waters families. When Vera returned to Wellington on a visit from Canada in November 1918, the ship she travelled in, the *Niagara*, brought the infamous post-World War One influenza outbreak to New Zealand. Vera herself arrived ill and both Harold and Uncle Val visited her on board ship. Both men then contracted the virulent virus. Harold and Vera recovered but Val was dead within a week. A window in St Mary's Church, Karori, commemorates the respected vestryman and choirmaster, with the inscription: 'To the glory of God and in / loving memory of / Frederick Valentine Waters / for thirty years a lay reader & / choirmaster in this parish. / Erected by the parishioners 1919.'[28]

Karori School was the only educational institution for miles around and children from all levels of society were taught together. At the time the Beauchamps attended, all the children walked to school; in bad weather the roads could turn into muddy swamps, and as a result children often stayed at home. In the Karori school register for 1895–7, KM is recorded as having come joint second at the annual inspectors' examinations. Chaddie was significantly further down the list, and bottom was Lily, the elder of the two McKelvey girls.

Many years later, a fellow pupil at the school recorded an incident involving KM, when she was ten years old. The class teacher allegedly had little regard for the poorer children and always favoured those from 'better' families. As the teacher was about to cane a boy for snoring in class, KM's hand came between the boy and the cane, as she told the teacher:

> You are not to hit Percy Jones. [. . . He] is up every morning at 3 o' clock. He helps his father to milk the cows and then he has to deliver the milk in the town, come back home, have his breakfast, and be here by 9 o'clock. That's why you are not to hit him.[29]

The teacher left Percy alone. In the playground at the end of the day, there were shouts of 'Three cheers for Kass Beauchamp.' This story presages, of course, KM's championing of the poor 'Kelvey' children in 'The Doll's House'. Her sense of injustice was marked for someone so young.

The school was the same as the one described in the story 'Mary'. Here is KM's description of it in 'The Doll's House':

> the fact was, the school the Burnell children went to was not at all the kind of place their parents would have chosen if there had been any choice. But there was none. It was the only school for miles. And the consequence was all the children of the neighbourhood, the Judge's little girls, the doctor's daughters, the store-keeper's children, the milkman's, were forced to mix together. Not to speak of there being an equal number of rude, rough little boys as well.[30]

Figure 4.13 Katherine Mansfield, aged 10.

Figure 4.14 Leslie Beauchamp, aged 3.

The stars of the story are the Kelvey sisters, Lil and Else:

> But the line had to be drawn somewhere. It was drawn at the Kelveys. Many of the children, including the Burnells, were not allowed even to speak to them. They walked past the Kelveys with their heads in the air, and as they set the fashion in all matters of behaviour, the Kelveys were shunned by everybody. Even the teacher had a special voice for them, and a special smile for the other children when Lil Kelvey came up to her desk with a bunch of dreadfully common-looking flowers.
>
> They were the daughters of a spry, hard-working little washer-woman, who went about from house to house by the day. This was awful enough. But where was Mr Kelvey? Nobody knew for certain. But everybody said he was in prison. So they were the daughters of a washerwoman and a jailbird. Very nice company for other people's children! And they looked it. Why Mrs Kelvey made them so conspicuous was hard to understand. The truth was they were dressed in 'bits' given to her by the people for whom she worked. Lil, for instance, who was a stout, plain child, with big freckles, came to school in a dress made from a green art-serge table-cloth of the Burnells', with red plush sleeves from the Logans' curtains. Her hat, perched on top of her high forehead, was a grown-up woman's hat, once the property of Miss Lecky, the postmistress. It was turned up at the back and trimmed with a large scarlet quill. What a little guy she looked! It was impossible not to laugh. And her little sister, our Else, wore a long white dress, rather like a nightgown, and a pair of little boy's boots. But whatever our Else wore she would have looked strange. She was a tiny wishbone of a child, with cropped hair and enormous solemn eyes – a little white owl. Nobody had ever seen her smile; she scarcely ever spoke. She went through life holding on to Lil, with a piece of Lil's skirt screwed up in her hand. Where Lil went, our Else followed. In the playground, on the road going to and from school, there was Lil marching in front and our Else holding on behind. Only when she wanted anything, or when she was out of breath, our Else gave Lil a tug, a twitch, and Lil stopped and turned round. The Kelveys never failed to understand each other.[31]

In 1931, Mantz met Else, still living in Karori. Mantz and her companion were invited into a ramshackle little cottage, with items strewn everywhere: "'The mantelpiece fell", said Our Else softly, "and we had to leave the things about". Things, Pampas grass, China knobs. Guilded willows. Seared wood.' Lil, she said, was now married with seven children:

> Our Else looked at the crowded walls. 'I never seemed to care for anything, only drawing; I had to give that up when father was ill'. She raised the

candle. A brownish castle tottered on brownish crags – like a chromo – surprisingly well done. [. . .] 'My husband isn't with us. He had an accident the first year and we put him away at <u>Porirua</u>'.[32]

Clearly, KM never forgot the young McKelvey sisters, and the young Kass Beauchamp / Kezia Burnell was moved by their situation in life. Another of KM's schoolfriends, Lena, remembered the doll's house well and especially the little lamp, 'with its white globe shade, a round bowl with colored liquid in it, and a round base'. When the family moved back to Wellington, she remembered the doll's house on the back of the dray,[33] and how unusual it was for anyone to move so quickly in and out of Karori, since most residents had been there for two generations.[34]

In his introduction to the 1933 biography, Murry makes an important point when he notes that

New Zealand is still a relatively small community, and Katherine Mansfield's memories of the people there which she used as material for her stories were sometimes such as to create resentment and heartburning. People still living were disturbed by the reflections of themselves which they found, or thought they found, in her crystal mirror. Further, it seemed to them that what she had done was very easy to do; it consisted in 'copying' the characters she had known.[35]

There are many recorded instances of family and acquaintances being openly put out by KM's very true-to-life portrayals of actual events and characters. Of course, details described can sometimes differ from historical fact, but overall her stories offer a clearer picture of her childhood than any of her notebooks or letters. Even names are barely disguised. Beauchamp becomes the literal translation – Fairfield, McKelvey – Kelvey and so on. There was no mistaking who was being depicted. Uncle Val Waters, portrayed as Jonathan Trout, speaks in the romantic, idealistic way that so marked him out from his brother-in-law, Harold Beauchamp / Stanley Burnell (Burnell being Annie Beauchamp's and KM's sister Gwendoline's middle name):

At that moment an immense wave lifted Jonathan, rode past him, and broke along the beach with a joyful sound. What a beauty! And now there came another. That was the way to live – carelessly, recklessly, spending oneself. He got on to his feet and began to wade towards the shore, pressing his toes into the firm, wrinkled sand. To take things easy, not to fight against the ebb and flow of life, but to give way to it – that was what was needed. It was this tension that was all wrong. To live – to live! And the perfect morning, so fresh and fair, basking in the light, as though laughing at its own beauty, seemed to whisper, 'Why not?'[36]

Looking at him as he lay there, Linda thought again how attractive he was. It was strange to think that he was only an ordinary clerk, that Stanley earned twice as much money as he. What was the matter with Jonathan? He had no ambition; she supposed that was it. And yet one felt he was gifted, exceptional. He was passionately fond of music; every spare penny he had went on books. He was always full of new ideas, schemes, plans. But nothing came of it all. The new fire blazed in Jonathan; you almost heard it roaring softly as he explained, described and dilated on the new thing; but a moment later it had fallen in and there was nothing but ashes, and Jonathan went about with a look like hunger in his black eyes. At these times he exaggerated his absurd manner of speaking, and he sang in church – he was the leader of the choir – with such fearful dramatic intensity that the meanest hymn put on an unholy splendour.[37]

While presented as fiction, this is also life-writing. KM's description here of her Uncle Val Waters would have been instantly recognisable to everyone who knew him. These passages, taken from 'At the Bay', written in 1921, were KM's homage to her dead uncle, who received only a passing mention in the first Burnell story, 'Prelude', published before his untimely death.

Chapter 5   Back to Thorndon:
75 Tinakori Road,
1898–1903

In early 1898 (KM had not yet turned ten), with the lease on Chesney Wold expiring later that year, Harold made the decision to move his family back to town, to Aunt Belle's immense relief, as suitors were hard to come by in Karori and she longed to be back in the city. Whilst they had all been living in Karori, Wellington's sewerage system had undergone a substantial upgrade; sewerage was no longer pumped directly into the harbour and the number of epidemics was now greatly reduced. It was a propitious time to return. Harold had never given

Figure 5.1 View over Wellington.

Figure 5.2 Entrance to the Botanical Gardens, Wellington.

Figure 5.3 Wellington Girls' High School.

up the lease on 11 Tinakori Road, the house where KM had been born, but as an increasingly prosperous businessman who now had five children to accommodate, as well as numerous relatives, that box-like house was clearly no longer suitable. Instead, he acquired a fourteen-room, two-storey mansion at 75 Tinakori Road, with formal gardens and tennis court, just up the road from no. 11 and a stone's throw from the Prime Minister's residence, further up the same road. The three girls were now moved from the little school in Karori and enrolled at Wellington Girls' High School, only a short walk from no. 75. Prior to the move back to town, the girls were to go to school every morning by horse-drawn bus.

These arrangements all made, in March 1898, Harold and Annie Beauchamp undertook the second of their trips 'home' to England, for both business and pleasure (Annie was always a keen sea-voyager), leaving the children once more in the care of Annie's mother, Grandma Dyer, and Aunt Belle, together with the handyman, Pat Sheehan, and Alice, the kitchen maid. In the parents' absence whilst they were still at sea, the organisation, packing and the move to no. 75 were undertaken in late April 1898.

Around this time, with Harold and Annie absent, Grandma Dyer, as a treat, would take the children to one of KM's favourite haunts, 'McNab's Tea Gardens' on the Woburn Road in Lower Hutt, not far from Wellington. A popular tourist attraction at the time, there were pleasure gardens, orchards and lawns, as well as monkeys, birds and squirrels. The gardens in particular were renowned for the prolific variety of plants they contained. KM would remember McNab's with fondness in the last year of her life. On 14 February 1922 she wrote to her friend Dorothy Brett,

> Do you know the scent of boronia? My grandma and I were very fond of going to a place called McNabs Tea gardens and there we used to follow our noses and track down the boronia bushes. Oh how I must have tired the darling out! It doesn't bear thinking about.[1]

And just five days later, with McNab's still impressed in her memory, she wrote to her youngest sister Jeanne about her friend, the author Walter de la Mare,

> I am so glad you like DelaMare. He is a wonderful person as well as poet. Do you know his book The Three Mullar Mulgars? It is the story of three monkeys – very nice monkeys – not like the ones in McNab's Gardens.[2]

Even Harold, in his *Reminiscences*, talked fondly of McNab's, when he and Belle would 'stroll' out there, 'have lunch and return to Wellington in the cool of the evening'.[3] That was some stroll: an approximate round trip of sixteen miles.

Annie kept a diary of the voyage on the R.M.S. *Ruahine* from March to May as a record for the children (aside from family letters, her only extant writing), with some entries made by Harold.[4] When they eventually arrived in London, the diary was posted back to the family. It was a long stay in England – they did not return until November. The diary entries begin on 19 March and end on 5 May, and comprise a daily record of events on board ship to amuse and inform the family back home. It is a fascinating document, for the biographical detail it offers, as well as for being a record of those long sea voyages undertaken by so many at that time. Ensconced in the 'First Saloon' (having paid the princely sum of £73.10.0, equivalent to over £7,000 today), Harold and Annie made a trip that was the acme of luxury and attentive service. They threw themselves into the on-board life, and Harold, ever the born leader, was made joint honorary secretary and treasurer of the Entertainments Committee. Annie was soon overcome with seasickness:

> The stewardess and Harold were most attentive. During the day I heard stray pieces of news through my porthole, which I can always keep open a little. My cabin is certainly the best in the ship, its so cosy and free from smells, and you feel the machinery so little. I only have to go downstairs twice a day, my lunches and afternoon tea is brought upstairs. [all *sic*][5]

On 23 March she celebrated her birthday with a cake and a tea party: 'I put the children's photograph on the table so they should be present too.'[6] Harold, always a strong singer, took part in many of the ship's musical events, as did Annie:

> Done a little practice on my guitar, the Dr. wants me to play Alabama Coon and Hal to sing it at the concert tomorrow night. Hal is singing in a glee with the Parsons and Mrs P. says he is a tenor and she wants him to take many parts.[7]

She noted: 'Tell Chad that there is a most lovely little cock canary on board that sings most beautifully and fancy he sings just as well at night. Sometimes we hear him sing after we have gone to bed, about eleven o'clock.'[8] It is tempting to think of KM remembering this little snippet, hurt that the little story was not meant for her and, in the last story she ever wrote, remembering that ship-board canary as she fashioned her own story about another one, seen during her stay in Paris in 1922. In fact, all the children were referred to specifically in the diary, except KM, which surely would have been noted by the sensitive nine-year-old.

At Montevideo, Annie left a few blank pages and these were filled by Harold. The difference in writing style and content is quite striking. Where Annie's entries were mostly about herself, her health, little tea parties and gossip about the rest of the First Saloon passengers, Harold's entry reads like a guide book:

> One of the principle places of interest is the cemetery, the statuary in which has cost several millions of pounds sterling.
> The population of the city is between 500,000 and 600,000. The climate,

which is, generally speaking, healthy, resembles that of Auckland, the latitude being about the same – the death rate is low, 14 in the 1000; whilst the birth rate is nearly 40 in the 1000.[9]

It is, in fact, possible that much of this long entry was copied verbatim from a guidebook on board ship to educate the children back home. Annie then resumed the entries from 9 April, and the talk reverted to social events on board, gossip and fashion:

> Everybody is dressed in the most summery garments, I am wearing my black skirt, green blouse, and brown hat, I am quite comfe and have nothing to get grubby, like the white blouse and skirt ladies, with stiff collar and cuffs which they grumble about being so fearfully uncomfe. [all *sic*][10]

It was perhaps from her mother that KM inherited her eye for the minutiae of daily life, and which would go on to become such a defining characteristic of her fiction.

Harold again resumed the entries as the ship approached Rio, with more factual information on their trip ashore with several of the other passengers. At this point in the journey, he went down with a fever, as did numerous others on board, and Annie looked after him, though, as she records, the role of nurse was clearly not one she relished: 'Unfortunately I am feeling a little tired after my efforts in looking after Hal yesterday.'[11] A fancy-dress ball brings the following entry: 'I have not told anyone but I am going as a New Woman in my <u>bloomers</u>, waistcoat shirt front and blue serge jacket.'[12] In the end – possibly at the behest of Harold, who, still weak after his illness, was unable to accompany her and guard her morals – she wrote, 'I am not going as a New Woman but as a little girl in short frocks';[13] 'I carried Rene's doll and looked about eight years old they all said mine was a splendid makeup. The Dr. went as a little girl of two, carrying a feeding bottle with him.'[14] To a modern sensibility, Annie's revised costume seems even more risqué than her first choice, but would certainly have amused her children, if not perhaps her mother and sister.

On 30 April, Harold once more made a few entries, noting, 'I had an awfully bad time for 14 days after leaving Rio, and think that I must have contracted a sort of malarial fever in that beautiful but disgustingly insanitary City, with which I never wish to renew my acquaintance.'[15] Ever practical, of the two parents, it was in fact Harold who wondered how the move to no. 75 was going: 'We are wondering whether our dear ones have left Karori, and are now comfortably ensconced at 75 Tinakori road, at any rate, we trust they are or will be within the next day or two.'[16] The ship arrived on 2 May in the

Figure 5.4 Katherine Mansfield with her family and Marion Ruddick, 1898, 75 Tinakori Road, Wellington.

Figure 5.5 Little George Street, Thorndon, Wellington, in flood, 1893.

Royal Albert Docks in London, where the couple were met by 'Uncle Henry' – Henry Herron Beauchamp, Harold's much-revered uncle – now in his seventies. Back in Wellington, the family's move to no. 75 was now complete.

In a notebook entry for the end of 1915 called 'Saunders Lane', KM recalled details of no. 75, which, six years later, would transmute into one of her most famous stories, 'The Garden Party' (1921):

> Our house in Tinakori Road stood far back from the road. It was a big white painted square house with a slender pillared verandah and balcony running all the way round. In the front from the verandah edge the garden sloped away in terraces & flights of concrete steps – down – until you reached the stone wall covered with nasturtiums that had three gates let into it – the visitors' gate, the Tradesman's gate, and a huge pair of old iron gates that were never used and clashed and clamoured when Bogey & I tried to swing on them.
>
> Tinakori road was not fashionable, it was very mixed. Of course there were some good houses in it – old ones like ours for instance, hidden away in wildish gardens, & there was no doubt that land there would become extremely valuable, as Father said, if one bought enough & hung on. It was high, it was healthy, the sun poured in all the windows all day long, and once we had a decent tramway service, as Father argued [. . .].
>
> But it was a little trying to have one's own washerwoman living next door who would persist in attempting to talk to Mother over the fence – & then just beyond her 'hovel' as Mother called it there lived an old man who burnt leather in his back yard whenever the wind blew our way. And then, just opposite our house, across the road, there was a paling fence & below the paling fence, in a hollow, squeezed in almost under the fold of a huge gorse-covered hill, was Saunders Lane. And further along there lived an endless family of halfcastes who appeared to have planted their garden with empty jam tins and old saucepans and black iron kettles without lids.[17]

Thorndon, as noted earlier, was indeed a very 'mixed' area of Wellington, with extremes of poverty and wealth living side by side. KM's sensitivity, even as a child, to those less fortunate than herself, is manifest in countless of her stories, and particularly in her New Zealand stories, 'The Doll's House' and 'The Garden Party'. All the children were forbidden to enter Little George Street ('Saunders Lane' in 'The Garden Party'), which the house overlooked on its western side: an ugly little street of poor workers' cottages, always prone to flooding (something which never affected no. 75, of course, built high up on the hill). Aside from class distinctions, the constant threat of epidemic and disease may have been another real factor in the children being told to avoid the area, just as in 'The Doll's House', the Kelvey children are said to be 'untouchable': that is, their poverty allies them to disease. 'Saunders Lane' is described thus in 'The Garden Party', the description now more muted and less condemnatory than the one KM had written six years earlier:

> They were little mean dwellings painted a chocolate brown. In the garden patches there was nothing but cabbage stalks, sick hens and tomato cans. The very smoke coming out of their chimneys was poverty-stricken. Little rags and shreds of smoke, so unlike the great silvery plumes that curled from the Sheridans' chimneys. Washerwomen lived in the lane and sweeps and a cobbler and a man whose house-front was studded all over with minute bird-cages.[18]

In Harold and Annie's absence, family life continued much as normal, though not perhaps for KM. In September 1898, there occurred a landmark moment in her life when her first short story was published in the Wellington Girls' High magazine, *The High School Reporter*. She was just nine years old. Coincidentally, in the same month, her father's cousin, Elizabeth von Arnim (Henry Herron's daughter), had published her first hugely successful book, *Elizabeth and her German Garden* (a copy was eventually brought home for the children by their parents). KM's story, called 'Enna Blake', is set in England: perhaps not a surprising choice, given her parents' voyage. The nine-year-old KM tries to imagine the countryside in England, assuming that ferns (one of the national symbols of New Zealand, where they grow prolifically) are a main feature of the flora:

> The next day was very fine. Mrs Brown proposed that they should go ferning. So soon after breakfast they started. 'It seems just the day for enjoy-ing one's self,' said Lucy, as they climbed the hill. 'Yes,' Enna answered, 'today is much nicer here than in London.' At about twelve o'clock the two girls sat on a log and ate their dinners. 'I think it would be very nice to get some moss,' Enna said; so off they trudged. The girls spent a very happy day, and got a great many nice ferns and some beautiful moss. And that night Enna said she thought it was the nicest day she had ever spent in the country.[19]

At the end of the published story, an editorial comment by one of the senior girls notes that the story 'shows promise of great merit', thus becoming in itself the first published critique of KM's fiction. In conversation with Mantz, Vera 'remembered Kathleen's excitement that night over her printed "story"'.[20] Years later, KM's childhood friend Marion Ruddick would remember how,

[t]he repast over, Kathleen drew me to the book case and producing the last number of the school magazine [. . .] invited me to read the foot-note [. . .] Kathleen looked at me triumphantly. When I reminded her of this, many years later in London, she said 'What a little horror I must have been.'[21]

Harold and Annie finally arrived back in New Zealand in November, and were quick to take up their old life but with more panache and style, as befitted his role of prominent Wellington businessman and her role as a charming – if frail – society hostess. Harold's *Reminiscences* for these years reveals not only a man devoted to his growing family, but also an important businessman, friend to politicians and judges, whose star was rising higher and higher, on the boards of numerous companies, Chairman of the Wellington Harbour Board and a justice of the peace. The Beauchamps were clearly now prominent members of a small, but nevertheless still class-conscious, young country.

On the return journey home from England, Annie and Harold had met a Canadian family called Ruddick, who were also sailing to New Zealand. They brought with them their young daughter Marion, who was enrolled at Wellington Girls' High. She and the friendless KM instantly became friends. In later life, after KM's death, Marion wrote down her memories of the now cel-ebrated writer in a long article called 'Incidents in the Childhood of Katherine Mansfield'. She recorded her first impressions of Harold and Annie on the boat trip home:

He had the fresh look of a man who, having recently emerged from a cold bath, had anointed himself liberally with Eau de Cologne or lavender water. When we went ashore at Honolulu or Fiji, Mr Beauchamp inevita-bly wore a bowler hat and carried an unfurled umbrella, despite a burning tropical sun and a cloudless sky.

Mrs Beauchamp was a languid woman with a weak heart. [. . .] She had a decisive way of speaking, and the definite views she held on most sub-jects contrasted strangely with her languorous and apparently indifferent manner. She had shown me a photograph of her five children standing in a row [. . .] I gazed long and often at the three, wondering which would be my friend. Mrs. Beauchamp however, in her decisive manner, completely overlooking Kathleen, decided that Chaddie was the one I would like best.[22]

KM's strangely ambivalent place in the Beauchamp family is affirmed in this portrayal. Her family did not consider her a particularly likeable child and she had no real friends at school: 'she was reserved, she sulked, she lied.'[23]

As the returning ship neared Wellington harbour, where the three eldest girls plus Grandma Dyer were waiting to greet the returning parents, Marion noted:

> I stood beside Mrs. Beauchamp as she gazed down in a detached way at the group and to my mind didn't seem as overjoyed as I thought she would be after such a long absence. Finally it was to Kathleen she spoke first, for everyone to hear.
>
> 'Well, Kathleen', she said, 'I see that you are as fat as ever.' And in my first glimpse of Kathleen I saw her eyes flash, and her face flush with anger as she turned away with a toss of her ringlets.[24]

The psychological effects of such a comment on KM cannot be underestimated. Time after time in this account of her childhood, KM is presented as an outsider, set apart, different, and clearly not 'belonging' in the same way as her better-behaved sisters. If Annie Beauchamp had deliberately set out to create a difficult child, she could not have made a better job of it. As Marion noted on her visit to no. 75, 'Kathleen alone was silent, as she so often was when her sisters were present. They didn't belong in the same world.'[25] Meanwhile, if young Marion needed any proof of KM's idiosyncratic personality, this would have confirmed

Figure 5.6 The Beauchamp children and Marion Ruddick at 75 Tinakori Rd, Wellington.

it: 'suddenly, during a pause she looked at me intently and in a low almost tense voice said, "Do you have any parrots in Canada?"'[26] The fascination with birds, the isolation, the sense of separation, all have their genesis in the events of KM's childhood.

The garden at no. 75, which would feature so prominently in 'The Garden Party', is described in detail by Marion:

> We were standing on a cinder path from where the grass sloped to the croquet lawn. In a depression between the lawn and the wall in front was what later, Kathleen and I were to call the lily lawn after the long bed of arum lilies at one side. The lilies were bordered with a row of tightly packed violets and at one end was an old pear tree. This lily lawn was to become later our favourite play ground.[27]

Once Marion was enrolled at Wellington Girls' High, she and KM became firm friends. Even aged ten, KM was writing poetry: 'We were often called upon to recite poems we had learned the previous week. One day Kathleen recited one of her own and although it was slightly difficult to understand, we were duly impressed.'[28] One can only feel for the plump, awkward young KM, with her ink-stained fingers, for whom school sewing lessons were sheer torture:

> There was one in the class who did not consider sewing a pleasant subject and that was Kathleen. Her fingers, usually inky, (it was in later years that she became fastidious,) seemed to be unusually inky on sewing class days, and when her fingers were hot as well, the ink was infused into the white material she was sewing with dire results. One day on top of her misery she pricked her finger which drew forth maledictions, whispered to me, on the head of the person who had invented sewing.[29]

The only enjoyable part of the sewing class was when the girls took it in turns to read out loud. Years later in March 1915, KM recalled her childhood delight in performing for an audience, and being the centre of attention:

> Jinnie Moore was awfully good at elocution. Was she better than I? I could make the girls cry when I read Dickens in the sewing class – and she couldn't, but then she never tried to. She didn't care for Dickens. She liked something about horses and tramps and shipwrecks and prairie fires – they were her style, her reckless, redhaired dashing style.[30]

As Marion remarked in her recollections, all New Zealand schoolchildren at this time were required to learn to swim, and she, KM and the other girls

Figure 5.7 Thorndon Esplanade and Baths, Wellington.

were taught at the Thorndon Baths, a wooden building overhanging the sea, inside which the tides ebbed and flowed, creating a large natural pool: 'Kathleen made hard work of it, alternately puffing and panting and holding her breath, but she persevered and triumphed in the end.'[31] The little girls would eat their lunch at the baths, shared with Pete the Penguin, the baths' mascot, brought to Wellington by a sailor and left behind, and who now lived at the baths, performing tricks as though he were in some sort of modern 'sea world' centre. An incident at the baths, recounted by Marion, tells us much about KM's developing character. On one particular trip Marion was talking to another young girl, whose family had for a while shared the same boarding house as the Ruddicks:

> Suddenly, someone bumped into me rather violently. To save myself from falling back into the water, I clutched the railing and turning discovered it was Kathleen [. . .] Kathleen was jealous of her friends; her likes and dislikes were intense, there was no half way.[32]

This intensity of emotion and likes / dislikes, present at such a young age, was certainly a trait carried over into adulthood, and also marked her out from her much more obedient, less demanding siblings.

KM turned Marion's boarding house and gardens at Golders Hill in Wellington into a fairy kingdom, peopled with gnomes, witches, nymphs and dragons:

We read and re-read Grimms and Hans Andersen's fairy tales, The Princess and the Goblins, Alice in Wonderland of course, and a book we liked very much called Christmas Tree Land. It was a German fairy tale about two children who, when visiting their grandmother in her German castle went daily accompanied by their nurse to a fir wood on a nearby hill; there while the nurse was overcome by sleep, the children entered a door in one of the trees and day after day had the most wonderful adventures.[33]

Mrs Molesworth's enormously popular children's book, *Christmas-Tree Land*, beautifully illustrated by Walter Crane, had first been published in 1884. Didactic in tone, its fantasy element nevertheless thrilled young readers – as it clearly did KM and Marion – who revelled in the fairy-tale adventures of its brother and sister protagonists, Rollo and Maia. The pine forest in which the castle was situated is the most dominant feature of the book: 'And far as the eye could reach stretched away into the distance, miles and miles and miles, here rising, there again sweeping downwards, the everlasting Christmas-trees!'[34] KM seemingly never forgot this book; though none of her extant writings mentions it specifically (as was the case with almost everything she read as a child), nevertheless, resonances are to be found scattered throughout her writing. She would not forget 'the feeling of mystery caused by the dark shade of the lofty

Figure 5.8 Miss Florence Holt's music pupils, including Katherine Mansfield, on a picnic.

trees, standing there in countless rows as they had stood for centuries, the silence only broken by the occasional dropping of a twig or the flutter of a leaf'.[35]

On another occasion, Marion told of how, on a picnic to Day's Bay, KM regaled the children present with her own rendering of 'Hansel and Gretel', holding her audience completely spellbound:

> We loved the part about the guardian angels protecting the children as they slept, and were thrilled when Gretel pushed the old witch into the oven and especially liked the part where they found the row of children stiff with honeycrust which fell off when Gretel touched them with a wand of juniper.
>
> We always listened to Katie's stories with interest. She not only could tell them but she could write them. When she told stories she drew on her store of fairy tales and legends.[36]

One day, they had an adventure of their own, when both girls pretended a fire-eating dragon called Bronzo lived in a mysterious garden near to Marion's house. Armed with plant-leaf spears, the two girls secretly entered the magical kingdom by way of a small side door, thinking perhaps to be greeted by a Red Queen and gardeners painting roses red, only to be immediately chased out by an irate, flesh-and-blood gardener. Wanting to go home but too scared to pass by the same garden door again, KM solved the problem by asking a kindly-looking man on a white horse if he would accompany the girls back up the hill, as they were too scared to go near the fire-eating dragon: 'The knight took his cue, "I shall consider it an honour to escort the fairy princesses to their castle."'[37] This life of the mind, pretending, playing at make-believe, steeped KM in the tools she would need for her future career – a lively imagination and a will to create imaginary worlds and characters. The two girls would also write poems, and one in particular, called 'Ode to a Snowdrop', was read to Chaddie and Vera, who scoffed at their efforts, which only served to make them even more determined to keep their friendship separate from KM's sisters.

As a Christmas treat for his young family in 1898, Harold took a small seaside bungalow at Island Bay, on the southern shores of Wellington Harbour, a few miles out of town. In her memoir of KM, Marion wrote of having met KM in London in May 1917, and the two women had reminisced about their childhood: 'We became steeped in the salty smell of the sea, in crunching the sands of the Bay under our bare feet, and in the cold days in "Windy Wellington", warming our frozen fingers at the class room fire.'[38]

During this first Christmas of their acquaintance, Marion had been taken in by the Beauchamps, as her mother wanted to take a water cure in the hot springs in the north of the island. The first week of her visit was spent at no. 75. She had bought Christmas presents for all the children, including a silver thimble in a green plush case for KM: a surprising gift, given KM's intense dislike of sewing. At this time, the girls ate in the schoolroom and were not permitted into the dining room to eat with the adults, not even Vera. Whilst the adults ate their dinner, the children worked at their studies, and were brought cocoa and buns to signal bedtime by the maid, Jennie. Early every morning, Harold insisted on his children taking a cold bath before school: 'Katie would emerge with a ruddy glow on her vivid face. She would try desperately to brush some of the corkscrew out of her ringlets, but the water she put on only made them curl more tightly.'[39] On the way home from school, the girls would sometimes walk over the little suspension bridge, which KM described so clearly in her story 'A Birthday'. For Marion,

> [t]he suspension bridge, swinging above a deep gorge lined with feathery trees was most exciting. While crossing we fearfully wondered if another earthquake like the one which cleft the earth and made the gorge below might be repeated and swallow us up, bridge and all.[40]

During the Christmas season, the Beauchamps would regularly put on a concert and refreshments at no. 75 for the sailors of a certain shipping line favoured by Harold. During the Christmas that Marion spent with the Beauchamps, it was decided that the children would perform instead of the adults. The large verandah downstairs, with a makeshift stage at one end, would serve as the concert room. Vera, a talented young pianist, opened the sometimes nautically-themed evening with a marching song; Chaddie sang a song about ships at sea in her sweet little voice; Marion gave a rather scratchy solo on her half-sized violin of Braga's 'Angel's Serenade'; and last of all the girls, KM recited one of her own poems concerning a missing fisherman: 'Katie, announced beforehand as the author of her poem, brought down the house. A fashionable audience would have appalled her but she liked these rough sailor lads.'[41] Here is early evidence of several marked facets of KM's adult life: her love of performance, as noted earlier, the importance of poetry in her life, and her preference for the 'common man' over 'society'.

Three days after the concert for the sailors, the family decamped in two horse-drawn landaus to the cottage at Island Bay, cutting the journey time by driving through the little city. Days of sea, sand, sunshine and shrimping followed, in a perfect New Zealand Christmas. After a bad bout of sunburn, KM and Marion had to spend a day indoors, making dolls' clothes:

> Neither Katie nor I liked big dolls, we much preferred tiny ones that we could make clothes for out of wisps of nothing. We found things in

miniature much more intriguing. Little jewel like flowers and the smallest of pink tinted sea shells gave us the greatest pleasure.[42]

On Christmas Eve, after a day spent shrimping and bathing dolls in rock pools ('Leslie in a burst of generosity donated his crab to Katie's pool'),[43] Vera read aloud Charles Dickens's *A Christmas Carol* and the children then walked the length of the bay to see the Italian fishermen hauling in their nets that groaned under the weight of the day's catch, a thrilling and unforgettable sight. KM, sensitive, and attuned to nature and flowers in particular, was the only one of the party who noticed the smell of dainty, pink-centred, white manuka flowers, and on the way home the children gathered armfuls of them.

Christmas Day was equally hot. As predicted, KM, on waking up and examining her stocking, declared indignantly: '"Someone has given me a thimble."'[44] Marion never did have the courage to say she was the culprit, so remorseful was she over her ill-judged gift. Marion's parents sent each of the two girls a greenstone tiki pendant and Harold lost no time in explaining the history of the little carved figures. His knowledge of Maori customs was exceptional for the time and he had learnt many words and phrases of Maori language, with which he liked to instruct the children. A letter from Marion's mother, read out on Christmas Day, recounted the details of her trip to the hot springs in the north and her encounters with Maori tribes, presaging an almost identical trip that KM would take at the end of 1907. Marion's recollections note that 'Katie took a special interest in my mother's letter as the Maoris were beginning to have a great fascination for her.'[45] Several of her early stories – for example, 'Rewa' (1908) and 'How Pearl Button was Kidnapped' (1912) – would feature Maori characters.

The family were surprised to receive a caller on Christmas Day, as Marion recorded:

'It's Mr Seddon', Katie cried, as we watched a big man laboriously descend from a carriage. 'Oh, I do hope he's wearing his diamond stud'.

I felt that if Chaddie had made the remark, there would not have been such a reproving chorous [*sic*] of, 'Kathleen!'[46]

Richard Seddon, also known as 'King Dick' for his rather autocratic manner, was New Zealand's longest-serving prime minister, dominating the then Liberal government for thirteen years. Quirkily dressed in top hat and tails, no matter what the occasion or weather, he had come to pay his respects to his great friend Harold Beauchamp on this Christmas Day in 1898, and KM was not disappointed, for on his shirt front, 'there was the diamond in all its glory, sending forth flashes of light.'[47] Who else but KM, with her beady eye for detail and her love of the

Figure 5.9 'The Glen', Muritai, Day's Bay.

Figure 5.10 Muritai, showing the gardens that ran down to the sand hills. Called 'Crescent Bay' in 'At the Bay'.

miniature, would have set such store by a small diamond tie pin? The main reason for Seddon's visit was to enquire whether his good friend would take on the role of Government Director on the Board of the Bank of New Zealand, a request that would eventually see Harold as Chairman of the Board for many years, and then knighted for his services in the year of KM's death, 1923.

Figure 5.11 Martin and Jones general store, Muritai.

Recognising how much his family enjoyed this seaside trip, and wanting a more permanent holiday home for his family, from 1899 to 1902 Harold leased The Glen, a little cottage nestled into the hillside on the landward side of the Muritai Road in Eastbourne, near Day's Bay, only accessible at that time by ferry. The native bush ran almost down to the sandy beach and the sea. It was a perfect little summer retreat and it was here that the Beauchamp children spent their summer holidays, looking out over paddocks and sand dunes, mostly cared for by Grandma Dyer; it was brought so vividly to life in the second long Burnell story, 'At the Bay' (1921), completed on 10 September 1921, just four weeks before 'The Garden Party'. The opening paragraphs of 'At the Bay' contain some of the finest prose KM ever wrote, a testament to the writer who was then at the height of her creative powers. The reader is immersed in the beauty of an early summer's morning (soon to be disturbed by Stanley Burnell as he makes his clumsy way from beach house to sea). The universe is holding its breath, and nature is preparing itself for what the day will bring:

> Very early morning. The sun was not yet risen, and the whole of Crescent Bay was hidden under a white sea-mist. The big bushcovered hills at the back were smothered. You could not see where they ended and the paddocks and bungalows began. The sandy road was gone and the paddocks and bungalows the other side of it; there were no white dunes covered with reddish grass beyond them; there was nothing to mark which was

beach and where was the sea. A heavy dew had fallen. The grass was blue. Big drops hung on the bushes and just did not fall; the silvery, fluffy toi-toi was limp on its long stalks, and all the marigolds and the pinks in the bungalow gardens were bowed to the earth with wetness. Drenched were the cold fuchsias, round pearls of dew lay on the flat nasturtium leaves. It looked as though the sea had beaten up softly in the darkness, as though one immense wave had come rippling, rippling – how far? Perhaps if you had waked up in the middle of the night you might have seen a big fish flicking in at the window and gone again. . . .

Ah-Aah! sounded the sleepy sea. And from the bush there came the sound of little streams flowing, quickly, lightly, slipping between the smooth stones, gushing into ferny basins and out again; and there was the splashing of big drops on large leaves, and something else – what was it? – a faint stirring and shaking, the snapping of a twig and then such silence that it seemed some one was listening.[48]

While writing the story, KM wrote to her friend, Dorothy Brett, on 4 August 1921:

It's called At the Bay & its (I hope) full of sand and seaweed and bathing dresses hanging over verandahs & sandshoes on window sills, and little pink 'sea' convolvulus, and rather gritty sandwiches and the tide coming in. And it smells (oh I DO hope it smells) a little bit fishy.[49]

This world of sand and rock pools was an integral part of KM's childhood memories and she never forgot them. Harold, too, derived great enjoyment from the rural life in the remote little colony at Eastbourne, swimming, fishing and hiking. His family never perhaps understood his love of nature and his sporting prowess, all born out of his impoverished, rural childhood.[50]

At the beginning of 1899, with Marion's mother still not well and unable to look after her, it was decided that she should be sent to boarding school in Nelson, then a little cathedral town in the north of the South Island. KM was bereft at the thought of losing her only real friend, and in the run-up to Marion's departure the two girls spent almost every day together. The Beauchamp girls and Marion all attended the same dance classes. KM was not a good dancer and disliked the classes, but was nevertheless enraged when she discovered that Marion and Chaddie had been chosen to dance a gavotte from Gilbert and Sullivan's *Gondoliers* at a large annual bazaar. Instead of attending the bazaar, 'she had decided to write an ode to something and was chewing her pencil down on the lily lawn, her place of refuge in moments of stress, when she was called in.'[51] Dressed up in 'smocked tussore', KM was dragged along with the rest of the family. Her eyes, which on arrival had been 'smouldering with resentment', were soon 'sparkling with excitement':[52]

> What do you think Molly, I was sitting with Gran and Aunt Belle, thinking I would like to be a hermit and live on wild honey and locusts like John the Baptist, when I saw our knight who rescued us from the dragon on Golders Hill![53]

He was, in fact, a knight in the strict sense of the word. His name was Sir Kenneth; in true chivalrous fashion, he sat the girls either side of him, and after they had told him about school, Pete the Penguin, and their Christmas holiday at Island Bay, he in turn told them the tale of a white dolphin called Pelorus Jack, who was reputed to meet and escort every ship that sailed through Pelorus Sound, the largest of the sounds (a system of drowned river valleys) that make up the Marlborough Sounds at the north of the South Island, and which KM knew well from her trips to Picton. The girls were entranced.

On the day of Marion's departure to her boarding school in Nelson, alongside her mother and father at the dock was KM, waving her handkerchief until the ship passed out of sight. The only consolation for KM was the fact that Marion was able to report in a letter that Pelorus Jack was most certainly real. The two girls wrote frequently but saw each other only briefly thereafter, and a year later Marion returned to Canada with her parents. The recollections of her friendship with KM remain a priceless record of the chubby little schoolgirl in 1898, who immersed herself in fairy stories and the world of the imagination: the misfit of the family, quick to love and equally quick to hate. In July 1921, ensconced in the Chalet des Sapins in Switzerland, KM wrote to John Ruddick, Marion's father, who had sent her two photographs of herself and Marion, via Chaddie: 'Does she remember Island Bay, I wonder, and bathing her doll in the rock pools with me.' And remembering delicious cream buns shared with Marion, she mocked her own childhood chubbiness as evidenced in the photographs: 'I must say I think the cream buns should have been withheld from me, though.'[54] A few weeks later, she wrote in a similar vein to Chaddie and Jeanne: 'And why was I stuffed – why wasn't I given lean meat & dry toast – [. . .] Even my curls were like luscious fried sausages.'[55] In 1896, KM had been presented with a copy of *The Book of Common Prayer* for her eighth birthday by her mother. After KM's death it passed to Vera, who subsequently gave it to Marion, in memory of those precious few months of friendship with KM.

During 1899, KM continued to attend Wellington Girls' High with her elder sisters, whilst all the time wishing for the 'glamour' of a boarding school in Nelson with Marion. Her second story, 'A Happy Christmas Eve', published in

Figure 5.12 The Beauchamp family, 1898.

the *High School Reporter* in 1899, concerns the plight of the poor from the point of view of a little rich girl, once more showing how the young KM was mindful of such disparities in society:

'As you break up today, I am going to take you with me to town, to get the presents for our tree.' For the Courteneys were going to have a tree for the poor children that year. [. . .]

    Such a funny crowd it was that came that night, ragged and dirty, but having a look of curiosity on their faces. When they had all come, the study door was thrown open and the Christmas tree was seen in all its splendour. I wish I could have let you see the delight on the faces of the children. Really it was a sight to behold. The tree was loaded with sweets, fruits and presents and there was a present for everyone besides the sweets. Then there were games, supper at which the children ate very heartily, more games, and then they went home.[56]

The father in the story is called 'Harry', and the largesse of the rich family towards the poor tantalisingly presages elements of 'The Garden Party'. Notwithstanding these early publications and their 'promise of great merit', when KM announced to visitors that she wanted to be a writer when she grew up, her announcement was almost always met with laughter and derision.

Figure 5.13 Members of the Beauchamp and Waters families.

Overall, KM's academic achievement at the school was sound, winning her prizes in English, arithmetic and French at a ceremony presided over by Sir Robert Stout, the Chief Justice and former Prime Minister. The subject of his address to the young girls was higher education for women, stating that 'parents who gave their children higher education gave them better dowry than money.'[57] Listening attentively in the audience was Harold Beauchamp. Always ambitious for his family, he would go one better than Stout's suggestion. His girls not only would enjoy the benefits of higher education, but also would do so back 'home' in London, something which only the wealthy few in Wellington could afford to do.

Lonely again, KM still was able to immerse herself in the joys of the large garden at no. 75, with its croquet lawn, lily lawn bordered with violets, tennis court and fruit trees, and, in the absence of Marion, she now found herself drawn to her amenable little brother, Leslie. In October 1915, following Leslie's tragically early death in Flanders just a few days before on 6 October, and remembering their conversations about life as children in Wellington whilst he was undergoing military training in London, she recorded part of their reminiscences about no. 75 in an achingly poignant notebook entry:

Figure 5.14 The Beauchamp children.

Do you remember the enormous number of pears there used to be on that old tree.
Down by the violet bed.
And how after there'd been a southerly buster we used to go out with clothes baskets to pick them up.
And how while we stooped they went on falling, bouncing on our backs & heads. And how far they used to be scattered – ever so far, under the violet leaves, down the steps, right down to the Lily Lawn we used to find them trodden in the grass. And how soon the ants got to them – I can see now that little round hole with a sort of fringe of brown pepper round it.
Do you know I've never seen pears like them since.
They were so bright – canary yellow, & small. And the peel was so thin and the pips jet – jet black.
First you pulled out the little stem & sucked it. It was faintly sour & then you ate them always from the top – core & all.
The pips were delicious.
Do you remember sitting on the pink garden seat.
I shall never forget that pink garden seat. It is the only garden seat for me.
Where is it now. Do you think we shall be allowed to sit in it in Heaven.
It always wobbled a bit & there was usually the marks of a snail on it.

Sitting on that seat, swinging our legs & eating the pears.

But isn't it extraordinary how <u>deep</u> our happiness was – how positive – deep, shining, warm. I remember the way we used to look at each other & smile – do you? Sharing a secret – what was it?

I think it was the family feeling. We were almost like one child. I always see us walking about together, looking at things together with the same eyes, discussing. I felt that again – just now – when we looked for the pear in the grass. I remembered ruffling the violet leaves with you. Oh that garden!

Do you remember that some of the pears we found used to have little teeth marks in them.

Yes.

Who bit them.

It was always a mystery.

He puts his arm round her. They pace up and down. A thin round moon shines over the pear tree & the ivy walls of the garden glitter like metal.

The air smells chill, heavy, very cold.

We shall go back there one day, when its all over.

We'll go back together.

And find everything.

Everything.[58]

In June 1900, Wellington Girls' High no longer considered quite socially elevated enough for his daughters, Harold moved all the children, including young Leslie, to Wellington's most prestigious private girls' school, 'Miss Swainson's', located at 20 Fitzherbert Terrace, again just a short walk from no. 75, and the best that Wellington had to offer in terms of girls' private education at that time, and which also had a little junior school for boys. A cousin of KM's described it more as a 'finishing school' for young girls, even though young Jeanne, also a pupil, was just eight when the girls were enrolled and hardly at an age to be 'finished': 'It was one of those snobby semidiocesan schools where the dear Vicar was always hanging round. Education was not so much of a feature but you didn't eat peas with a knife or dip your bread in the gravy.'[59] Many years later, in 1921, KM would fictionalise the school in an unfinished story called 'Weak Heart', with herself as the young fourteen-year-old character of Edie Bengel (the name itself almost identical to a close friend from 1907–8, Edie Bendall):

Was it possible that in a week's time she would be one of Miss Farmer's girls, wearing a red and blue hat band, running up the broad steps leading to the big grey painted house that buzzed, that hummed as you went by? Their pew in Church faced Miss Farmer's boarders. Would she at last know the names of the girls she had looked at so often?[60]

Figure 5.15 Girls from Fitzherbert Terrace School, Thorndon, Wellington, including Katherine Mansfield and Maata Mahupuku.

Figure 5.16 Staff of Fitzherbert Terrace School, Thorndon, Wellington.

Set up in in 1878 by her mother, the school in which the Beauchamp children were now enrolled had been run by Miss Mary Swainson for three years. Mrs Henry Smith was the headmistress; a tiny, determined woman, she was a stern disciplinarian who made the children march like soldiers and rise whenever she entered a room. Mr Robert Parker taught music, and Miss Eva Butts taught elocution, arithmetic and geography, whilst Miss Swainson herself took the girls for their singing lessons. Miss Butts was young and attractive, the object of adoration for many of the girls; indeed, in echoes of Miss Jean Brodie, she cultivated a little circle of six or seven girls who rebelled against narrowness and provincialism. She found KM amusing but noted that her English compositions were not always on the subject requested and that overall she was 'untidy and careless and lacking in concentration'.[61] Later, she remembered KM as 'dumpy and unattractive – not even cleverly naughty'. At the age of thirteen, KM came to Miss Butts after school to ask her opinion of 'free love'. But she could not shock Miss Butts, who told her 'that for a man it was all right. He had protection. A woman hadn't. "Ask your mother what she thinks of it". Kass said "Yes", and dashed off, but I knew well enough she wouldn't ask her.'[62] According to Miss Butts, she was 'shabby and inky', and 'unambitious in the school'.[63] KM was the right age, at thirteen, for puberty to have taken a hold, with its ensuing physical changes and emotional extremes. It was at this point in her life that she started to keep little notebooks, presaging the sort of writing that readers would come to appreciate after her death.

KM soon became a class rebel, to the consternation of the headmistress, Mrs Henry Smith, who ruled the school with a rod of iron and expected absolute obedience and discipline. She certainly met her match in KM, who became the leader of a group of girls who formed a secret club with literary aspirations, and who started a little magazine called *The School*:

> Kathleen was the leader of a group that met upstairs, under the eaves (rather influenced by *Little Women* perhaps) and keeping the 'literary club' and its activities secret. *The School* was composed of jokes collected from grown-up papers and 'original' stories. Kathleen's was a story [called 'In-Flu-Enza'] about a dog: 'The door opened and in-flu-enza'. The first issue (for club members only) was copied in Kathleen's irregular, rather distinctive hand, on large double sheets of foolscap.[64]

The club was called the A. R. Club (the ante-room), and a school rhyme of the time begins: 'A. for A. R. Club confined to the fair'. There was certainly a cachet attached to the girls who belonged, amongst whom were KM, a young Maori princess called Maata Mahupuku (also known as Martha Grace), and another friend of KM's called Marion Tweed. According to Pat Lawlor, 'it was Maata

Figure 5.17 Maata Mahupuku, also known as Martha Grace.

who wrote on the foolscap sheets at Katherine's dictation, because [. . .] she "could write more legibly".'[65]

Episodes from KM's life at Miss Swainson's would be fictionalised in later life. One particular feature of the walk to school was having to dodge 'Ole Underwood', a homeless old man who used to hide in the bushes on Fitzherbert Terrace and jump out at the children. As a justice of the peace, Harold, after hearing one too many stories of his girls arriving dishevelled and flushed at Miss Swainson's, having been chased by Ole Underwood, had him '"charged as a rogue and a vagabond, to serve some time in jail"'.[66] In KM's story, 'Ole Underwood' (1913), he is described in all his outlandish glory, a perfect subject for *Rhythm*, the avant-garde magazine edited by John Middleton Murry and KM, where the rawness of life was celebrated:

Down the windy hill stalked Ole Underwood. He carried a black umbrella in one hand, in the other a red and white spotted handkerchief knotted into a lump. He wore a black peaked cap like a pilot; gold rings gleamed in his ears and his little eyes snapped like two sparks. Like two sparks they glowed in the smoulder of his bearded face.[67]

The headmistress, Mrs Henry Smith, described KM as 'a thundercloud' compared to her sisters:

> The family was very conventional; Kass was the outlaw. No one here saw that the unconventionality and rebellion had something behind it. Nobody, I think, understood that or her. They just tried to make her conform: reprimanded her for errors in spelling, carelessness, and poor writing. But that was 'the method' in those days.[68]

KM was

> 'a very unpolished diamond, while the others were too polished'. She was 'plain,' 'a surly sort of a girl' and 'imaginative to the point of untruth.' Even the other girls used to say of her stories: 'Oh, wait till to-morrow and it will be different!'[69]

Like Miss Butts, the headmistress found much to criticise in her English compositions due to their excessive length and because they were often about her school life: '"no girl should write about school girls: she put *herself* in too much."' Even at the tender age of thirteen, KM was to be found overtly fictionalising aspects of her own life, a defining feature of her work as a mature writer.

Ever the showman, one of the highlights of KM's time at Miss Swainson's was being allowed to arrange and direct a school benefit for the Polynesian Missions, organised by Miss Butts and titled *Mrs Jarley's Wax Works*, with KM herself in the role of Mrs Jarley.[70] Her comedic talents and flair for impersonation won her many admirers for her performance, not least a visitor from England, the Reverend Charles Prodgers, who was so delighted he wrote in her autograph book: 'With every good wish for "Mrs Jarley's" future success.'[71]

The piano teacher, Mr Robert Parker, taught KM for two years at Miss Swainson's and later revealed that her story, 'The Wind Blows' (1920), was very much taken from real life. The description here of his music room (where his name is now Robert Bullen instead of Robert Parker) is completely accurate and only embellished by a made-up inscription on the photograph of Rubinstein:

> How funny he is. He doesn't exactly laugh at you . . . but there is just something. . . . Oh, how peaceful it is here. She likes this room. It smells of art serge and stale smoke and chrysanthemums . . . there is a big vase of them on the mantelpiece behind the pale photograph of Rubinstein . . . à mon ami Robert Bullen. . . . Over the black glittering piano hangs 'Solitude' – a dark tragic woman draped in white, sitting on a rock, her knees crossed, her chin on her hands.[72]

Not all names in the story were fictionalised:

> Marie Swainson runs into the garden next door to pick the 'chrysanths' before they are ruined. Her skirt flies up above her waist; she tries to beat it down, to tuck it between her legs while she stoops, but it is no use – up it flies.[73]

There is clearly no mistaking the origins of this story. KM and her father (who liked to keep up his music) shared Mr Parker as a piano teacher. He was kind and courteous, he was sentimental, but above all, he made all of his pupils feel special – and not even prominent businessman Harold Beauchamp was immune to that kind of flattery. Mr Parker would carry on teaching, both at Miss Swainson's and privately, charming his pupils until his eightieth birthday.

Maata Mahupuku (Martha Grace), who helped KM with the first issue of *The School*, was a strikingly good-looking young girl, with a Maori father and English mother; she was the granddaughter of Wiremu Mahupuku, chief of the sub-tribe of Ngati Kahungunu, which technically made her a 'princess'. She was rich (being the sole heiress of her uncle's considerable fortune) and glamorous, and although two years younger, KM instantly became besotted with her, the obsession continuing long after adolescence. In 1913, KM started a novel, *Maata*, never completed, in which her remembered sensual feelings for Maata are clearly evident. The two girls became close, in that all-encompassing way that was to be such a feature of KM's life. You were either one of 'her' special people or you were not. A family member noted:

> Martha was constantly at the Beauchamps' House. The girls who were not allowed much money were pop eyed with the amount Maata always had to spend. All the same she was very pretty, bright and generous and nothing of a snob herself. She and Kathleen were particularly friendly.[74]

This was a relationship that would last for several more years, with its after-math lingering on into adulthood. For the moment, KM's passions were all-consuming, her newly burgeoning sensuality seemingly untrammelled by the conventions of her family and society.

In 1901, the Duke and Duchess of Cornwall, the future King George V and Queen Mary, visited New Zealand as part of an antipodean tour. As Chairman of the Harbour Board, Harold not only was a member of the party that greeted the royal couple on their arrival, with little Jeanne presenting a bouquet to the Duchess, but also was given the role of bidding the royal couple farewell as they boarded the gangway on to their departing ship. Unfortunately, the rain was

Figure 5.18 The Beauchamp family.

torrential at the moment of departure, but Harold was not going to be denied his moment in the spotlight. In his own words,

As the Duke stepped on the gangway leading to the *Ophir* I said to him: 'Sir, the heavens are in keeping with our feelings to-day. They are weeping at your departure'. He replied, as he shook hands, 'Thank you; you are very kind.'[75]

It was a time, as Harold noted in his *Reminiscences*, when his three eldest girls were now 'beginning to appear with their parents in public and were all busy with their music and other accomplishments'.[76] Vera and Kathleen were taking piano lessons and Chaddie singing lessons. They made for a fetching trio at Beauchamp family soirées. But underneath the outward veneer of familial happiness, KM's adolescent mood swings led to quite terrifying fits of temper that affected the whole family. One of her friends at that time recalled how 'she was very excitable in those days and often in a furious rage. I remember one day she gave a squeel [*sic*] of rage and pinched her sister Vera for some small trifle.'[77] In *Juliet* (1906), KM's unfinished novel written when she was just eighteen and

Figure 5.19 Katherine Mansfield and her sisters on the deck of a ship.

Figure 5.20 Katherine Mansfield and her sisters on the deck of a ship, 1900.

started whilst still at school at Queen's College, she paints a warts-and-all portrait of herself at this time:

> 'We've told Father all about it, Juliet,' said Margaret. 'And Father's fear-
> fully angry,' Mary added. Juliet slipped the Byron down in the front of her
> sailor blouse. She had no definite idea of what she had been reading but
> her head was full of strange unreasonable impulses. She was feeling slightly
> sorry for her absence of self control in that it incurred a long interview with
> her Father, and in all probability some degrading issue – no jam for a week,
> or to go to bed at seven o'clock until she apologised. She walked slowly to
> the house, up the broad stone steps, into the wide hall, and knocked at the
> morning room door.
>   At two o'clock in the afternoon Juliet had thrown a heavy book at her
> eldest sister Margaret, and a bottle of ink at her elder sister Mary. At six
> in the evening she was summoned to the morning room to explain these
> offences. After her two wholly successful acts of violence she had retired
> to a sloping lawn at the extreme end of the garden where she lay down
> comfortably and read Don Juan – – –
>   Margaret and Mary, still smarting from the shock to their sensitive little
> systems, had rather rejoiced in the search for her, and more especially in the
> knowledge that Mr Night was pacing up and down, up and down. They
> were both virtuous enough to take a keen enjoyment in the punishment of
> others.[78]

Vera's middle name was Margaret and Chaddie's was Mary. Reading Byron
secretly reveals KM's precocious – if illicit – literary tastes at this time. This was
quite some distance from Mrs Molesworth's *Christmas-Tree Land*. The passage
also reveals her distaste for her perfect sisters, with whom she shared little
affinity. And yet, in typical contrary fashion, she recorded on the flyleaf of her
prayer book on 3 November 1901:

> Went with E K Bendall and Vera to St. Mark's Church to hear the Rev.
> Fred Bennet preach a sermon on Mauries [*sic*]. The most heavenly thing
> possible. He also read the Second lesson. The Betrayal of Jesus. I never
> enjoyed myself so much. I am going to be a Mauri missionary.

A drawing and little note in KM's autograph book at the end of 1901 also
confirm the fact that KM met Edie Bendall long before 1907, as supposed by
other biographers. The Reverend Frederick Augustus Bennett (1871–1950), of
Maori / Irish descent, became New Zealand's first Maori bishop in 1928. He
was a passionate speaker on Maori affairs and may well have met KM in 1907

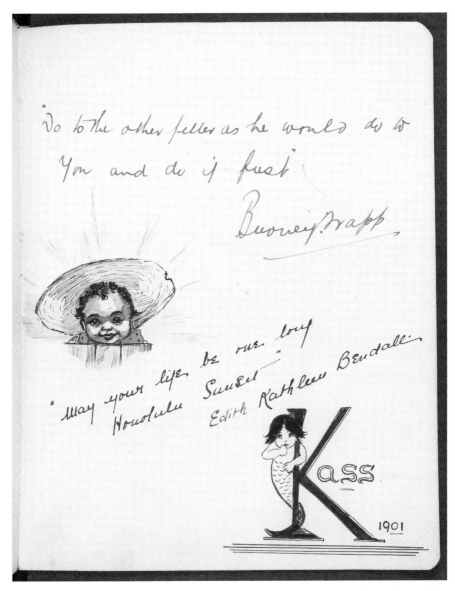

Figure 5.21 Katherine Mansfield's autograph book. Drawing and inscription by Edith Bendall,
1901.

during her trip to Rotorua, where he was then working as Superintendent of the
Maori mission.

A more lasting legacy of 1901, and one which would have ramifications for
the rest of KM's life, was meeting the Trowell family through her piano teacher,

Figure 5.22 Mr Thomas Trowell with, from left to right, Tom, Garnet and Lindley.

Figure 5.23 Tom (Arnold) Trowell playing the cello, 1901.

Figure 5.24 Garnet Trowell playing the violin.

Figure 5.25 The Trowell family house, 18 Buller Street, Wellington.

Robert Parker, who was a close friend of the father, Thomas Trowell, having conducted him in numerous concerts. Mr Trowell was a music teacher who had emigrated from England in 1882. His family consisted of his wife Kate; his twin sons Thomas Arnold and Garnet Carrington; and his ten-year-old daughter Muriel Dorothy, known as Dolly. (Another son, Lindley, had died tragically from pericarditis in 1894, aged just eight, and was buried in Karori cemetery.) The red-headed twins, who, having been born on 25 June 1887, were a year older than KM, were musically very gifted, especially Tom, the more dominant twin, who played the cello, though shy Garnet was also highly proficient on the violin. A strange tale would appear in the New Zealand press in 1907, of how

> when about nine years old, the two, travelling through the bush of the North Island, were taken by the Maoris and worshipped. The heads of golden-auburn hair, which the boys possessed, so attracted the natives, that certain of them carried off the boys at night to worship as Children of the Sun God.[79]

It was perhaps this tale which influenced KM's own story of Maori taking a Pakeha (white settler) child in 'How Pearl Button Was Kidnapped (1912). The Trowells, who lived at 18 Buller Street, were definitely 'her' kind of people: artists, bohemian and informal, penniless yet entrancing. KM, as was her wont, was soon obsessed with the whole family but quickly reserved her main passion for Tom, sometimes referred to as 'Caesar', who, at this early point in their friendship, was flattered and responsive.

Musically, the young twins were already making their mark on the cultural life of Wellington:

> On Tuesday 13 November 1900, Maughan Barnett directed the Wellington Orchestral Society in a concert at which Garnet played violin and Thomas [Arnold] played cello. It was held at the Opera House and included Mendelssohn's Italian Symphony and overture to A Midsummer Night's Dream, Rubinstein's Toréador et Andalouse and Mélodie by Paderewski.[80]

In December 1902, KM appeared on the same programme as the Trowell twins, in a concert organised by Robert Parker at the Sydney Street Schoolroom, in order to raise funds for St Paul's Sunday School Library. Mr Trowell was also a resident conductor at the Opera House, where his young son Garnet frequently led the violin section.

Both boys attended St Patrick's College on Cambridge Terrace, where Mr Trowell was a violin teacher. They made steady progress but it was in music that they excelled, especially Tom. When Jean Gerardy, the renowned

Belgian cellist, visited Wellington in 1901, he heard Tom play. A Wellington social column described the meeting:

> It is said that a Wellington boy, a son of a musician all too little known save in his own immediate circle, played before M. Gerardy on the 'cello, and the great musician was delighted with the youngster. He declared that he had 'soul' in his playing, and that that was the one thing needful to become a great musician. Technique might be acquired, but soul was inborn. The boy 'cellist has reached his flood-tide that leads on to fortune, for in a year M. Gerardy is coming back, and will take him to Europe, and keep him under his own supervision, so delighted is he with the promise the child displays.[81]

In time, several subscription funds would be set up, to which Harold personally donated the considerable sum of £25, in order to pay for the boys' musical education in Europe. Together with benefit concerts and other fundraisers, the grand total of £802 was collected. It is clear that Harold and Annie's musical family were soon caught up in the excitement over the talented twins and thus began a relationship that was to prove one of the most important of KM's adolescent life. Immediately, of course, KM had to start learning the cello with Mr Trowell in Buller Street. Harold was delighted, and an instrument was purchased without delay. KM's own musical talents now developed rapidly; she practised hard and was soon a proficient player, eventually playing a repertoire not dissimilar to that of young Tom himself.

As a result of the success of the trust fund, the twins finally left Wellington on 4 August 1903, initially staying with an uncle in London, and finally arriving in Frankfurt to begin their formal musical education on 30 September 1903 at the Hoch Conservatory. In the autumn of 1904 they moved from Frankfurt to Brussels, to study at the Royal Conservatory, where, '[a]ccording to Pablo Casals' biographer H. L. Kirk the cello class in Brussels was considered the best in Europe.'[82] By February 1905, Tom would have his own little music column, 'Music in Brussels', in *The Strad*, a London-based classical music magazine about string instruments, founded in 1889 and still going today. KM read the columns avidly; they almost certainly acted as a catalyst for her desire to see some of her own work in print, following her return to New Zealand from Queen's College in 1906. Meanwhile, in June 1905, Tom won the Premier Prix de Concours in the Royal Conservatory's cello competition, to joyous acclaim in the papers back home, where it was rather breathlessly reported that 'young Trowell is the first student for twenty years to win this prize at the age of seventeen [. . .] He is believed to be the first Englishman to win the Concours, and is certainly the first colonial.'[83]

Figure 5.26 Tom and Garnet Trowell before leaving New Zealand in August 1903, with their sister Dolly.

In the first chapter of *Juliet*, KM recreates the first meeting between herself and Tom and then follows it with her first experience of hearing him perform at a concert given in her own home:

> There was the usual amount of very second rate singing concerning Swallows and 'Had I Known'. Margaret played several nondescript pieces on the piano – and at last David's turn came. Juliet watched him with great pleasure and curiosity. A bright spot came into her cheeks, her eyes wide opened – but when he drew his bow across the strings her whole soul woke and lived for the first time in her life. She became utterly absorbed in the music. The room faded, the people faded. She saw only his sensitive inspired face, felt only the rapture that held her fast, that clung to her and hid her in its folds, as impenetrable and pure as the mists from the sea – – –
>
> Suddenly the music ceased, the tears poured down her face and she came back to reality – – – She put her handkerchief to her eyes and when she looked round became aware of the amused glances of the company, and heard the steady, almost prophetic sounding voice of David's Father: 'That child is a born musician.'
>
> The rest of the evening passed she knew not how. Something had come to life in Juliet's soul and it shone in her transfigured face. For that night she was brilliantly beautiful – not with the beauty of a child, but the charm

of a woman seemed to emanate from her. David was conscious of this, conscious too that he had never played before as he was playing. They avoided each other strangely, but Mr Wilberforce praised the boy and said 'You might come and give my little daughter a few lessons, and see if she has any talent.' She never forgot their leave-taking. The wind was furious, and she stood on the verandah and saw David turn round and smile at her before he passed out of sight.[84]

This account was written four years after the events it described; there is a marked difference of maturity between a girl of thirteen and a young woman almost eighteen years old. However, her 'crush' had remained intact during all that time, and indeed in 1906, when the above passage was written, was as profoundly real as ever, though sadly no longer reciprocated.

Chapter 6   Queen's College, London: 1903–1906

Meanwhile, life at no. 75 continued, albeit with a renewed enthusiasm for all things musical. By the end of 1902, Harold's three eldest daughters had been at Miss Swainson's for over two years. Perhaps motivated by the talk of sending the Trowell boys to Europe, Harold conceived the bold plan of sending his girls 'home' to England to be educated. Now a wealthy man, this considerable expense could be easily met and there was no better way to show Wellington society how far his star had risen. In his opinion, New Zealand could not offer the necessary cultural stimulus for his daughters. KM and her sisters were thrilled. Queen's College, at 45 Harley Street (which took both boarders and day pupils), was chosen on the recommendation of Annie's cousin, Joseph Frank Payne, whose mother, Eliza, was the sister of Annie's father. When the latter had emigrated to Australia, Eliza had stayed behind in London. Joseph Payne was a physician in Wimpole Street, just around the corner from Harley Street, and his own three daughters were all happily enrolled at Queen's College. The fees were twenty-two guineas per term for boarders, in addition to nine guineas for tuition. Multiplied by three, the total came to ninety-three guineas per term – around £100 – which, in those days, was a considerable sum, given that the average weekly wage was then little more than £1. Nevertheless, the businessman in Harold would have been pleased to take the fee discount on offer for three girls from one family. In addition, and possibly to avail himself of the discount, in order to have KM registered in the senior school with her two sisters, her date of birth was advanced by two years to 1890.[1]

VOYAGE TO ENGLAND

The whole Beauchamp family – a party of nine – made the outward journey to England, with Harold, the proud patriarch of his good-looking and distinguished brood, in an expansive gesture, taking the entire passenger accommodation of the S.S. *Niwaru* to accommodate himself and Annie, their five children, and his two in-laws: Belle, who would remain in England to chaperone the girls, and Sydney Dyer, Belle and Annie's brother. As Harold recorded in his *Reminiscences*, with a certain degree of pride:

> What we did was to take the whole passenger accommodation in the Tyser liner *Niwaru* (10,000 tons), for my wife and myself, our whole family of four daughters and one son, and the two in-laws. It was really a glorified yachting cruise, beginning with calls at Gisborne and Auckland and then via Cape Horn and Las Palmas, the whole voyage occupying 47 days. My wife was very fond of sea-travelling and always accompanied me on my trips, which added very much to their enjoyment.[2]

They left Wellington on 29 January 1903. Annie, always conscious of her delicate health, had just written her will. KM was fourteen, her hormones cranking up a gear, in love and eager to embrace 'life'. The ship offered many comforts to its only passengers, including a clavichord and sewing machine for the women, and a little caged canary. At every stop – Montevideo, Mexico, Las Palmas – KM sent love letters to Tom Trowell.

During the voyage, KM, the budding writer, put together a little booklet of verses in her own hand, called *Little Fronds*. It comprises seventeen poems; two of them, 'Love's Entreaty' and 'Night', would subsequently be published as songs in 1904, with music composed by Vera (Harold's money being put to showy use). The other poems, with titles such as 'Evening', 'The Sea' and 'In the Darkness', offer an enticing glimpse into the first long voyage of KM's life, with all the sights and sounds of shipboard life. 'The Sea' reveals the might of the ocean waves, as the *Niwaru* ploughed its way across the oceans:

> When fiercely rage the tempests o'er the deep
> And all the slumb'ring world is waked from sleep
> When the sea sobs, as if in sad distress
> And none are there to cheer my loneliness
> I feel for thee O Sea.[3]

At the same time, however, the poem reveals KM's (perhaps subconscious) imaginative response to her environment, stemming from the influence of that powerful, pantheistic 'oceanic consciousness' in the arts (poetry, music, painting) in the mid- to late nineteenth century. A flowery, sentimental poem, 'To M', was almost certainly a response to her separation from her close friend, Maata:

> For me, O love, thine eyes like stars are shining
> For me, thy voice is all the sound I need
> O love, dear love, dost know how I am pining
> My heart to plead.[4]

The S.S. *Niwaru* carried another passenger, in addition to the Beauchamp clan, described in the poem, 'The Chief's Bombay Tiger' – a delight for the children, if not the adults:

> Since leaving New Zealand
> I grieve to say
> A great Bombay tiger
> Has come to stay.
>
> He is kept by the chief
> In the No. 2 hold
> And is famous for doing
> Whatever he's told.
>
> And at night when the ladies
> Have gone to bed
> This great Bombay tiger
> Prowls round overhead.
>
> At six and seven, he's heard to roar
> At the ladies' porthole or cabin door
> But the lady passengers venture to say
> They never feel safe till that tiger's away.
>
> Now your pardon I beg, dear chief, to intrude
> And if you don't think me most horribly rude
> Just keep your dear tiger in No. 2 hold
> And your pardon I beg for being so rude.

Many years later, KM wrote to her father concerning a sea voyage he was about to take, reminiscing about this first trip to England:

> I envy you your voyage in the 'Aquitania.' It must be a most interesting experience to travel in one of those huge liners – very different to the good

old 'Star of New Zealand.' Still, I have a very soft corner in my heart for the 'Niwaru', for example. Do you remember how Mother used to enjoy the triangular-shaped pieces of toast for tea? Awfully good they were, too, on a cold afternoon in the vicinity of The Horn. How I should love to make a long sea voyage again one of these days. But I always connect such experiences with a vision of Mother in her little seal skin jacket with the collar turned up. I can see her as I write.[5]

On the final stop before England – Las Palmas, in the Canary Islands – the Beauchamps, together with the Captain, took a ride around the island in two carriages, finally stopping for lunch in a hotel, where a photographer took a rather grand photograph of the entire party, with Captain W. P. Fishwick centre-stage, and Aunt Belle with a rather conspicuous rose adorning her chest. KM stands slightly apart on the left at the back, her unbecoming wire-rimmed spectacles now a thing of the past, looking every inch the young lady, with her straw boater (a relic of her Miss Swainson's school uniform, soon to be replaced in London 'by a big soft navy felt, which her father paid £3 for at Swan and Edgar's'),[6] and with a slightly wistful expression on her face. KM wrote a post-card from Las Palmas to Lulu, one of her Dyer cousins: 'This is such a lovely

Figure 6.1 The Beauchamp family at Las Palmas, 1903.

place, darling, & we are having a very good time';[7] it was not posted, however, until the family finally reached Plymouth on 17 March 1903.

BEAUCHAMP RELATIONS

In England at last, the next month was spent in a dizzy round of Beauchamp / Dyer family visits, before the three eldest girls became boarders at Queen's College in Harley Street on 29 April, with Aunt Belle close at hand, eventually assisting their housemistress when a member of the boarding staff retired. Harold, Annie and young Leslie and Jeanne stayed on in England for several months until 28 September, when they left Southampton to return home to New Zealand, the parents content that their daughters were settled and in capable hands.

One of the first things to get used to was the topsy-turvy seasons; instead of April being in autumn, it was now spring. On 16 April, KM wrote a delightful letter home to a schoolfriend from Miss Swainson's; KM playfully addressed her as Marius (possibly Marion Tweed) and signed herself as Kassius. In the letter she describes her sense of wonder and excitement at all that London had to offer an impressionable young girl:

> I wish that I could give you an idea of London. It is totally beyond description. It is most marvellous!!! The traffic is so astounding. There is none other way to have a really splendid view, than to sit on the top of a bus, with a piece of strong elastic on your hat; Then it is superb!! The bus drivers are such cures. They look most beautifully comfy wrapped up in gloves and rugs, and are most talkative. My dear, I wish that you could see Westminster Abbey. It is so lovely!! It is utterly impossible to rush the Abbey, because immediately you enter you are held enthralled by some marvellous work of sculpture, and so it is the whole time that you are there. I fell in love with Sophia, daughter of James I, (I mean, I fell in love with her tomb.) She died when she was three days old. The tomb is of white marble. It is a baby's basinette with a hood and deep curtains, and a little child asleep inside. I bent over and kissed the baby; it looked so sad! Are you laughing dear? It was not funny. We went to St. Paul's Cathedral last Good Friday. What charmed me most was the beautiful paintings the exquisite arches, & the magnificence of the mosaic work. The service was fearfully impressive. The church was dim, and there was a wonderful anthem. It seems to go right through you, and made you quite choky. The building of St. Pauls is very fine but I don't like all the pigeons that are constantly flying about. They remind me of the time that Christ came and turned the dove merchants

out of the Temple. How interested you would be in the British Museum. My dear you could see enough Julius Caesar's to last you a lifetime, with noses, and minus noses, according to B.C. & A.D. All the sculpture everywhere, was a huge revelation, to me. O the indescribable beauty of form and attitude, that can be hewn out of a block of marble. And, O Marius, the pictures. My dear they take away all my adjectives!!!!!! I have fallen in love with all Watts pictures in the Tate Gallery. The most marvellous originality of colour is so striking, the depth of his reds, the calm peace of his blues, and his figures!!!! I think that the two most beautiful I saw were 'Love and Life', & 'Hope'. On Bank Holiday Father & I did the correct thing & went to 'Appy 'Ampstead 'Eath. When we arrived there it grew most fearfully cold, and we had a bad snowstorm. I loved it. The whole place looked like a picture postcard. A place I am very fond of going to is Hyde Park. The carriages, horses and babies are most lovely, especially the last named. In their perambulators they remind me of little bits of wedding cake tied up with white ribbons. The motor cars are very fascinating. You see hundreds dodging about everywhere.

I never saw such beautiful curtains as the English have. Silk & silk lace of the most exquisite quality!!! I would just love some of them for dresses!!!

We three girls go to school on the 29th of this month (April.) We are going to Queen's College Harley Street. W. It is a most delightful school. The school headmistress is a Miss Croudace, and the house mistress a Miss Wood. They are both exceedingly nice. The school is most superbly furnished. The room where we study is carpeted with thick Turkey carpets, great armchairs everywhere, neat little tables, rugs, and charming pictures. Even Latin would be interesting in this room.[8]

So much of this enchanting, breathless letter presages KM the grown woman, particularly the eye for detail. It is doubtful whether Vera or Chaddie would have noticed or talked to the bus driver, wrapped up in gloves and rugs. KM's love of the miniature is here, in that poignant description of the tomb of the baby daughter of James I. There is a little bit of Harold talking too, when she shows off her knowledge of the 'magnificence of the mosiacs' in St Paul's. Her intoxication with the sculpture in the British Museum and the art in the Tate Gallery is palpable. And in the Bank Holiday visit, alone with her father, to 'Appy 'Ampstead 'Eath, we see KM the born mimic, replicating a Cockney accent and revelling in it. Hampstead Heath was renowned for its Cockney Carnivals on Bank Holidays, the biggest in London, when enormous crowds would gather. Harold was certainly up for the visit, but apparently only KM was keen to accompany him to see the rowdy sights on offer. It could also be dangerous: in 1892, nine people had been trampled to death in a rush to escape a rain storm. The phrase ''Appy 'Amstead 'Eath', which KM replicates in her letter, was nationally known, and celebrated in a song by Albert Chevalier and the cartoons of Phil May. On 26 August 1918, KM and Murry would move into a house in Hampstead: 2 Portland Villas, East Heath Road, where she would undoubtedly have remembered this first visit to Hampstead Heath and all the excitement of the fair.

As well as enjoying the sights and sounds of London, the family visited their Beauchamp relatives and Harold's favourite uncle, Henry Herron, and his wife Louey at their home, The Retreat, in Bexley, Kent. Uncle Henry's children – Harold's first cousins – had all done well for themselves. Mary had transformed herself into 'Elizabeth' von Arnim, married a German count, and become a hugely successful, best-selling author. Charlotte (Chaddie) had married a stock-broker (it was her son, Sydney Waterlow, a civil servant in the Foreign Office, who hankered towards a more artistic life and hung around the fringes of Bloomsbury, and who would eventually introduce KM to that intellectual and artistic circle). Sydney had become a successful doctor, and Henry (also known as de Monk in some biographies) was a music teacher at the London Academy of Music and an accomplished cellist and singer. It was this last cousin who Harold chose as the girls' official guardian for their stay in England, a popular choice with his daughters, who thereafter referred to Henry as 'Guardy'. He would go on to become Professor of Singing at the Royal Academy of Music from 1907 to 1937, with a distinguished career, conducting the choir as well as many opera productions.

Most holidays, and especially Christmas, were spent with Great-Uncle Henry Herron and the Beauchamp clan at The Retreat. Henry Herron himself seemed to enjoy the girls' company. In his regularly kept diaries, he noted their visits. On Christmas Day 1903, he wrote:

> Three Harold Beauchamp girls in residence at 'The Retreat' since last Tuesday, very nice young things, cheered our day. Dined at 1 [. . .] and a High Supper at 7 p.m. – added a bottle of Champagne which immediately developed the dear girls young spirits and we became rather 'royal' – with 'Tol-de-Rol' etc., etc., and recitations afterwards by Vera & Kathleen the latter's very good.[9]

For Christmas 1903, KM received a parcel from Tom Trowell, which contained a German edition of Heinrich Heine's *Buch der Lieder*. Inside he wrote, 'To dear Kass, wishing you the most prosperous of New Years from Tom. Xmas. 1903.'[10] It was one of the few instances when Tom seemed to demonstrate some affection for KM. It was not to last, however, and until KM finally moved on from Tom (though only as far as his twin, Garnet), it would be KM doing all the running, her miserable infatuation barely acknowledged by the object of her affection. KM was still annotating the Heine in 1908, and kept it all her life.

Due to sickness in the household in Bexley, KM and Chaddie left on 3 January 1904, leaving Vera and now Aunt Belle who took their place, and who could be more of a help than the younger Beauchamp girls. KM and Chaddie were sent northwards to Wortley, near Sheffield, to stay with the Broughtons, relatives by marriage of the Beauchamps (Henry Herron's brother Cradock had married Harriet Broughton, and it was to her family that the girls were sent). KM wrote from there to her cousin Sylvia Payne:

> Chad and I came here [. . .] because Bertha, Aunt Louey's maid has been very ill, and there were so many in the house [. . .] Really, I am not enjoying it at all, but I have to pretend I am. [. . .] At present I am sitting in a small room with a large fire and
> 3 dogs
> 1 cockatoo
> 1 canary.[11]

A year later, they were all back in Bexley as normal. On Boxing Day 1904, KM wrote to Sylvia:

> So far, I have enjoyed myself immensely. The days have flown past, without one dull moment. There has been so much to do. I have had some good practices too, and my cousin who is staying here has a glorious tenor voice.[12]

Great-Uncle Henry's diaries for the same Christmas period recorded: 'the three Harold Beauchamp (Maori) girls came on Friday to form our Christmas Party. Much feeding! [. . .] After supper much Tol-de-rol, recitations etc by the gifted Kathleen and general jollity.'[13] He continued to refer to the three sisters as the Maori girls in his diary, no doubt a family joke for the amusement of all.

QUEEN'S COLLEGE

Queen's College was an unusual, avant-garde educational institution for women, and without the recommendation of Joseph Payne, one wonders whether Harold would have come to choose the school of his own accord. It was certainly a bold choice for his precious daughters. What started out as the Governesses' Benevolent Institution had become, by 1848 (the same year that 'pa-man' Arthur Beauchamp, Harold's father, had left Hornsey Lane), Queen's

Figure 6.2 Katherine Mansfield with cello.

Figure 6.3 The main corridor, Queen's College.

Figure 6.4 Staff at Queen's College. Prof. Hall Griffin, Miss Harper, Miss Croudace.

College – a bold experiment, and the first of its kind in England – providing further education for young women (and most definitely *not* a 'finishing school'), set up by social reformers Frederick Denison Maurice and the author Charles Kingsley. (Its original governess roots would be remembered by KM when she wrote her story 'The Little Governess' in 1915.) There was also a junior school, catering for younger girls up to the age of fourteen, who would then transfer to the college. Camilla Croudace had been one of the college's earliest students, and by the time the Beauchamp girls arrived, she had been the headmistress – or to give her the correct Queen's College title, the Lady Resident – since 1881. She was a formidable woman and perfect for the institution: firm but fair, with a sense of humour and not easily shocked. It was not uncommon for girls to develop crushes on one another (known as 'D.V.'s' after the initials of one of Miss Croudace's own infatuation-prone nieces); such instances were dealt with swiftly and with good humour. Favoured girls, both past and present, were invited to weekend at Ridge Cap, her cottage in Haslemere, Surrey,[14] and KM was a visitor on at least one occasion, writing in the visitors' book: 'I have never

Figure 6.5 The Office, Queen's College. Miss Harper, Miss Croudace with Sylvia Payne.

spent happier holidays. Is there anything more beautiful than English woods in spring?'[15]

Miss Croudace would retire in 1906, before the Beauchamps left, and her place was taken by Miss Barbara Harper, who, when the Beauchamps arrived, was a dynamic and exciting English teacher. KM wrote a poem with the following rather bizarre title – 'An Escapade Undertaken by A Green Raspberry, & A Kidney Bean' – in tribute to her, possibly as a poetry exercise devised by Miss Harper herself, her name being the refrain of all six stanzas:

> Two girls asleep in the office chair
> waked by Miss Harper who found them there
> Look up at her with sleepy eyes
> And mutter – with a vague surprise
> Miss Harper.[16]

Miss Harper reciprocated by writing in KM's autograph book on 11 November 1903:

> When God looked out upon His Earth,
> How fair it was to see!

And still the flowers spring to birth,
And still it seems to me,
That Early fragrance lingereth
Upon the rosemary . .[17]

The Lady Resident, however important, still reported to a man, known as the Principal, and this would not change until 1931. There were two principals during KM's time: the Rev. T. W. Sharpe, a former Chief Inspector of Schools, and then from 1904 to 1912, Canon G. C. Bell, former Master of Marlborough College, and the one KM would remember in later life.

Miss Clara Finetta Wood, 'Woodie' to the boarders, leased and ran the hostel, which comprised no. 41 and the top half of no. 43 Harley Street, next door to the school at no. 45, catering for around twenty students in shared rooms. Now elderly, she was a true Queen's College institution, renowned for her eccentricities. She dressed only in her favourite colour, purple, except when she went to the opera, when she favoured the colour violet. Her ink was also violet in colour. When she had first applied to the college in 1873, she had given her address as 'Violet Cottage, Felixstowe'. Her sparse hair was concealed by the addition of a large coil, worn on the crown of her head, surrounded by a velvet band which was decorated with a bow for everyday wear but adorned with sequins and beads in the evening, to the fascination of her charges. Four overworked maids and two assistants helped Miss Wood with the boarders. When her assistant, Miss Robinson ('Robin'), left to marry one of the local tradesmen, Aunt Belle secured her position. The second assistant was Miss Hatch ('Hatchet'), a rather pathetic creature whose own cubicle was a curtained-off portion of the one and only bathroom, which also contained the boarders' piano.

Another female teacher, outdoing even Miss Wood for eccentricity, was Mademoiselle Séguin, who taught French at Queen's from 1878 to 1911. She had an obsession with germs, which resulted in her keeping all windows closed, whatever the weather, and her neck and face wrapped up in scarves. All her pupils were called 'Dolly' and any girl who dared to use a germ-laden handkerchief in her presence was instantly given the order 'Pocket Dolly'. Exercise books were returned by throwing them. Extremely popular with the girls, she was, by all accounts, an excellent teacher. KM would remember her in the name of a Geneva boarding house in 'Epilogue I: Pension Seguin' (1913).

School-age girls normally took a four-year 'course' of study, although the college was celebrated for its provision of free evening classes, taken by women who were beyond school age and known as 'Non-Compounders' (the boarders being known as 'Compounders'). Lectures were given, university-style, with no registers or class marks, and the girls were treated as young adults; they were free to wander in and out of classes, or not go at all. Although they were required to write papers twice a year on their chosen subjects, it was very easy for a lazy girl to coast her way through the system: 'Each girl was the assessor of her own progress, not a competitor. The object was to learn how to learn rather than to amass facts.'[18]

The staff list boasted some renowned scholars in 1903. Firstly, there was the notable historian John Adam Cramb (1861–1913), who taught at the college from 1893 until his death. A brilliant man and somewhat of a polymath, being not just an historian but also an authority on philosophy, divinity, French literature and the medieval romance, he also wrote novels under the pseudonym J. A. Revermort. In the autumn of 1903, Cramb became the personal tutor of Lady Ottoline Morrell (later to become one of KM's close friends). He was a lonely man by all accounts, with an invalid wife and crippled son; by February 1904 he had become Ottoline's regular companion, and soon developed a romantic obsession for her. Ottoline, having never encouraged such frantic passion, ended the friendship a year after it had begun, though Cramb carried a torch for her for the rest of his life.

Other prominent members of staff included literature expert William Hall Griffin (1857–1907), who wrote a celebrated biography of his friend Robert Browning.[19] There was also Richard Gregory (1864–1952), the school's Professor of Astronomy, who would be knighted in 1919.[20] The Professor of Theology was the Rev. E. H. Pearce, occasionally helped by his sister, Miss Pearce:

> He had a parish in the city and his sister worked amongst the factory girls; he ran a club for them and tried to arrange 'evenings'. On one such evening the Beauchamp sisters and I were invited down: Katherine's 'cello, my fiddle, Chaddie's voice and Vera's piano. I don't know how much pleasure the girls derived from our activities, but I gathered two strange pieces of information there: that old women spent their time cutting wood into tiny bits to be used as raspberry seeds in the factory jam, and that the workers drank large quantities of vinegar.[21]

It says something for the young girls that they agreed to go to such an 'evening'; it was certainly an experience for KM.

However, it was Walter Rippmann (1869–1947), the brilliant young German Professor, born in London of a German father and an English mother (and who changed his German name to the more anglicised Ripman during World War One), who, of all the teachers at the school, would have the greatest influence on KM. He became Professor of German at Queen's in 1896, aged just twenty-seven, and stayed for nearly twenty years. One of the students, Ruth Herrick, noted that he 'was rather young for a girls' school', and indeed he

Figure 6.6 Professor Walter Rippmann.

did go on to marry a former pupil, a Canadian girl called Connie Greer, in 1905. Evelyn Payne, KM's older cousin, who left Queen's College in the summer of 1903 to study at the all-female Oxford college, Lady Margaret Hall, was even less impressed, claiming he was 'rather fat and flabby, with very well-oiled hair, and his voice had a thick lisp'.[22] Nevertheless, he was a brilliant scholar, having taken the Tripos Examinations at Cambridge in Classics, Medieval and Modern Languages, *and* Indian Languages:

> [He] was an admirer of Oscar Wilde, of Walter Pater, and of *art nouveau*. In contrast to most of the other professors, he was 'young and ardent', and a man of great social charm. With his more able original students, he was ready to spend time in stimulating conversation, introducing them to new ideas and encouraging them to discover their own potentialities. A select group was invited to visit his house in Ladbroke Grove, where he would talk to them of his literary heroes, show them his collection of Japanese prints, and introduce them to an exciting new world.[23]

KM would become one of Rippmann's favoured students, and was invited to his bohemian home at 72 Ladbroke Grove, which he shared with a journalist and an artist, decorated in an art nouveau style, as well as with Japanese prints, which were then hugely popular. There he would give 'rose teas', with rose petals scattered in the hearth, under the soft rose glow of his art nouveau lamps. KM would never have seen anything quite like it. In *Juliet*, she fictionalised her first visit to the strange and wonderful house, in a section called simply 'The Man', whose name happens to be Walter:

> When she reached the long tree-lined avenue, the rain had ceased and great splashes of sunlight lay across the road. As she neared the house she stopped and repeated the Dorian Grey [*sic*]. Her heart was beating almost unbearably. She pressed her hand against her hot face. 'This is gloriously unconventional' said Juliet, 'but I wish I was less frightened.'
>
> Walter opened the door. 'Ha – you've come at last' he said, his voice full of intense hospitality. 'Come along into the smoking room – second door to the right.' She pushed aside the heavy purple portière.
>
> The room was full of gloom but vivid yellow curtains hung straight and fine before the three windows. Tall wrought-iron candle-sticks stood in the corners – the dead whiteness of the candles suddenly brought back a memory of Saint Gudule at dusk and Juliet caught her breath. There were prints of beautiful women on the walls, and the graceful figure of a girl holding a shell in her exquisite arms stood on a table. There was a long low couch upholstered in dull purple, and quaint low chairs in the same colour. The room was full of the odour of chrysanthemums. The blossoms were arranged in high glasses on the mantel shelf – – –
>
> 'I am afraid,' said Walter, closing the door and speaking slightly apologetically, 'it's not very – – –'
>
> 'Please I like it,' Juliet said, smiling at him and pulling off her long gloves.[24]

It is probably not an exaggeration to state that in introducing the impressionable KM to the works of Wilde, Pater and other writers of the fin-de-siècle and Decadent movements (especially Arthur Symons, Ernest Dowson, Paul Verlaine and Nietzsche), Rippmann would alter the course of her reading – and writing – life. At this time, KM was an open vessel, absorbing every influence that came her way.

KM had not long been at the school when, on 29 June 1903, Rippmann wrote a long entry in her autograph book, with quotations from S. A. Tipple and Maurice Maeterlinck:

Figure 6.7 Katherine Mansfield in her room at Queen's College.

Ah! how we think sometimes that much is going to be done by organizing committees, and appointing officials; or fondly hope to regenerate society with new franchises, new political arrangements, better legislation; when the real need is, that there should be some making and remaking of men, and the truest work would be to seek to promote the culture of individual minds and hearts. Nor let us doubt that <u>that</u> is always the divinest work – to get at a man, and be the means of ministering in some way to his healthier growth or finer inspiration; of helping him in some way to juster thought or loftier feeling. Get at a man, and send him from you into busy street and market-place, into the circle of which he is the centre, into the midst of his neighbours and friends with a greater spirit, with a breath of higher life in him, and who can tell what good you have not started and provided for in doing that? – who can predict whereunto that may not grow? – you have wrought, anyhow, for once in your life, an immortal work. The noblest sculptures and pictures will perish; the noblest utterances, the noblest poems may be forgotten; but any purifying or elevating effect which they have had upon a human soul, – that remains and dies not until the heavens be removed. S.A.T.[25]

It is just beauty and no more which again and again has saved us, putting us into a finer mood, giving us inspiration, sweetening us to our healthening, soothing us to our increase in vigour.

Have we not been more deeply, subtly benefited often in looking at a picture than in hearing a sermon, in strolling through a summer wood than in listening to a botanical discourse? Has not God drawn nearer to us at times and spoken with us more intimately or healingly in a wonderful sunset than in any words of the preacher? S.A.T.

Qu'il y ait bonheur ou malheur, l'homme le plus heureux sera toujours celui dans lequel la plus grande idee vit avec la plus grande ardeur. Maeterlinck.[26]

All very appropriate and above board, of course, with just a hint of aestheticism for KM to carry away with her, Tipple being a favourite of Ruskin. How thrilled she must have been with this long two-page entry in her autograph book, written in a neat, round hand. Many years later, when Murry became editor of the *Athenaeum*, KM suggested Rippmann as a reviewer of foreign literature. In 1932, following a request by Mantz for information on KM, Rippmann replied, rather enigmatically: 'my memory does not seem very clear as regards the rather remote period about which you enquire.'[27]

KM was soon smitten with Rippmann. She wrote to her cousin, Sylvia Payne, on 24 January 1904:

I am *ashamed* at the way in which I long for German. I simply can't help it. It is dreadful. And when I go into class, I feel I must just stare at him the whole time. I never liked anyone so much. Every day I like him more. Yet on Thursday he was like *ice*![28]

One can only imagine poor Rippmann, confronted with such an obvious crush by one of his young students, having to choose to ignore the staring colonial girl in the corner. Even so, having seen and admired KM's poems, he invited her to contribute some for an English language textbook for foreigners that he was writing. Sadly, none was used in the end; her disappointment must have been considerable, since it would have been her first opportunity for commercial success with her writing. In a letter to her friend, S. S. Koteliansky, written in May 1917, a memory of one of Rippmann's classes came to her:

Two lovers came and hid behind a tree and put up an umbrella. Then they walked away, pressed against each other. It made me think of a poem that our german professor used to read us in class.

Ja, das war zum letzenmal
Das, wir beide, arm in arme
Unter einem Schirm gebogen. – –
Alles war zum letzenmal.[29]

And I heard again his 'sad' voice (so beautiful it seemed, you know) and I
saw again his white hand with a ring on it, press open the page![30]

'A Fairy Story', written at the end of 1910 and published in the *Open
Window* under the pseudonym Katherina Mansfield, is replete with allusions to
Rippmann and all he taught her. The central character, 'The Wanderer', is based
on Rippmann himself:

'Well?' he said sharply, as the Girl stood by the door.
'I want to look at your books,' said she.
He glanced at her curiously. Her wonderful face gleamed strangely at
him, from billow and billow of white pinafore.
'I'm – I'm quite exceptional,' she said, hastily, "I'm very advanced.'
'Oh, are you?' said the Wanderer.
'Don't think of what I *look* like; as Mr. Shaw says, 'You Never can Tell.'
'Hang thee, sweet wench,' said the Wanderer, 'come along here – you
know the "Open Sesame" and I'll show you the books.'
And two hours later, they were, both sitting on the floor – And he was
reading her Omar Kháyyám, and she was looking into Arthur Symons.
[. . .]
And he told her of London, of Spain, of Paris, of Brussels, and again
London.
And he taught her his ethics of life, and that unselfishness signifies lack
of Progress – and that she must avoid the Seven Deadly Virtues. And she
printed a little text, and hung it above her washstand – '*The strongest man
is he who stands most alone.*'
[. . .]
And the Wanderer did not forget her. He sent her a post-card of Maxim
Gorki, and a little book 'The Virgins of the Rocks'; she did not understand
it, but it gave her beautiful dreams.[31]

The story is based on a heady mix of the fairy stories of the Grimm brothers
and Hans Christian Andersen, the fantasy delights of *Christmas-Tree Land* by
Mrs Molesworth, and the Decadent literature introduced to the impressionable
fourteen-year-old by Rippmann, remembered seven years on and fictionalised.
It was also in this year that one of KM's close friends, Vere Bartrick-Baker,

lent KM the original Lippincott's magazine serialisation of Wilde's *The Picture of Dorian Gray*. Vere herself had received it from one of the younger mistresses, Miss Messenger, 'with many injunctions to secrecy'.[32] KM was hooked and soon obtained a copy of the book itself, which became almost a sacred tome for her during the next few years. She filled her notebooks with quotations from it and tried to imitate the wit in aphorisms of her own. For some time, KM would refer to herself as the 'White Gardenia', referencing one of the preferred flowers of Oscar Wilde.[33]

It was also at this time that KM started writing in notebooks. Whether this activity was inspired by Rippmann or not, towards the end of 1903, we find a list of German phrases and their translations, and the draft of a letter sent to Tom Trowell. On 13 July 1904, below the note 'Private!', she began what would become a lifetime's habit of list-making, beginning with 'Books I have read', then 'Music I have studied', followed by 'Letters I have written' and 'Writing I have done'.[34] All offer a fascinating glimpse into KM's daily life at this time. Books she particularly enjoyed were marked with a star. These included the *Life and Letters of Byron*, James Lane Allen's *The Choir Invisible* and *Aftermath*, Anthony Hope's *Dolly Dialogues*, and *Poems* by Jean Ingelow. Several of the books listed focus on the short story or sketch form. Indeed, KM's first foray into sketch-writing came on 18 August 1904, when she wrote down the following short piece in her notebook, taking the persona of a man writing to an old schoolfriend:

> Dear old George – I'm going to write you a letter. I guess you have forgotten all about me, and the times I had with you. Well, I haven't. I'll tell you who I am. Do you mind the red-haired boy with the big freckles who was in your form at school. One day you stuck wet varnish on his seat. God! how my Mother swore, and how you fellows laughed. Have you forgotten how you taught me to swim in the old bathing hole down in the 3rd meadow? Don't say you have, old man – I mind it all as though it were yesterday.[35]

There is a clever twist in the writing since the jovial tone belies the hurt of the young schoolboy who put up with such bullying. This unfinished short paragraph demonstrates the experimental nature of her writing at this time.

Life at Queen's College suited KM. For the first time in her life she experienced emotional and intellectual freedom, and relished it. A poem written in 1903 expresses her delight in the gentle, studious, creative environment of her room in college (even if she did have to share it with Vera and Chaddie):

> This is my world, this room of mine
> Here I am living – – – and here I shall die

All my interests are here, in fine
– – – The hours slip quickly by.

Look on these shelves – just books, you would say
Friends I can tell you, one and all
Most of them sorrowful – some of them gay – –
And my pictures that line the wall.

Yes, that is a Doré, from where I sit
At night with my books or my work, I see
The light that falls and glorifies it – – –
And I gaze and it strengthens me.

Ah! in this cupboard, my miser's store
Of music finger it sheaf on sheaf
Elixir of life – – it is something more
It is Heaven to me, in brief.

And that is my 'cello, my all in all
Ah, my beloved, quiet you stand
– – – If I let the bow ever so softly fall,
– – – The magic lies under my hand.

And on winter nights when the fire is low
We comfort each other, till it would seem
That the night outside, all cold and snow
Is the ghost of a long past dream.

This is my world, this room of mine
Here I am living – – – here I shall die
All my interests are here in fine
– The hours slip quickly by.[36]

A typical college day would see her and the other boarders go into no. 45 and the college dining room, where they would have their breakfast, followed by some fresh air, with a walk, crocodile-fashion, either to the nearby Park Square gardens, or over to the grandeur of Regent's Park, where they could feed squirrels and ducks. Each girl then undertook her lectures for the day; there was no prescribed number or compulsory subjects. The students could take as many – or as few – lectures as they chose, though they were expected to be in classes for a minimum of ten hours per week, in addition to an hour's private study per subject. In this sense, it resembled a university far more than a school – if you did not want to work, there was no one to force you. In addition, having been 'Kathleen' to her teachers at Miss Swainson's, KM suddenly became the much

Figure 6.8 The library, Queen's College.

Figure 6.9 The waiting room, Queen's College.

Figure 6.10 A lecture room, Queen's College.

Figure 6.11 The Pfeiffer Hall, Queen's College.

more grown-up 'Miss Beauchamp'. Of course, all this did not come without its difficulties. Girls as young as fourteen, as KM was in her first term, were not always equipped for this type of intellectual freedom.

There was a beautiful library, where the girls could work in silence, and which, as KM described in a letter home, 'was thick Turkey carpeted, great armchairs everywhere, neat little tables, rugs, and charming pictures'.[37] The library was well stocked, but even so, provision had also been made for girls to have lending rights at the enormous London Library in St James's Square. In addition there was a 'waiting room', with a large bay window and comfortable chairs, where they might pass the time in between lectures. A more informal space for the girls to relax, where staff rarely ventured, was the Bun Shop, run by old Mrs Brown. Dark, yet cosy and warm, with its own built-in stove, it had a useful noticeboard where messages could be left for friends, and its wooden tables bore fifty years' worth of student graffiti.

At the end of the day, the girls might take another walk to the Park Square gardens for some fresh air, then return to change. The girls loved to look down through the 'giraffe hole', where boarders, on an upper landing linking the hostel with the school, could stare down through the railings to the main school corridor below:

> younger members of the boarding house would look down through it and watch the older girls, wearing posies from their young admirers in the lower forms, walking along the corridor with their brothers and friends to the hall at the end where the dances were held.[38]

There were endless college dances in the Pfeiffer Hall:

> These consumed a surprising amount of emotion and surplus energy, considering that they were merely school affairs. Except on rare occasions, the girls had only each other to dance with; but the lights, the dresses, the fires flaring on either side of the Hall, the bonbons thrown down the Giraffe Hole by special friends to special friends – all made an exciting, a thrilling ball.[39]

For an hour before dinner there was silent study. Following dinner, Miss Wood would come to collect her charges, and more often than not, they would go into her cluttered, overheated sitting room and relax whilst she read to them from a suitably edifying novel, Charlotte M. Yonge being a favourite author. Weekends were reserved for trips to museums and other culturally approved venues, but on these occasions the girls were allowed to go off in pairs. Wandering through the streets of London was an exhilarating pastime for the young KM.

A fellow pupil at Queen's frequently remembered seeing KM, generally alone, in the dining room:

> She as the senior would pass the time of day with us, and laugh at the intenseness of our gossip. I did not think her pretty by my schoolgirl standards, but she had a sweet expression, and usually a little smile [and] an exquisitely clear complexion. [. . .] I thought of her as a quiet girl, more inclined to listen than to talk. [. . .] But although she was often by herself she never seemed to be lonely.[40]

It was mostly the boarders whose parents forced them to take proper lunches in the formal dining hall. Day girls had much more freedom, and could bring in their own sandwiches and eat them downstairs in the Bun Shop.

Much later on, whilst in Bandol on the Riviera with Murry in early 1916, KM took the time to reflect over her Queen's College life, in a fascinating record of those three precious years:

> I was thinking yesterday of my <u>wasted wasted</u> early girlhood. My college life, which is such a vivid and detailed memory in one way might never have contained a book or a lecture. I lived in the girls, the professor, the big lovely building, the leaping fires in winter & the abundant flowers in summer. The views out of the windows, all the pattern that was – weaving. Nobody saw it, I felt, as I did. My mind was just like a squirrel. I gathered & gathered & hid away for that long 'winter' when I should rediscover all this treasure – and if anybody came close I scuttled up the tallest darkest tree & hid in the branches.
>
> And I was so awfully fascinated in watching Hall Griffin & all his tricks – thinking about him as he sat there – his private life, what he was like as a man (he told us he & his brother once wrote an enormous poem called The Epic of the Griffins) etc etc. Then it was only at rare intervals that something flashed through all this busyness – something about Spenser's Faery Queene or Keats Isabella & the Pot of Basil. Those flashes were always when I disagreed flatly with H.G. & wrote in my notes – this man is a fool.
>
> And Cramb – wonderful Cramb! The figure of Cramb was enough, he was 'history' to me. Ageless & fiery, eating himself up again & again, very fierce at what he had seen but going a bit blind because he had looked so long. Cramb, striding up & down, filled me up to the brim. I couldn't write down Cramb's thunder. I simply wanted to sit & eat him. Every gesture, every shifting of his walk, all his tones and looks are as vivid to me as though it were yesterday – but of all he said I only remember phrases – 'he sat there & his wig fell off'. 'Anne Bullen a lovely <u>pure</u> creature stepping

out of her quiet door into the light and clamour', & looking back & seeing the familiar door shut upon her with a little click as it were – final.

But what coherent account could I give of the history of English Literature? Or what of English History? None.

[. . .]

[. . . Why] didn't I listen to the old Principal who lectured on Bible History twice a week instead of staring at his face that was very round, a dark red colour with a kind of bloom on it & covered all over with little red veins with endless tiny tributaries that ran even into his forehead & were lost in his bushy white hair.

He had tiny hands, too, puffed up, purple, shining under the stained flesh. I used to think looking at his hands – he will have a stroke & die of paralysis. They told us he was a very learned man, but I could not help seeing him in a double-breasted frock coat, a large pseudo-clerical pith helmet, a clean white handkerchief falling over the back of his neck staring and pointing out with an umbrella a probable site of a probable encampment of some wandering tribe – to his wife, an elderly lady with a threatening cerebral tumour who had to go everywhere in a basket chair arranged on the back of a donkey, & his two daughters in thread gloves & sand shoes smelling faintly of some anti-mosquito mixture.

As he lectured I used to sit, building his house, peopling it, filling it with curious ebony & ivory furniture, cupboards like tiny domes & tables with elephants legs presented to him by grateful missionary friends . . . I never came into contact with him but once when he asked any young lady in the room to hold up her hand if she had been chased by a wild bull & as nobody else did I held up mine (though of course I hadn't). Ah, he said, I am afraid you do not count. You are a little savage from New Zealand – which was really a trifle exacting – for it must be the rarest thing to be chased by a wild bull up & down Harley Street, Wimpole Street, Welbeck Street, Queen Anne, round & round Cavendish Square.

And why didn't I learn French with M. Huguenot. What an opportunity missed! What has it not cost me! He lectured in a long narrow room that was painted all over – the walls, door & window frames a charming shade of mignonette green. The ceiling was white & just below it there was a frieze of long looped chains of white flowers. On either side of the marble mantelpiece a naked small boy staggered under a big platter of grapes that he held above his head. Below the windows, far below, there was a stable court paved in cobblestones – one could hear the faint clatter of carriages coming out or in, the noise of water gushing out of a pump into a big pail, some youth clumping about & whistling. The room was never very light & in summer M. H. liked the blind to be drawn half way down the window . . . He was a little fat man.[41]

KM was perhaps unjustifiably hard on herself in the above notebook entry, since her achievements at Queen's were very creditable and she did well in most areas, though the subjects she studied became gradually more limited. Students were given free rein to drop subjects they did not enjoy. As a consequence, in the last term of 1904, KM stopped taking theology, chemistry, geography, ancient history, drawing and arithmetic, which left her with just German, French, English, singing and cello. Her worst subject had been arithmetic; in one paper she received the ignominious mark of 0/150, one assumes because she simply chose not to show up. Her best subjects were French and German, with reports in these subjects ranging from good to excellent. In her Christmas 1905 report, Professor Cramb noted that her English language was 'unsatisfactory', and literature 'disappointing';[42] perhaps more was expected of her, given the stories written for the school magazine, but there may have been laziness on KM's part too, hinted at in the above notebook entry.

The memory of M. Huguenet's French class, as described above by KM, would be replicated almost exactly in 'Carnation' (1918), one of her most sexually charged stories. The lyricism of the words in the story owes much to the Symbolists and Decadents, with their notion of expressing the inexpressible. Even the title of her story pays homage to the Decadent movement, since a dyed-green carnation, the preferred lapel flower of Oscar Wilde, was the potent symbol of both decadence and homosexuality at the turn of the new century. On 4 July 1906, just before KM left Queen's College, M. Huguenet wrote in KM's autograph book:

> Years pass, one after another, and soon we arrive at a moment where we have only memories of youth. But the memory which will never fade from our mind is that of our school years and we always look back with the greatest pleasure to those who shared our studies and our labours.[43]

The only real blot on KM's life at this time was Aunt Belle, who had taken up the position of assistant to Miss Wood, and was thus inescapable. This was of no great concern to Vera and Chaddie, but to KM she represented parental restriction, both emotional and physical, and the rows between them were frequent and loud. Fortunately, Aunt Belle's attention was given only partly to the girls: '[She] was young and hard and more interested in her own affairs than in attempting to understand an evolving artist.'[44] Aged twenty-eight when they made the trip to England, Belle was more than conscious of the fact that her prospects for finding a suitable husband from the small number of available men in Wellington were almost non-existent. She was a good-looking woman and she knew it; she used to enjoy placing a scarlet rose in her thick auburn hair, which made her appear striking. The complex, restless character of Aunt Beryl from the Burnell stories was more or less based on Aunt Belle. Here she is, in 'Prelude' (1917):

> And then, as she lay down, there came the old thought, the cruel thought – ah, if only she had money of her own.
> A young man, immensely rich, has just arrived from England. He meets her quite by chance. . . . The new governor is unmarried. . . . There is a ball at Government house. . . . Who is that exquisite creature in eau de nil satin? Beryl Fairfield. . . .[45]

> In the dining-room, by the flicker of a wood fire, Beryl sat on a hassock playing the guitar. She had bathed and changed all her clothes. Now she wore a white muslin dress with black spots on it and in her hair she had pinned a black silk rose.[46]

Part of Belle's determination to go to England was to find a husband in London, and find one she did. In September 1905, she married a stockbroker, Harry Trinder, at St Marylebone parish church, with Vera, Chaddie and KM as bridesmaids, all dressed in white silk and chiffon, and with Miss Wood providing the reception. Harold could not have been more pleased with his sister-in-law's choice, noting proudly in his *Reminiscences* that Harry Trinder owned two fine properties in Lyndhurst and on the Isle of Wight.[47]

FRIENDSHIPS

In the unfinished novel *Juliet*, started in 1906 whilst she was still at Queen's College, KM provides us with a detailed record of her complex juvenile self at this time. The plot (such as it is) involves a young woman eager to move from Wellington to the London she yearns for, especially after David, the musician she is infatuated with (that is, Tom Trowell), travels there to study. Once in the metropolis, she becomes close to Pearl (based on her close Queen's schoolfriend, the worldly Vere Bartrick-Baker), a fellow student at a women's hostel, with whom David falls in love, while Juliet is seduced by his friend, Rudolf. Following a pregnancy and her refusal to consider returning home, she lives in some degree of squalor (with the suggestion of an abortion), and a relationship is hinted at with another man called Walter (the Rippmann character). She is desperately ill when found by David, taken to live with him and Pearl, and dies at their home.

It is ironic that KM to some degree anticipates the misery of the year 1909 and the still-born child from her relationship with Garnet Trowell, but all that was in her unknowable future. Here she is, remembering the events of 1903 and her arrival at Queen's, being shown around the boarding hostel on her first day:

Juliet looked round her room curiously. So this was where she was to spend the next three years – three years. It did not look inviting. She noticed two texts ornamented with foxgloves and robins – – – and decided that they must come down. The three large windows looked out upon the Mews below – the houses built all round in a square. She wondered who would share this sanctum. Some English girl, stiff and sporting, who would torture the walls with pictures of dogs and keep a hockey stick in the corner. Heaven forbid, she thought. She sat down by the side of the bed and pulled off her long gloves. How strange and dim the light was.

She was alone in London – glorious thought. Three years of study before her. And then all Life to plunge into. The others were actually *gone* now.

She was to meet total strangers. She could be just as she liked – they had never known her before. O, what a comfort it was to know that every minute sent The Others further away from her! I suppose I am preposterously unnatural, she thought, and smiled.

Then the porter brought in her two large boxes, and behind him Miss Mackay hovered and told Juliet she must have everything unpacked before teatime – it was quite one of the old customs. Did the glory of England rest upon old customs? She rather fancied it did. When to start overcoats and when to stop fires, hard boiled eggs for Sunday supper, and cold lunches. She knelt down on the floor and unstrapped her luggage. From the pocket of her suitcase she drew out David's picture and looked at it seriously, then bent forward and kissed it.

'Here we are, dear,' she said aloud. 'Boy of mine, I feel that life is beginning – write [*sic*] now.'

When the old custom had been sustained and she had undressed she suddenly longed to write just a few lines of her impressions. So she slipped into her kimono and drew out her notebook.

'If I could retain my solitude' she wrote, 'I should be profoundly happy. The knowledge that sooner or later I shall be hampered with desirable acquaintances takes away much of the glamour. The great thing to do is to start as I mean to continue – never for one moment to be other than myself as I long to be, as I never yet have been except with David.' She laid down her pen and began braiding her hair in two thick braids. There was a knock at the door and immediately afterwards Miss Mackay entered with a tall thin girl beside her.

'My dear' the old lady said, 'Juliet', positive Maternity in her tone, 'this is your roommate, Pearl Saffron — new like yourself so I hope you will be friends.'[48]

There is much to dwell on in this fragment: firstly, KM's recognition at an early age of her solitude — always seemingly apart from others, singled out as different and yet *wanting* to be different. Also revealed is the need to jot things down in a notebook — impressions, ideas — a trait that would stay with her all her life, and 'slipping on a kimono' anticipates, even at this early age, KM's fascination with the Orient, developed and encouraged by Walter Rippmann, which again would continue to the end of her life. This extract also portrays the meeting between KM and the young girl who would go on to be her life-long friend and companion, and witness to many of the most notable events in her subsequent life: Ida Constance Baker.

Ida, born on 19 January 1888 (and therefore nine months older than KM), came from a family dedicated to colonial service. Her father, Colonel Oswald Baker, was a doctor in the Indian army; two months after Ida's birth, the family moved to Burma, where May, her younger sister, would be crippled by an

Figure 6.12 Ida Baker and Gwen Rouse, Queen's College.

accident in infancy. (There was also a younger brother, Waldo.) In 1895, when Ida was seven years old, the family returned to London and a house in Welbeck Street, stuffed full of Oriental carvings, where her father had set up a medical practice. Both Ida and May attended the junior school at Queen's College, moving to the senior college in 1901 as day students. Ida had thus already been at the college for almost two years when the Beauchamp girls arrived.

In the spring of 1903, at about the same time that the Beauchamps arrived in England, Ida's mother died of typhoid fever. Colonel Baker (who would shoot himself whilst in Rhodesia at the end of World War One, leaving his three offspring parentless) was a strict and undemonstrative father, lacking in any obvious parenting skills. He was prone to moods, had a vicious temper, and had 'ruined his digestion on curries'.[49] In the wake of his wife's death, he took the decision to move to the family's recently acquired country house with May and Waldo, leaving Ida to board at Queen's College on her own. To modern-day sensibilities it seems a cold and heartless decision; it does not take a trained psychologist to understand Ida's subsequent idolisation of, and attachment to, KM, to fill the emotional void the death of her mother and the almost immediate removal of her entire family had created. By 1904, however, she had become a day girl again. Her father and siblings were now living just off Baker Street in Montagu Mansions; Colonel Baker had found the isolation of country life unbearable without his wife.

When the Beauchamp girls arrived at the boarding house for the first time, Miss Wood chose Ida to show them up to their top floor room at no. 41, with its view into the courtyards below, where the sounds of the carriages and horses could be heard mingled with the voices of the Cockney grooms and the splashing of water. KM recalls all of this vividly in 'Carnation', that story based on a French lesson at Queen's:

> Down below, she knew, there was a cobbled courtyard with stable buildings round it. That was why the French Room always smelled faintly of ammonia. It wasn't unpleasant; it was even part of the French language for Katie – something sharp and vivid and – and – biting!
>
> Now she could hear a man clatter over the cobbles and the jingjang of the pails he carried. And now *Hoo-hor-her*! *Hoo-hor-her*! as he worked the pump, and a great gush of water followed. Now he was flinging the water over something, over the wheels of a carriage, perhaps. And she saw the wheel, propped up, clear of the ground, spinning round, flashing scarlet and black, with great drops glancing off it. And all the while he worked the man kept up a high bold whistling, that skimmed over the noise of the water as a bird skims over the sea. He went away – he came back again leading a cluttering horse.[50]

The girls' beds were separated by curtains to create small cubicles, but these were soon removed to make the room seem less claustrophobic. KM chose her bed first, the one between the door and the bay window, thus giving her instant access to the view described above. Ida would later note, 'I would sometimes watch Katherine lean out of the window, breathing, listening, absorbed and dreaming,'[51] and when it rained, she would spread a towel on the sill and lean on it, looking out at the view, exclaiming, 'Don't bother me, girls: I'm going to have a mood.'[52]

That most liminal of all spaces – a window – was to be such a feature of KM's fiction that it is hard not to view the three years she spent in this room as critical to an almost subconscious desire to place her characters in a similar position, within the confines of her stories' domestic arenas. In her stories, characters as insiders, self-absorbed in their own reflections, frequently position themselves in liminal spaces such as staircases or stare out of windows, allowing her to engage with altered perceptions of interiority. Indeed, within KM's domestic arena, in so many of her stories, at least one character will, at some point, be looking out of a window. This view from a window – a *place-in-between* – can alter perceptions from the present to the past, from the past to the future, and invite the crossing of a metaphorical threshold to an event yet to be realised or understood.

An intensely personal series of little scenes, published as 'Vignettes' (1907) following her return to New Zealand, are redolent of KM's life at Queen's College in that top-floor back room in the boarding hostel:

I lean out of the window. The dark houses stare at me and above them a great sweep of sky. Where it meets the houses there is a strange lightness – a suggestion, a promise

   Silence now in the Mews below. The cry of the child is silent, even the chiming of the bell is less frequent, no longer so persistent. But away beyond the line of the dark houses is a sound like the call of the sea after a storm. It is assuming gigantic proportions. Nearer and nearer it comes – a vast incontrollable burst of sound.[53]

Another story which exemplifies this liminal place is 'The Tiredness of Rosabel' (1908): 'Rosabel [. . .] knelt down on the floor, pillowing her arms on the win- dowsill . . . just one little sheet of glass between her and the great, wet world outside!'[54] In this liminal position, Rosabel reflects on the harsh reality of the events of the day, as well as dreaming of an alternative fairy-tale scenario of those same events. And, of course, in 'Bliss' (1918), Bertha Young's first epiphany comes as she looks through a window at the moonlit pear tree, in the presence of Pearl Fulton.

Even in her early forays into poetry, KM placed her characters at windows, as in a poem from 1903 called 'Friendship':

> He sat at his attic window
> The night was bitter cold
> But he did not seem to feel it
> He was so old – so old –
> [. . .]
> He moaned as he sat at the window
> And moved as though in pain
> 'O dream of my happy boyhood
> Come back to me again.' – – –
> [. . .]⁵⁵

It is a curious piece, in standard ballad form, and the first of KM's poems to suggest the influence of Heine's ballads, which figures in the notebook she was using at the time, since the poem appears just four pages after her transcription of 'Der Tod, das ist die kühle Nacht' ['Death is the cool night'], a poem by Heine from 'The Homecoming' in his *Book of Songs* (1827). It also presages the developing fixation in her prose writing with death. My discovery in 2015 of a cache of poems written by KM in 1909/10 reveals that she took her poetry writing seriously from an early age, and resonances between her fiction and her poetry show her according equal importance to both genres and using techniques and themes. KM was a short-story writer *and* a poet.

Initially, it was Vera who was the object of Ida's affection: 'I used to find her lying on the floor outside my room, waiting to ask if she could help me undress.'⁵⁶ But KM must also have felt some sort of connection to Ida, the tall, shy, fair-haired young girl with the size nine feet, who showed them around, or perhaps KM wanted to spite her sister and steal her admirer. Whatever the intention, a few weeks later, whilst walking in Regent's Park, KM asked Ida simply, 'Shall we be friends?,'⁵⁷ and thus began a relationship which dominated and defined Ida's entire life, and which would support KM until her own untimely demise. Not everyone thought the friendship a wholesome one. KM was seen as dominating Ida, telling her what to do, and treating her in a dismissive fashion at moments when she had no need of her. Hour after hour was spent in KM's room, where Ida started the habit of photographing her adored subject, a hobby she continued throughout KM's life. Ida noted in her memoirs, 'Looking back, I feel I must have abandoned many friendships during that period; but that was because Katherine absorbed all my time and thought.'⁵⁸ Many years later, Vera remarked that Ida was KM's 'walking shadow',⁵⁹ and Ruth Herrick went even further, claiming she '"was not impressed by Ida's intellect" and was sickened by the adoration of the "lymphatic lump of humanity", whom Katherine treated like a slave'.[60] What onlookers never understood, however, was that Ida, much of whose life had been spent looking after an invalid sister, relished and lived for the idea of 'service' to a loved one. KM, in a non-sexual sense, was the love of Ida's life and she remained faithful and true to her beloved 'Katie' until her own death in 1978. She was also far from stupid, even if Ruth Herrick had not been 'impressed by Ida's intellect'. She competed for the very prestigious Queen's College Professors' scholarship in 1904 and won it. On 16 March 1906, KM gave Ida a copy of Poe's *Tales of Mystery and Imagination*, with the dedication in (inaccurate) French: 'A mon ami de ton ami Kate', indicating that she thought Ida would enjoy such a book.

It was during their early friendship that the idea of changing their names had its genesis. At the time, KM – desperately believing herself to be in love with Tom Trowell, whose photograph had pride of place on her dressing table, and to whom she was writing regular, passion-filled letters – had thought that she would become a professional cellist. She had acquired a new cello, bought from the highly regarded purveyors of musical instruments, W. E. Hill and Sons of Bond Street. Ida was also a musician, playing the violin very competently. Both girls considered that their names were wholly inappropriate for professional use. Tom Trowell had started using the name 'Arnold' professionally, and KM's cousin Mary Beauchamp was now the celebrated author Elizabeth von Arnim. KM decided that when she became a professional cellist she would drop the very dull-sounding Kathleen and become Katherine instead, taking her middle name, Mansfield, as her new surname. Poor Ida, whose name, KM had decided, was the ugliest on earth, had decided to rename herself Katherine Moore, after her dead mother, but her choice was blocked by the forceful KM. They could not possibly both be called Katherine, KM firmly pointed out, and so she chose 'Lesley' (the female version of her brother's name, Leslie) for Ida, who thus became 'Lesley Moore', eventually shortened to LM (the name by which she would be known for most of her relationship with KM).

Ida described KM at Queen's College, noting how

> she adapted herself quickly to the new life; the delicately waving hair disap-
> peared, turning into the then fashionable pads of back-combed rolls; the
> high stiff collars and leg-of-mutton sleeves successfully hid the shape of a
> young girl's shoulders; small waists and full skirts followed; and Kass of
> New Zealand became Kathleen Mansfield Beauchamp written in large firm
> writing across her exercise book.[61]

There were other friendships, of course, during these Queen's College years. In particular, KM became very close to Vere Bartrick-Baker (known as 'Mimi'),[62] who was petite, dark and sophisticated. Her unconventional background was a particular attraction for KM, whose own solid, colonial family seemed dull by comparison. Vere's parents were divorced – rare at that time – and her mother lived alone in Surrey, having declared herself a widow, and wrote poetry. Ida wrote of Vere that '[s]he has left me with the impression of a bunch of choice flowers – roses and carnations';[63] 'curious Eve', one of the protagonists in KM's only Queen's College-based story, 'Carnation' (1918), is a portrait of Vere, as is Pearl in her unfinished novel, *Juliet*. Most importantly, it was Vere who lent KM the copies of *Lippincott's* magazine, where that salacious text, Oscar Wilde's *The Picture of Dorian Gray*, had first been serialised (KM thus reading the book in its first, unexpurgated version). In return, KM lent her Wilde's *The Ballad of Reading Gaol*. The two girls would huddle together in corners before and after lectures, looking suitably mysterious and intense, deep in conversations about Wilde, Tolstoy and Maeterlinck. Vere later told Mantz, '[we] were suspected of immorality. Miss Croudace was *stupefied* when, asking what we talked about, I told her.'[64] Vere considered KM had 'a stocky build [. . .] Her appearance [. . .] did not attract me. She interested me very much, but that's different.'[65] Vere would remain in KM's life, though they kept a certain distance from each other, KM always wary of their previous intensely close relationship and the 'hold' that this situation had on her, given that the girls must have exchanged many letters during the period of their intense friendship. In 1933, Murry (who had once proposed to Vere after KM's death) wrote to Vere stating that, later in her life, KM had been afraid of her, believing that one day she would somehow strike back at her. But KM need not have worried; the potentially incriminating letters never surfaced, having presumably been destroyed. In 1928 Vere married J. W. N. Sullivan, who had been one of KM and Murry's closest friends.

Another close Queen's College friend was Ruth Herrick, also a New Zealander, and 'wild', according to Ida: 'She was younger than Katherine but shared her comings and goings in No. 41.'[66] Ruth became KM's cello accompanist and, as such, '[t]hey went to concerts together in large, floppy black ties, and wide, soft felt hats and assumed a rather slouching walk, imagining themselves to be young bohemian musicians.'[67] Even though the two girls knew barely more than a few French phrases, KM would insist on them speaking French together, which Ruth would later regard as affectation. For Christmas 1904, KM presented Ruth with a copy of Robert Herrick's *Flower Poems*, inscribed: 'A mon ami Emile De ton ami Jean. Xmas, 1904. "That age is best, which is the first" Herrick.'[68]

Many years later, Ruth wrote an article for the *New Zealand Listener* recalling her Queen's College schooldays and portraying KM in a rather unflattering light:

Most of [the professors], I'm afraid, thought her troublesome. She was certainly very lazy. [. . .] She was a strange girl, and she had an intensity beyond the understanding of most of her schoolfellows. [. . .] Mimicry was her strong suit and her sense of drama was faultless – she could think herself into any part.[69]

On one occasion, dressed up and using her impressive acting skills, KM even fooled Miss Croudace into believing she was the mother of a prospective parent. Elsewhere, Ruth stated that other students at Queen's disliked her moods and her determination to be different to everyone else:

> If she wanted you to like her she could be utterly charming, that was part of the enormous vitality, she could be great fun to be with. On the other hand, she could be moody and morose for days on end.[70]

Indeed, KM's moods became quite notorious, and college girls who were not her friends found her tiresome – and occasionally even unwholesome – in the way she would cut herself off, or just stare blankly with an air of complete indifference. But this detachment from normal school life, and the erection of a barrier between herself and others, provided her with the means to try out different personalities and, most importantly of all, to *observe* quietly. Her eye for the most minute detail, even at this early age, was already a feature of both her fiction and her personal writing, and solitude allowed for reflection, which in turn led to creativity, as in this diary entry from 1904 reveals:

> *April 1* Today the weather has been very dull and gray. I woke this morning at four and since then I have heard nothing save the sounds of traffic, and feel nothing except a great longing to be back in the country, among the woods and gardens and the meadows and the chorus of the Spring orchestra. All day during my work, I have found myself dreaming of the woods, and the little secret nooks that have been mine, and mine only, for many years. A girl passed under my window this morning, selling primroses. I bought great bunches of them, and untied their tight chains, and let them stretch their little poor tired clamped selves in a sky-blue dish that had been filled with primroses every year. But they were not like country primroses. As I bent over them, their weary, pale faces looked into mine with the same depth of wondering, strange, fearful perplexities that I have sometimes seen on the face of a little child. It was as though Spring had entered my room, but with her wings broken and soiled and her song quiet – very quiet.
>
>   This evening I have sat in my chair with my reading lamp turned low, and given myself up to thoughts of the years that have passed. Like a strain of minor music they have surged across my heart, and the memory of them, sweet and fragrant as the perfume of my flowers, has sent a strange thrill of comfort through my tired brain.[71]

In both their poetic intensity and their artifice, these lines offer a glimpse of the mature writer to come.

In another swipe at KM, over the latter's relinquishing the cello in favour of writing, Ruth noted, rather pragmatically, that it was probably because 'her fingers were too short.'[72] She said that she had never known when to believe KM, who once claimed to have been 'raped', believed herself to be pregnant, and wanted Ruth to visit a female doctor with her.[73] There may be some dissembling here and scores to be settled; Ida recalls that '[w]hen college days were over the friendship faded: something must have happened, some unavoidable break and I don't think Katherine met her again.'[74] And of course, KM delighted in not telling the truth when it suited her, sometimes to shock, but more often because she lived partly in a fantasy world of her own making, where she really could be anything or anyone. The attraction of Ida was that she accepted all of KM's selves, never questioning or judging. In that sense she was KM's 'perfect' friend.

Gwen Rouse was a girl from the Isle of Man; tall and graceful, she was much quieter and less boisterous than the 'wild' Ruth Herrick, but KM felt she could be herself with Gwen and valued her as a friend. On 24 January 1904, KM wrote to Sylvia Payne:

Figure 6.13 Katherine Mansfield and Gwen Rouse outside Queen's College.

[i]s not the condition of the Poor just now awful. Miss Wood told us all about [it] the other afternoon, so I have arranged a Celebrity Evening for next Thursday night. Admission sixpence. Gwen Rouse is going to help me, and the money is to be sent to a poor parish.[75]

No record exists of how much money was raised but the sentiment was certainly a noble one, and Gwen a willing helper.

Gwen remembered how KM used to stammer slightly when she was very excited and could not get her words out quickly enough, and that her cello was

the great thing. She was to play in London and appear as a cellist. She gave me a solo performance on the landing outside the 'Giraffe Hole' [. . .] I thought it extremely good, but should have done the same, no doubt, if it had been extremely bad'[76]

Of course, both music and story writing offered KM an escape, when she needed it, from the claustrophobic atmosphere at Queen's. Music – her cello – was particularly important at this time. Indeed, she persuaded 'Guardy' to recommend that she should have additional music lessons at the London Academy of Music, where he taught, KM dragging Ida along for extra violin lessons to keep her company, though the latter could ill afford them. Undoubtedly, KM thought that these lessons would provide her with added cachet in the eyes of Tom Trowell, currently studying at the Brussels Conservatoire: whilst they took their lessons, KM and Ida called the London Academy 'The Conservatory'. The relationship with Gwen would eventually turned sour, however; having introduced her close friend to Tom Trowell in 1906, he and Gwen would later start a relationship, which was in full bloom during the autumn of 1908, following KM's return to London.

Eileen Palliser was another New Zealand girl studying at Queen's. Her bank manager father Charles, now working in London and with a second home in Cornwall, had been a friend of Harold Beauchamp's when young. KM adored him; even as late as 1915, she was still meeting and corresponding with him,[77] and in December 1917, she wrote to her friend Anne Drey, who was in Cornwall, 'If you should meet a tall man with a pointed grey beard, Irish eyes, and a voice like the sky at evening, salute him from me. His name is Charles Palliser, and he was a love of my salad days.'[78] Mr Palliser took the girls to concerts at the Queen's Hall in Langham Place, London's principal concert venue, which could hold 2,500 people and was less than a five-minute walk from the college. It was known as the musical centre of the British Empire; many of the most renowned musicians of the late nineteenth and early twentieth centuries performed there, including Claude Debussy, Edward Elgar, Maurice Ravel and

Richard Strauss. From 1895 until 1941, when it was destroyed by German bombing in the London Blitz, it was also the home of the celebrated promenade concerts. Whenever Palliser came to the college to collect his daughter and her friend, Miss Croudace would ask him, defensively, 'What do you want with Miss Beauchamp.'[79] (KM and Ida would also often go together to Queen's Hall on their own, in the early evenings, and wait for the cheap seats high up 'in the gods' to be released.)

Isobel Creelman, a young Canadian girl, was another student at Queen's whilst the Beauchamps were there. When she returned to Canada in April 1904, KM wrote her a poem. The second stanza conjures up the picture of the boarders' bathroom and their only practice piano:

Think of the bathroom, warm and filled with light
With strains of 'Orchid' and sweet music rare
And Norway singing songs with all her might
– Then wish that you could be transported there.[80]

Although not one of her particular friends, Isobel nevertheless recalled that KM appeared reserved and 'different'. A particular stanza of poetry that KM wrote at the time (the final stanza of her poem 'Night') seemed so morbid that, even after many years, she could still recite it:

I hope I may die in the darkness
When the world is so quiet and still,
And my soul pass away with the shadows,
Ere the sun rises over the hill.[81]

It is such memories of KM that bring to light how unusual she appeared to some of the students at Queen's; the morbidity of fin-de-siècle and Decadent writers, the solitude, that notion of death permeating everything were not shared with many of her peers.

There were also KM's cousins, the Paynes, who lived just around the corner from Queen's in Wimpole Street. KM developed a rather unusual attachment to Sylvia, who, by all accounts, was a strange girl with long red hair and wire spectacles. She left Queen's in the summer of 1905 but returned to attend some lectures during 1906. Both girls were members of the 'Swanswick Society', the college's poetry-reading circle. A dozen or so of the earliest extant letters of KM's are those sent to Sylvia, who kept them all her life. The second one, written on 23 December 1903 from The Retreat, Great-Uncle Henry Herron's house, where the Beauchamp girls were spending Christmas, must have surprised the recipient with its intensity, though the friendship seemed to survive it:

Figure 6.14 Sylvia Payne, 1906.

I like you much more than any other girl I have met in England & I seem to see less and less of you. We just stand upon the thresholds of each other's heart and never get right in. What I mean by 'heart' is just this. My heart is a place where everything I love (whether it be in imagination or in truth) has a free entrance. It is where I store my memories, all my happiness and my sorrow and there is a large compartment in it labeled '*Dreams*'. There are many many people that I like very much, but they generally view my public rooms, and they call me false and mad and changeable. I would not show them what I was really like for worlds.[82]

Of course, it was a letter designed to show off a little, and to demonstrate to her older cousin how sophisticated she really was, but it is also remarkable for its perceptions about her own personality, and for that notion of 'rooms' and compartmentalisation, which KM retained throughout her life; it was rare, even as an adult, that anyone saw all of her 'rooms'. The deep friendship does seem to have been reciprocated. On 14 February 1905, Sylvia sent KM a Valentine's card, the very first one she ever received. Ida had known Sylvia since she was seven, for the Baker sisters and the Payne sisters had all started together at Queen's College junior school. Ida explained KM's attraction for Sylvia, noting her intelligence and her artistic sensibility but also her high spirits and general naughtiness:

> She seemed to revel in gathering 'conduct marks', and since she was always in a hurry, she could never be bothered to formulate an explanation to put everything right. When frustrated she would murmur to herself something like 'jug jug' or 'tch tch', which gave her the name of 'Jug'.[83]

In 1920, KM would immortalize both Ida and Sylvia in one of her most celebrated stories, 'The Daughters of the Late Colonel'. Its original title was 'The Non-Compounders', that term referring to older women who attended some of the lectures at Queen's College (but which would have meant nothing to anyone else). Constantia (Con) and Josephine (Jug) are two middle-aged spinster sisters, who have had their wants and desires so subjugated by those of their domineering father that, after his death, they find themselves unable to make the simplest decision for themselves. Ida's middle name was Constance and 'Jug', of course, was Sylvia. The story also preserves something of the Baker family circumstances whilst growing up, when Ida and her sister May (together with their brother Waldo) lived with their widowed and dominating father, Colonel Baker. The 'Daughters of the Late Colonel' is also an indictment of the patriarchal society in which KM lived, where the bullying of women – and particularly spinsters, as here – was commonplace. In the utilisation of two middle-aged spinsters at the centre of her narrative, who have had no life to speak of and done nothing of any importance, KM fashioned one of her most powerful yet humorous stories:

> Father would never forgive them. That was what they felt more than ever when, two mornings later, they went into his room to go through his things. They had discussed it quite calmly. It was even down on Josephine's list of things to be done. *Go through father's things and settle about them.* But that was a very different matter from saying after breakfast:
> 'Well, are you ready, Con?'
> 'Yes, Jug – when you are.'
> 'Then I think we'd better get it over.'
> It was dark in the hall. It had been a rule for years never to disturb father in the morning, whatever happened. And now they were going to open the door without knocking even. . . . Constantia's eyes were enormous at the idea; Josephine felt weak in the knees.
> 'You – you go first,' she gasped, pushing Constantia.

But Constantia said, as she always had said on those occasions, 'No, Jug, that's not fair. You're eldest.'

Josephine was just going to say – what at other times she wouldn't have owned to for the world – what she kept for her very last weapon, 'But you're tallest,' when they noticed that the kitchen door was open, and there stood Kate. . . .

'Very stiff,' said Josephine, grasping the door-handle and doing her best to turn it. As if anything ever deceived Kate![84]

The celebrated twentieth-century critic, David Daiches, viewed the story as

a landmark in the history of the short story [. . . where] everything has reference to the mood of the story, everything is organised so as to bring "the deepest truth out of the idea". That so much should be achieved by such an economy of means is the greatest tribute to Katherine Mansfield's technique.[85]

SCHOOL LIFE

Thus, with friendships, schoolwork and a variety of trips, KM relished her life at Queen's College. There was certainly plenty to keep her busy. One of the extra-curricular activities she particularly enjoyed was the Debating Society, in which she took an active part during 1904–5. Reports on the debates were written up in the *Queen's College Magazine*, which thus provides a fascinating account of KM's activities. Motions proposed included 'Free Trade v. Protection', 'Pessimism is better than Optimism' and 'The Experience of Old Age is better than the energy of Youth'. KM spoke in all the above debates, and in the motion regarding free trade stood up for the colonies, in a speech which would have made Harold proud, decrying Britain's preference for foreign goods over those produced by its colonies.[86] On the motion that 'Dickens holds the first place in the great novelists of our literature,' KM opposed, stating that 'Thackeray is much more refined than Dickens who always gloats over death.'[87] She seconded the proposer of the motion 'That the Poet should be more esteemed by his country than the Statesman', with an impassioned speech on the importance of poets:

Many people cling fast to the idea that a poet is impractical, dreamy and egotistical. But a fine poet does not tell us only to dream [. . .] If poems and poets were not in existence, we should never become great, we should grow mean and sordid.[88]

Figure 6.15 Katherine Mansfield at Queen's College.

Figure 6.16 Theatrical group, Queen's College, including Katherine Mansfield.

And on the motion 'that the public prefer Tragedy to Comedy on the Stage', KM seconded the motion, with a very Wildean statement: 'A great love for comedies shows a degeneration of the English people.'[89]

However, KM's debating career came to a rather abrupt end in February 1905, when she proposed the motion that forcing children to study Shakespeare when young spoilt any future pleasure in the Bard's work. The actual wording of the motion was as follows (apparently derived from *The Times*): 'That pastors and masters, parents and guardians, commentators and cranks have done their best to spoil the taste of Shakespeare for us by making a duty of it instead of a pleasure.' Opposing the motion was none other than Ida. Much of the debate was recorded verbatim for the college magazine and KM is seen in full rebellious mode:

K. M. B., proposing said: 'When the average boy goes to school, he is plunged into the most magnificent of Shakespeare's works. If a person has a tendency early in life to be literary, the very idea of being *forced* to learn Shakespeare deadens the sense of the appreciation of the beautiful – a true schoolboy never appreciated the beautiful at all, so he considers Shakespeare in the same way as anything else that is forced upon him. The most glorious pieces in Shakespeare have been read and re-read, quoted and misquoted by cranks and commentators till they have lost all true significance. There is so short a step from the sublime to the ridiculous!'

'A foreigner said to me, "Nearly all foreigners love and appreciate Shakespeare as much as you English."

"Why is this?" I asked.

"Oh, of course we do not read Shakespeare till we have had some experience of life – Shakespeare is not for a child." I felt a little crushed!

'It is impossible for a student to form an original opinion for himself, for he is always more or less biassed by what he has been forced to learn in his youth. Why should Shakespeare be employed in schools as a spelling book or reading book? Of a surety this is what happens when we come to consider how we are recommended to the Clarendon Press as an authority to find the correct spelling of the word "cousin" in 1680. After laborious references to other plays of Shakespeare we have to take recourse to the researches of a certain Dr. Faulkner, folio ix, end of sect. v! The predominating element in a teacher is duty. The satisfaction of finding that a pupil can quote 50 lines of Shakespeare without faltering is to them far greater than finding that a pupil appreciates the intrinsic value of the speech. Even the divine Shakespeare himself, would writhe in his grave should he hear a fat, podgy little boy roll off a long farewell (with appropriate or seemingly appropriate gesticulations). Why should Shakespeare be made the bogey of the schoolroom?'

Ida Baker, opposing the motion said: 'At home you are first of all given a story book with several tales from Shakespeare, perhaps illustrated and so you learn the story of the plays. Later, when you are older, you discover that Shakespeare made the people talk and to gratify your curiosity to know how they talked – what sort of things your favourite hero or heroine said, you read the plays, and with a certain amount of extra pleasure (though of course you didn't realise it then) in watching the developments. That is the result of forcing at home. At school it is stronger. If a play is chosen for that term, you know you are doomed to learn by heart at least five or six long speeches. But when you are older, it is wonderful what pleasure you get in finding how immense, how vast, is the meaning which you failed to appreciate when you first read it. You may suggest that however good it may be to force children to read Shakespeare, yet it would be better to leave them alone. But, I say, if that were so, half, if not more of the children would never open a Shakespeare at all! Finally, I offer my deepest gratitude to all or any who taught me to read Shakespeare.'

K. M. B. summing up, said: 'In reply . . . unless we followed the advice of others, we should choose by covers and gilt edges. If you have a boy to stay in the holidays he would choose to go to see "The Orchard" sooner than a play of Shakespeare – and why? Because at school they have made it a duty instead of a pleasure!'[90]

This should have been an easy victory for KM, but somehow once the debate was opened up to the floor, her points were attacked on all sides, Ida's were upheld, and the opposition votes defeated the motion, by twenty-one to one. It must have been a crushing humiliation, especially when every embarrassing detail was recorded in the college magazine. Nevertheless, all was not lost; in the same issue, Ida's report on the Senior Party (a concert / dance for students and staff) was a chance for her to boost her dear friend's morale. Praised above all other performances at the event was the cello playing of KM, 'who in her artistic and beautiful rendering of Tchaikowsky's *Chanson Triste* quite delighted her audience. She also played a *Caprice* by Noel Johnson and therein showed her command over her instrument.'[91]

Another musical highlight from the previous year had been the publication (with Harold proudly picking up the bill) of two songs, 'Night' and 'Love's Entreaty', with KM writing the words and Vera the music (and a copy, of course, proudly sent to Tom in Brussels). A few months later, Uncle Val Waters would go on to sing the songs at one of Harold's Wellington Harbour Board dinners, when the latter was able to extol the virtues of his gifted daughters, currently enjoying their expensive education in London. KM's own commercial skills, no doubt inherited from Harold, were also made full use of during an auction at the school's bazaar in 1906, as reported in the magazine:

All the stalls sent their various produce to be sold by the hammer, generally at ridiculously low figures, though Kathleen Beauchamp, who next took the hammer, occasionally succeeded by her determined and most professional air in really doubling the price of some things, the Colonial jams especially going at prices far exceeding what had been asked for them at the stalls [. . .] enquiries were anxiously made, when at last everything had been disposed of, after the voices of the two brave auctioneers, which showed that women's inferiority is not extended to that branch of professionalism in any case.[92]

Harold would have been proud of this facet of KM's character. Her business acumen would also be needed several years later in 1912, when working on the little magazine *Rhythm* with Murry; it was KM who helped to balance the books and who touted for advertisement revenue to help the magazine survive.

There were many other college activities KM enjoyed participating in, including croquet, tennis, swimming at the Marylebone baths and theatre visits. In another letter to Sylvia, written from Bexley on Boxing Day 1904, she was already voicing her concerns about having to leave:

Figure 6.17 Queen's College boarders holding tennis racquets, including Katherine Mansfield.

Isn't there a strange fascination about College? I am always thinking of it. It seems to be quite part of one's life in time. I don't know what I shall do when I leave, and think of it going on in the dear old way, and new girls coming and the old ones all gone away.[93]

In the meantime, there was a minor operation on her foot in February 1905, which necessitated a stay in cousin Connie Beauchamp's nursing home in John Street, W1. (This was the same Connie Beauchamp who would later come to her rescue in Menton, looking after her in her luxurious villa and then renting her the Villa Isola Bella.) It was KM's first operation, and a great fuss was made of her in the absence of her parents, with visits from Beauchamp relatives and friends from school. KM lapped up all the attention, which she described in a letter to Sylvia:

Well, here am I in bed propped up with pillows, surrounded with flowers & books and feeling quite 'perky' – Still I *long* for College, and for 2 *whole* feet! My first operation is an event that I shall ever look back to with horror *and* amusement – It is amusing to think of such an old carthorse as I am being in such a condition as not even able to do my hair!

The Nurses are all dears – I am quite D.V. on the matron – What a day it is! The sparrows are having a Vocal Class outside my window, & the sky is blue.

There is a cab stand below my window – I never knew such cheerful souls as cabbies are – they do nothing but *shriek* with laughter. Sometimes I wake up in the night, and a cab comes, alone – 'Allo, Bill, 'ow are yer? calls a cab man, and straight way the whole number scream & guffaw. What dears they must be. I have had numbers of visitors, and that blessed Ida writes to me every day, & tells me about College. My head is full of plots for stories – I have not written any down yet, because it is so difficult in bed –[94]

Even at the age of sixteen, KM considered herself a writer of stories, and what is more, her fellow students also considered her a writer. That mind, full of plots for stories waiting to be written down, was something she mentioned regularly in letters and notebooks written as an adult. They were clearly waiting for her even at this young age.

STORY-WRITING

Between 1903 and 1906, KM had five stories published in the *Queen's College Magazine* (in which Professor Rippmann took a special interest), and she became its editor for a short time. She also wrote stories in her notebooks that were not published in the college magazine, demonstrating how her twin loves at this time – music and writing – were equally important to her. During 1903, she wrote a few additional little pieces, mostly unfinished. 'A True Tale' is just a fragment, but is the first time she brings New Zealand as a country into her fiction and, more importantly, its indigenous people, the Maori:

> Many, many miles from here, my little Saxons, many many years ago, there was a beautiful island. All round it lay the lovely laughing sea, and there were tall, green, 'smelly' woods, the like of which you have never seen, down to the water's edge.
>
> There were no white people living there, but tall, stately, copper coloured men and women, who sailed all round their country in great, carved canoes, and hunted in the woods for game, and very often, I am afraid, human people, whom they killed with aké-akés. They were always having wars among themselves, and it is about one of these wars that I am going to tell you. Let us come closer to the fire, dear children, and be glad that you did not live in the time that Motorua did.[95]

Although incomplete, it remains important for the way it demonstrates KM's confidence in discussing the country she was born in, its language and its indigenous people. Another fragment offers, for the first time, KM's description of Chesney Wold, which she would go on to fictionalise many times in her later stories:

> It was a big bare house surrounded with pine trees. A wilderness of a garden stretched away on all sides – no settled beds of flowers, but the whole overrun with weeds, and tall, long grass. At the back of the house were high thickly wooded hills. Beautiful hills where the tui sang all day in summer and the morepork cried aloud in the evenings. But the house looked desolate. There were no dainty window curtains, no creepers to soften its outlines. It was painted white. There was a broad verandah at the back, that was the only 'nice' thing about it.[96]

Again, the writing shows a New Zealand influence in its unusual bird imagery of tuis and moreporks (small owls).

'The Pine-Tree, the Sparrow and You and I' was KM's first story published in the school magazine, in December 1903. It is a story that Mrs Molesworth herself might have written, so closely does it resemble that fantasy forest of pines from *Christmas-Tree Land*, where magical things happen and trees are anthropomorphised into living beings:

He was a tall, stately pine-tree. So tall, so very tall, that when you stood underneath and looked right up through the branches you could not see the top. How very fond you were of that pine-tree. We used to go and see it every day. He sang the most beautiful songs and told the most lovely stories; but he always seemed a little sad, somehow.[97]

It was the first of KM's 'baby' stories – with little children as protagonists, and meant for a specific audience. It is also, however, the first story by KM in which the narrator is male – in this case the father of the little girl:

'No-o-o-o' you said, crying much harder. 'Its about zem poor 'icle spawows.' I sat right down on the bed and felt like Mummy feels when the cook says she's going to leave, 'dinner-party or no dinner-party.'

We went to see them the first thing next morning. Alas! As soon as I saw our old friend, I knew something must be the matter. He was crying and moaning – and then – and – then, you found three little dead sparrows. Poor, poor little darlings. You held them in your pinafore, and I quite forgot Mummy would be cross.[98]

The emotional state of the father at that precise moment is beautifully portrayed, and there is humour here too, in the reported speech of the cook and the ensuing headache of the mother.

KM ended 1903 writing a story whilst staying at Great-Uncle Henry Herron's for Christmas. The untitled story, dated 27 December, is quite different from anything written up to that point. Aged just fifteen, KM delivers a scathing attack on the Modern Woman:

[We] soon found ourselves in a most draughty room, on the most hard chairs, surrounded by the most Physical Cultured men and women. I shuddered at the women. Great tall gaunt looking figures, and all angles. They seemed to be seized with a mania to appear masculine. Men's boots, men's gloves, men's hats, men's coats. They walked with long strides and spoke in low tones. Poor benighted dears, I am sure in their heart of hearts they were very sorry for themselves. They had a hungry look in their eyes. I longed to take them home and show them my babies and make their hair soft and fluffy and put them in tea gowns, and then cuddle them. I think they would never have gone back to their Physical Culture or their Society for the Promotion of Women's Rights.[99]

If Virginia Woolf had sought inspiration for the 'emancipated' character of Miss Kilman in *Mrs Dalloway*, she would have found much to use here. KM reserves particular scorn for the Modern Woman's desire to remove play and imagination from the lives of children, and replace such fripperies with science and reason (echoing Thomas Gradgrind in Charles Dickens's *Hard Times*):

> Why teach an infant the entirely foolish and senseless rhyme of Jack Horner for instance. How much better it would be for him to learn the position of his heart and the Circulation of the Blood.
>
> [. . .]
>
> On, On, went that female. She pulled down, and cast into the fire, all the little things that seem to be part of our childhood. And where the little rose-covered summer houses had stood for so long, she erected great dull stone buildings and parallel bars. O Mothers of this generation let us rise in a great body and blunt the tools of these women before it is too late. Let us, with renewed fervour, impart to the babes Little Jack Horner and all his contemporaries.[100]

Whether KM had, in fact, been to any such 'Lecture on Physical Culture' is not recorded, but the wealth of detail in the story points to such a conclusion. It is interesting to speculate as to why this story was not published in the college's magazine, or, if it was submitted, why it was rejected. It was certainly the most mature, complete story she had written up to this point.

Early in 1904, KM reverted to a more typical, rather sentimental unfinished story called 'Misunderstood' about a musical orphan child, set in a poor London hospital, the medical theme possibly influenced by her stay in cousin Connie Beauchamp's nursing home in February 1904 for her foot operation, which, however, in its luxurious accommodation and West End location, was a world away from the one depicted in the story. Another story, 'She', written in 1904 and this time completed, is of much more interest. It is a hallucinatory story, steeped in KM's reading of Wilde and the Decadents, with the godmother from *Christmas-Tree Land* now transformed from childhood fantasy figure to a fin-de-siècle goddess of Death:

> One day, he walked by the river. The sun was hidden behind the clouds. The wind moaned as though in pain. The tall trees shook their branches in despair. Winter was at hand. But the river flowed on, calm and restful. And his heart was desolate. It moaned with the wind – Ah, for one sight of Her!!! Then a thought flashed across his brain. Why not go to the river and bury himself in its depths, and see her again, for always and for ever. And he gave one hoarse cry, and then ah, he saw her again. She stretched out her arms, with her lips parted, with her eyes luminous, and clasped him to her heart. She held [him] in her arms as she would a little child, but as her arms

touched him, he felt all his sorrows, his tears and his bitterness fade away into the past, become buried with the past. Then he looked up at her. 'Take me with you' he moaned, 'take me with you.' And she looked at him and smiled at him, and clasped him still more tightly in her arms and took him.

Death. Death. And her name was – ah! how well we know her you and I. She who came with our Forefathers, and will stay while this little universe will remain. Too often do we bar our doors against her, and watch her entrance with blinding tears. Her name was Death.[101]

The image of a mystical river is a popular one in literature – another liminal space acting, like a window, as both a boundary and a threshold. Another influence for this story is Ernest Dowson's prose poem, 'The Visit', whose dreaming protagonist is also taken by Death.[102] Dowson was another writer introduced to the impressionable KM by Rippmann, via her reading of Arthur Symons's *Studies in Prose in Verse*,[103] which had recently been published and which contained a whole chapter on Dowson, as well as a fascinating chapter on Wilde. KM's notebooks, as late as 1909, contain numerous quotations from this book, a particular favourite. Close to this story in her notebook, KM copied out, in the original German, Heinrich Heine's lyrical poem 'Der Tod' ('Death'), on the themes of death, love and dreaming:

Our death is in the cool of night,
Our life is in the pool of day.
The darkness glows, I'm drowning,
Day's tired me with light.

Over my head in leaves grown deep,
Sings the young nightingale.
It only sings of love there,
I hear it in my sleep.[104]

In 1904, then, KM was steeping herself in fin-de-siècle literature and poetry, and, more importantly, reflecting this influence in her own literary endeavours.

The second story printed in the *Queen's College Magazine* – and the most outstanding – was 'Die Einsame' ('The Lonely One'), published in March 1904. Its German-language title was taken straight from cousin Elizabeth von Arnim's latest best-seller, *The Adventures of Elizabeth in Rügen*, which had only just been published a few weeks before, and where 'Die Einsame' was the name of a resort on the beautiful Rügen Island, famous for its sandy beaches, chalk cliffs and lagoons. More importantly, the German title also hints at her obsession with Walter Rippmann and her desire to be liked by him, whilst the contents, replete

Figure 6.18 Elizabeth von Arnim and Count Henning von Arnim.

with Decadent, Symbolist and fin-de-siècle motifs, reveal just how much she had absorbed from Rippmann's suggested extra-curricular reading, as well as her memories (perhaps subconscious), yet again, of the pine-forest, flower-laden landscape in Mrs Molesworth's *Christmas-Tree Land*:

> All alone she was. All alone with her soul. She lived on the top of a solitary hill. Her house was small and bare, and alone, too.
> All day long she spent in the forest, with the trees and the flowers and the birds. She seemed like a creature of the forest herself, sometimes.
> [. . .]
> In the forest, in the forest, silence had cast a spell over all things. She plucked a great bouquet of daffodils and snowdrops, and tenderly held them to her, and tenderly kissed their fresh spring faces.[105]

The repetitive phrases add to the hauntingly poetic, lyrical, almost mythical quality of the prose. The magical silence of the forest, the bouquets of sweet-smelling flowers, both are taken from Mrs Molesworth's fantasy story. And who better to write about isolation and loneliness than KM, that moody, difficult adolescent, whose frequent preference for her own company, together with her notorious 'moods', marked her out as different. Alienation and loneliness were to become themes that KM would pick up time and again in her mature stories. There is another theme here, too – death – prevalent in KM's adolescent and early adult stories, where the anonymous protagonist, part wood nymph, part sea nymph, in the end almost seems to have her wishes fulfilled in going to her death:

> Now the water was creeping, higher to her waist, and now it was at her throat. She could barely stand. 'Take me,' she cried piteously, and looking up she saw – the boat and the figure had gone.
>   [. . .]
> Then a great wave came, and there was silence.[106]

In December 1904, another story, 'Your Birthday', was printed in the *Queen's College Magazine*. Another of KM's 'baby' stories (which she seemed to be able to toss off at will), it features a little four-year-old girl, who makes herself ill by finding her birthday cake and secretly eating the icing from the top; unremarkable in itself, it is, however, the second story by KM where the narrator is male – once again, the father of the little girl, who discovers the spoilt cake but pretends to the contrary. The difference between stories such as these and those Dowson- / Wilde-influenced offerings such as 'She' and 'Die Einsame' creates a marked dichotomy in KM's prose fiction at this time: experimental and dark, versus lightweight and simple. In essence, this dichotomy would also define her adult writing, where she mixed modernist, complex stories such as 'Je ne parle pas français' (1918) with much more commercially viable stories such as 'A Cup of Tea' (1922). This pattern was set, it seems, at a young age.

On 26 December 1904, during the second of the Beauchamp girls' Christmas holidays spent with Great-Uncle Henry Herron, KM wrote to Sylvia Payne about her 'baby' stories:

> Among my Xmas presents I got a photo of the blessed German baby. [. . .] I was so devoted to her. I have written another little tale about her. It is better than the others, so I am going to send it to the Mag. Some people seem to like those 'baby' stories, and I love writing them.[107]

The German baby in question was Felicitas Joyce von Arnim, the fourth daughter of her cousin Elizabeth. At some point during the Beauchamp girls' frequent visits to 'The Retreat', they did briefly meet their famous relation, the glamorous – and now aristocratic – Elizabeth, though sadly no written record

Figure 6.19 Katherine Mansfield and her sisters at 'The Retreat', Bexley.

Figure 6.20 Katherine Mansfield and her sisters at 'The Retreat', Bexley, with Great-Uncle
Henry Herron, Aunt Louey and Felicitas.

of such a meeting exists. Vera later recalled how she brushed them aside as if they were 'little colonial frumps'.[108] Much later, of course, KM's friendship with Elizabeth would be one of the defining relationships of the final two years of her life. 'One Day' was the third 'baby' story based on Felicitas and was printed in the July 1905 edition of *Queen's College Magazine* (with KM now acting as sub-editor and Ida as treasurer). Another influence for the story was Esterel Beauchamp, their guardian Henry's daughter:

> There is another baby here. She is four and a half. Her name is Estherelle. She is beautiful, with long gold hair far past her waist, and great blue won-derful eyes. [. . . She] sings in a little shaky voice about a black-bird, and says the drollest things. [. . .] Are you very fond of small children? They always will captivate me.[109]

It is clear that KM derived some enjoyment from writing such stories, whilst at the same time experimenting with other styles and themes.

The final story published in *Queen's College Magazine*, in December 1905 (with KM now officially the main editor), was called 'About Pat', that fiction-alised, affectionate account of the Beauchamps' Irish handyman at Chesney Wold, which ends:

> I should dearly love to show him the sights of London, and take him to the 'Carlton' for a slice of German sausage and a bath bun, and see once again the way in which the Dukes of Ireland balanced their salt on their knives.[110]

Pat, of course, would go on to make a notable reappearance in 'Prelude' (1917), KM's first long 'Karori' story.

FINAL YEAR

As well as her writing, KM's main preoccupation during these three London years was, of course, music and, by extension, Tom Trowell. For Christmas 1905, KM sent Tom a beautifully decorative edition of that tragically romantic tale, *The Story of Tristan and Iseult*, signed 'To Tom from Kass'. She saw the twins intermittently during these three years, as they occasionally came to London, and she introduced them to all her closest friends: Ida, Vere, Eileen, Ruth and Gwen. Ever eager to impress him, KM practised diligently on her expensive new cello, with lessons taken at Queen's College with Professor Hahn,[111] as well as at the London Academy with her guardian. Tom's photograph stared up at her every

Figure 6.21 Katherine Mansfield with cello, Queen's College.

day from her school dressing table, and many long letters were sent to Brussels –
and a few, far briefer ones, returned. Sadly, none on either side appears to have
survived, except for the rough copy of a letter in a KM notebook, written from
The Retreat on New Year's Eve 1904, and which presumably was meant for Tom:

> *New Years Eve.* It is 12.30. All the bells in the village Churches are pealing –
> Another year has come. Now at the entrance of this New Year, my dearest,
> I propose to begin my book. It will not be at all grand or dramatic but
> just all that I have done. You, who are so far away, know so little of what
> happens to me, and it is selfish of me not to tell you more – I have just
> returned from a Midnight Service – It was very very beautiful & solemn.
> The air outside was cold and bracing, and the Night was a beautiful thing.
> Over all the woods & the meadows, Nature had tenderly flung a veil to
> protect from the frost, but the trees stood out, dark and beautiful, against
> the clear, starry sky. The church looked truly very fit for God's House,
> tonight – It looked so strong, so invincible, so hospitable – [. . .] It was
> only during the Silent Prayer that I made up my mind to write this – I
> mean this year to try and be a different person, and I want at the end of this

year, to see how I have kept all the vows that I have made tonight. So much happens in a year. One may mean so much good, and do so little – I am writing this by the light of a wee peep of gas, and I have only got on a dressing gown – so dearie, I am so tired, I think I must go to bed. Tomorrow will be the 1st of January. What a wonderful and what a lovely world this is. I thank God tonight, that I am.[112]

The letter is rather forced, with parts of it written in a strained prose-poem style, and with KM's youthful ego very much in evidence. The sexual innuendo of the description of being in just her dressing gown was surely intended to titillate the recipient.

In a notebook entry for early 1906, KM described going to a concert by the Austrian virtuoso violinist and composer, Fritz Kreisler:

There are a more or less large number of weak minded looking females waiting here – the slightly mushroom hat type, the flannel coat & skirt type. I feel rather self-conscious so doubtless look arrogant. Not a man to be seen. What must the feelings of Kreisler be. In two hours he will be playing. Does that excite him – is he too blasé for excitement. Is he looking at his fiddle calling to it, lifting the lid of the case – you know how – or he is eating the proverbial sausage with his Frau – Pour quelque raison I am interested. It is because one day Caesar shall be in the same position. Inside at last, we ate apples & chocolate while waiting & I read the book of the lady in front. Flat to let opposite. Programs now.[113]

Kreisler had been an acclaimed concert performer since his American début in 1901 and spent much of his time in England from 1902 until 1906. KM had attended one of Kreisler's many recitals given in London at this time. Here, however, we see her mind turns towards 'Caesar' (Tom) as she daydreams about how, one day, Kreisler's life will be his life, and the role of Kreisler's wife could possibly, in the future, be *her* life.

Two poems written on the same day – 2 March 1906 – demonstrate both her affection for Queen's College and her inner turmoil as the time for departure drew near. She portrays an outwardly joyful self, while all the while the words and adjectives offer a very different reading:

'The Students' Room'

In the students' room the plain and simple beds
The pictures that line the walls, of various excellence thrown together
And the students with heads bent low, silent over their books.

'What, think you, causes me truest Joy'

What, think you, causes me truest joy
Down by the sea – the wild mad storm of waves
the fierce rushing swirl of waters together
The cruel salt spray that blows, that beats upon my face.
Wet grey sand, straight paths of it, leading far and away
And showing never a sign of where man's foot has trod
Till only the sky overhead peers at itself in the mirror
The flying clouds, silently screaming, shudder and gaze at themselves
– – –
The song of the wind as I stretch out my arms and embrace it
This indeed gives me joy.[114]

The softly silent cocoon of her room in college in the first poem is contrasted with the strength of the waves by the sea, which are 'mad' and 'fierce', the salt spray is 'cruel' and 'beats upon' her face, and the clouds are 'silently screaming'.

Towards the end of March 1906, and prior to Harold and Annie's arrival in England on Friday 13 April, Aunt Belle took the girls abroad for a short vacation. It was from Paris that KM sent Edie Bendall a postcard, depicting a statue of a young John the Baptist by Paul Dubois. KM also bought herself a mounted photograph of the Greek statue of Venus, which she would eventually give to Edie as a parting gift before leaving New Zealand in 1908.

After Paris, the party then moved on to Brussels, where Tom, now officially using his middle name, Arnold (to distinguish him from his father, Thomas), was to give a solo recital at the Salle de la Grande Harmonie on 27 March, paid for with £25 from the twins' New Zealand trust fund. Aunt Belle had taken them to Germany – to Bollendorf – in 1904, to see the twins, but this visit was so much more exciting. The recital was an enormous success and garnered some excellent reviews in the European press. In a piece subsequently written for a New Zealand paper, Garnet himself described the occasion in detail:

The 'cello recital here was a triumph in the highest sense of the word. The Salle was crowded – people standing three deep in the gallery and round the hall, being unable to obtain seats. At 8.30 Arnold walked on to the platform (where he had seen so many famous artists), followed by one of the finest accompanists living (Mr Georges Lauweryns), and thirdly, his namesake to act as turnover. Amidst a storm of applause he greeted his audience with a slight bow of the head, bent over his Strad, waited a moment for silence, and so commenced the concert [. . .] the excitement

Figure 6.22 Statue of John the Baptist. Postcard from the Musée du Luxembourg, Paris, sent to Edith Bendall.

Figure 6.23 Tom (Arnold) Trowell.

increased with every number. He had flowers, and laurel wreaths, and bunches of violets by the hundred (thrown by the ladies). After the concert the artist's room was rushed with people – mostly women – trying to hug him, and everywhere was excitement. The students formed up behind our carriage and followed singing and cheering to the echo, till we reached home; and then they would not leave the front of the house, but continued to sing his praises.[115]

KM would surely have been one of the violet throwers, and afterwards, one of the many that greeted the young seventeen-year-old boy-prodigy backstage. The magnificent success of the occasion would have done nothing to quell her ardour for Tom and she basked vicariously in his triumph. The twins were alluring, too, fuelling KM's passion even more, with their red hair, huge black hats and immensely long, continental cigarettes. Their bohemian ways entranced her; she wanted to be a bohemian too and Tom taught her how to smoke, fuelling a life-long addiction that not even tuberculosis could weaken. KM wrote several letters to Ida from Brussels, none of which survives, but Ida recalled some of their contents in her own memoirs:

> I remember her account of one 'daring' episode, when she and her two sisters went down to a sheltered seashore and bathed naked, having no bathing dresses with them. Such behaviour, unusual for those days, seemed to fit the romantic bohemianism of student life in Brussels.[116]

One is tempted to think of this episode as one of KM's tall stories; firstly, it is difficult to think of a suitable beach en route to Brussels; secondly, it is hard to imagine Vera or Chaddie bathing naked; and thirdly, where was Aunt Belle?

KM's absorption in music, and the recent contact with Tom, now gave her the fanciful idea of becoming a professional musician (which, for women in those days, had a similar social stigma to putting your daughter on the stage). Annie may have enjoyed the thought of dressing as a 'Modern Woman' for a fancy-dress party on board ship but that was as far as modernity went in *their* household. When Harold and Annie arrived from Wellington, KM must have broached the subject but her father soon put a stop to any such fanciful notions. It was one thing to give your daughters the benefit of music lessons to enhance their marital prospects but quite another to think of them making a career out of it.

The entire family was now installed in the luxurious surroundings of Fripp's Hotel, 30 Manchester Street (less than a ten-minute walk from the College), as part of the girls' Easter break. KM wrote to Sylvia from there on 24 April 1906:

> A great change has come into my life since I saw you last. Father is greatly opposed to my wish to be a professional 'cellist or to take up the 'cello to any great extent – so my hope for a musical career is absolutely gone. It was a fearful disappointment – I could not tell you what I have felt like – and do now when I think of it – but I suppose it is no earthly use warring with the inevitable – so in the future I shall give *all* my time to writing.

And then, echoing words that surely must have come from Harold himself, she notes:

> There are great opportunities for a girl in New Zealand – she has so much time and quiet – and we have an ideal little 'cottage by the sea' where I mean to spend a good deal of my time. Do you *love* solitude as I do – especially if I am in a writing mood.

The whole letter is fascinating for what it reveals about KM at this time. A little further on, she talks in a very 'modern' fashion about her attitudes to women and matrimony (which would be replicated in a passage in *Juliet*), as well as some of her thoughts on books she has recently read:

> I am so keen upon all women having a definite future – are not you? The idea of sitting still and waiting for a husband is absolutely revolting – and it really is the attitude of a great many girls. [. . .] I picked up a small collection of poems entitled 'The Silver Net' by Louis Vintras – and I liked some of them immensely. The atmosphere is so intense. He seems to me to belong to that school which flourished just a few years ago – but which now has not a single representative – a kind of impressionist literature school. Don't think that I even approve of them – but they interest me – Dowson – Sherard – School.[117]

Of course, the Decadent writers Ernest Dowson and Robert Sherard (the latter, Wilde's first biographer) had been introduced to KM by Rippmann, but even so, for a seventeen-year-old girl, the comments demonstrate a mature grasp of some of the then current social and literary trends.

In the meantime, duty called, and the entire Beauchamp clan went to Bexley to The Retreat to pay their respects to Great-Uncle Henry Herron, who wrote in his diary on Sunday 29 April: 'Harold Bs came in force yesterday and dined.'[118] When Tom and Garnet arrived in London in May, having completed their studies in Brussels and elsewhere on the Continent, Tom visited KM at Queen's College, and of course his presence now made the idea of having to return to England all the more painful. KM was also told of how the Trowells' musician

Figure 6.24 Rudolf Bottermund.

friend, Rudolf Bottermund – handsome, though easily excitable and tempera-
mental – whom KM had only recently met on her trip to Brussels, had recently
committed suicide by shooting himself; she was profoundly affected by the
news. Rudolf, it was suggested, had been a homosexual, and this was the reason
he had taken his life. This was her first personal experience of the death of
someone her own age and, what was more, someone close to dear Caesar; the
news left her bewildered and unsettled.

Tom's arrival in London did not quite play out to KM's romantic plans,
however. KM's see-sawing emotions made her an unattractive prospect for the
overwhelmed Tom, who started to cool down the relationship – such as it was.
It would appear that, during the visit to Brussels, 'there had been a tacit agree-
ment between them practically amounting to an engagement.'[119] If true, this
may go some way to explain the histrionics which were to follow.

Eileen Palliser was now sharing a room with KM and Chaddie at no. 41
because KM had quarrelled with Vera. KM, undoubtedly to spite Vera, produced the following poem, dated Sunday 13 May 1906, which extolls the pleasures of the sisters' intimacy, and shows Vera, 'with her face all red', away with
the grown-ups instead:

'A Common Ballad'

Outside is the roar of London town
But we have pulled the sun blinds down
And are as snug as snug can be
Chaddie and me.

She lying on the empty bed
Her book half covering up her head
And *very* much 'en déshabille'
Chaddie – *not* me.

I – sitting here to write to you
And looking like a stocking blue
We both are longing for our tea
Chaddie and me.

But we're not really learned tho'
This poem sounds as if we're so
And with our grammar we're most free
Chaddie and me.

Our sister – with her face all red
Has gone to see her Ma instead
Well – she is she, and we are we
Chaddie and me.

Far better here to quietly stay
And eat and yawn away the day
We'll end by going to the d – – –
Chaddie and me.

She now is very fast asleep
God grant her hair in waves will keep
But no one is so sweet as we
Chaddie and me.[120]

Eileen, who, in addition to being a witness to the Beauchamp girls' bickering, also told of meetings with Tom when KM would return to college in a state of high anxiety, throw herself on the bed and weep inconsolably. KM also started talking and walking in her sleep – hallmarks of a troubled state of mind – and apparently visited fortune-tellers to try to find out what her future would hold. She also started going to séances (a very fashionable fin-de-siècle custom), which left her even more distressed:

One day she announced to the girls that she was 'going to have a séance'; and when they prepared for the table rapping, she 'went into a trance' – as one of them remembers – 'and talked so wildly that we were frightened out of our wits, and had to shake her violently to bring her back to herself'.[121]

Coupled with her torment over her 'relationship' with Tom was the anguish of the impending move back to New Zealand. KM had no desire to return. Her life – Tom's life – was in London. What on earth would she do back in that colonial backwater at the other end of the earth? Harold was left speechless by such ingratitude and vowed that young Leslie and Jeanne would be educated in New Zealand; an expensive education at 'home' had not proved quite the success he had envisaged.

Yet another New Zealand friend now entered this emotionally fraught cocktail: Maata. She had been sent to a proper finishing school in Paris and was briefly staying in London. Her chic, polished presence entranced KM; for a short time she forgot how miserable Tom was making her and fell into the arms of the beautiful and glamorous Maori princess, rekindling their close, almost passionate friendship of old (something which would play out more physically after their return to Wellington). In 1907, she remembered this moment together in London in a notebook entry, renaming Maata both 'Ariadne' and 'Carlotta' (and presaging the story 'Vignette: Summer in Winter' [1907]):

> In the pocket of an old coat I found one of Ariadne's gloves – a cream suede glove fastening with two silver buttons. And it has been there two years. But still it holds some exquisite suggestion of Carlotta – still when I lay it against my cheek I can detect the sweet of the perfume she affected. O, Carlotta – have you remembered. We were floating down Regent Street in a hansom, on either side of us the blossoms of golden light, and ahead a little half hoop of a moon.[122]

The emotional turbulence stimulated by the presence of Maata and the Trowells, and her own sexuality, as well as the fate of Rudolf, would all subsequently be poured into her unfinished novel, *Juliet*, which she now began on 18 May and which she carried on writing intermittently until early 1907, when it would be abandoned. Similar characters and themes would subsequently be resurrected in her second unfinished novel, *Maata* (1913). There was an unfortunate complication to Maata's visit. She had been introduced to the Beauchamps' dressmaker, 'Madame Louise', and ordered a large number of outfits, but then left without paying the bill, which was immediately sent to Harold; he reluctantly paid up, but subsequently, to his daughter's indignation, demanded that KM stop seeing Maata.[123]

Vere later revealed that KM had become so desperate to remain in London that she had seriously entertained the idea of finding a flat and trying to manage alone; at this point, Vere's sister, apparently in jest, said that perhaps they could flat-share and KM fruitlessly spent some time looking into such a proposition. All of this angst was poured into the pages of *Juliet*, where she sometimes even forgot to fictionalise names, so that on numerous occasions Pearl was written as 'Vere' and David as 'Caesar'. The following passage offers a view into KM's troubled mind-set at that time:

For days the rain had been falling steadily monotonously over London until it seemed to be suffocating her, beating into her brain. She had slept very little at night and her face [was a] little worn and set. At Vere's remark she stopped walking and said 'I – I beg your pardon. I did not quite realise what I was doing.'

Vere laid down her pen and pushed back her chair. 'Got a mood?' she said.

'Yes' said Juliet, 'it's the very Devil. While it lasts I think it is going to be eternal and I'm contemplating suicide.'

'It's sure to be something physical. Why don't you sleep better Juliet? Are you – you're not . . . repenting?'

'Good Heavens, no. The truth is, my dear girl, well I hardly like to own it to myself even, you understand. Bernard Shaw would be gratified.'

'You feel sexual.'

'Horribly. And in need of a physical shock or violence – perhaps a good smacking would be beneficial.'

'Don't laugh so much at yourself, Juliet. I'm sorry dear – you look wretchedly ill.'

[. . .]

'Our friendship is unique' said Vere, folding her arms and staring at the light. 'Nothing could separate us, Juliet. All the comforts of matrimony with none of its encumbrances, hein?'

'My word yes! As it is we are both individuals. We both ask from the other personal privacy, and we can be silent for hours when the desire seizes us.'

'Think of a man always with you. A woman cannot be wholly natural with a man – there is always a feeling that she must take care that she doesn't let him go.'

'A perpetual strain.'

'Also I should inevitably want to fly very high if I was certain that my wings were clipped.'

'Ugh' said Juliet, going over to the wardrobe and reaching for her coat and hat, 'I loathe the very principle of matrimony. It must end in failure, and it is death to a woman's personality. She must drop the theme and begin to start playing the accompaniment. For me there is *no* attraction.'

Vere suddenly laughed. 'I was thinking of your past affaire de coeur with David Méjin,' she said.

'Please don't,' cried Juliet. 'To think of it makes me feel overwhelmingly sick. When I think how he filled, swayed my whole life, how I worshipped him – only I did. How jealous I was of him! I kept the very envelopes of his letters for years, and he – to say the least – raised his hat and passed on.'[124]

It was a good job KM did not offer Harold and Annie her manuscript to read, with passages like this peppering the text. Deep down, however, below the showy, hard exterior designed to shock, and the emancipated talk resembling Shaw's very modern character, Vivie Warren, from his play *Mrs Warren's Profession*, whose mother is a prostitute and who wants to lead a life of freedom akin to a man's,[125] many of the sentiments were false. Of course, one way to recover from a broken heart is to pretend indifference but the truth was that KM still believed herself in love with Tom. The sexual impulses portrayed (which, a hundred and so years after they were written, still surprise) do, however, hint at the adolescent KM's difficulties in coming to terms with her feelings of sexual desire, which had no obvious outlet, at least in a conventional, heterosexual sense.

And so KM led almost a double life at this time, writing about feeling 'horribly sexual', needing a 'spanking', loathing 'the very principle of matrimony' on the one hand, whilst lectures at college and the daily routine carried on regardless, and with her parents' presence in London a constant and visible reminder of her hopeless situation. At about this time KM wrote a final poem, 'Shadows', to a schoolfriend, Hilda Nathan Salinger (also known as 'Diddy'), the mood of the poem reflecting her feelings, and the dedication reading 'To my Friend – in Memory – in Trust – and in Hope':

Shadows of days long past,
Come back again!
Never again – ah me! – the leaves may fall
Soft o'er the grass, and the Winter Pall
Darken the world – I shall call you in vain –
Shadows of days long past![126]

Occasionally, KM was able to escape to Ida at Montagu Mansions, where, curled up in the corner of a sofa, she 'bewailed the fact that she had no one on her side, that no one understood'.[127] KM grew more and more dejected as the departure date grew closer and Ida was needed more and more to bolster her up:

I was seeing more and more of her as the time for departure approached. I went every evening to the French class-room upstairs, where I knew I would find her changed for the evening meal and practising the 'cello; she would be playing her heart out. We talked of everything but chiefly of her hopes and plans to come back to London as soon as possible.[128]

KM's frustrations were vented on the depictions of her parents in *Juliet*:

The Mother was a slight pale little woman. She had been delicate and ailing before her marriage and she never could forget it. [. . .] Mr Wilberforce [was] a tall grey-bearded man with prominent blue eyes, large ungainly hands, and inclining to stoutness. He was a general merchant, director of several companies, chairman of several societies, thoroughly commonplace and commercial.[129]

Harold had, in fact, attended the sixth congress of the Chambers of Commerce of the British Empire during this trip, noting, incidentally, that he 'was one of the thirty members of the congress who were chosen to be received by King Edward VII, at Buckingham Palace':[130] another experience to regale colleagues with back in Wellington. In *Juliet* there are also conversations between the protagonist and her father, which must have come close to replicating the increasing frustration on both sides:

Juliet passed a sleepless night. She lay still in the darkness staring at the dim outline of the roofs outside the window, thinking, thinking. Each moment her brain seemed more awake. If I do once go back, she thought, all will be over. It is stagnation, desolation that stares [me] in the face. I shall be lonely. I shall be thousands of miles from all that I care for and once I get there I can't come back. I can't do it. If they choose to behave like devils they must be treated as such. On one hand lay the mode bohème – alluring, knowledge-bringing, full of work and sensation, full of impulse, pulsating with the cry of Youth Youth Youth. Pearl with her pale eager face and smiling ripe mouth, crying to Juliet, 'Here I am – here we both are. Trust me dear, live with me. You and I to reach for things together, you and I to live and prove our new Philosophy.'
    On the other hand lay the Suitable Appropriate Existence. The days full of perpetual Society functions, the hours full of clothes discussions – the waste of life. 'The stifling atmosphere would kill me,' she thought. The days – weeks – months – years of it all. Her father, with his successful characteristic respectable face, crying 'Now is the time. What have I got for my money. Come along – deck yourself out, show the world that you are

expensive. Now is the time for me to sit still and have my slippers brought for me. You are behaving badly. You must learn to realise that the silken cords of parental authority are very tight ropes indeed. I want no erratic spasmodic daughter. I demand a sane healthy-minded girl. It is quite time for you to put up the shutters upon this period.'

In the darkness Juliet smiled at the last expression. It was so exactly like him – an undeniable *trade* atmosphere.[131]

This was a battle that would play out once the family returned to New Zealand; it was a battle KM was determined to win, at all costs.

Meanwhile, Harold was more than happy to help Tom with his musical career (though not KM's) now that both he and Tom were in London, and did his best to secure him an agent. His choice was Laurence Rainbow, a celebrated agent who represented many well-known musicians, including Pablo Casals. A personal blow for Harold during this trip was the death, on 10 June 1906, of his great friend Richard Seddon, who had done so much to boost his career. He had suffered a massive heart attack and died suddenly, while returning to New Zealand from a trip to Australia. Of course, as the family were in London, attending the large state funeral at St Paul's Cathedral in Wellington was impossible, but the family went to the special memorial service held in his honour in London. Seddon's Liberal Party successor – and another friend of Harold's, Sir Joseph Ward, had also been in London at the time but immediately returned to New Zealand and became the country's next prime minister.[132]

In the last few weeks of their stay in England, Harold, accompanied by Vera (rewarding her good behaviour in the face of her belligerent younger sibling), made a short trip to Paris, since he had become the French consular agent in Wellington; this was followed by a brief tour of Switzerland, where he extolled the virtues of Swiss tourism but not its agriculture, believing they were considerably behind New Zealand in their farming methods.[133] The family also made numerous visits to their Beauchamp relations, and especially to the family favourite, Great-Uncle Henry Herron, whose diary records that, on 16 September 1906, '3 Beauchamp girls came yesterday for weekend. Delightfully natural,' and on 30 September, 'Harold B and his wife Saty to Monday here.' On Monday 1 October he wrote, 'Appointed Holy! This day – 68 years ago – I went as a "boy" to S^t. Baker, Phillpotts & Co at 106 Fenchurch S^t. Made a "pious pilgrimage" there to-day with Harold Beauchamp.'[134] Harold was always interested in his London roots and such visits with his favourite uncle always gave him enormous pleasure. On KM's birthday, 14 October, the three girls were once again his visitors.

The final meeting with Henry Herron took place on 17 October at Fripp's:

Lunched – with Loey – at Harold B's at 36 Manchester S[r]. The 3 dear girls came in later. We all bade each other very sincere adieus as they start per 'Corinthia' (over 12,000 tons) on their return to New Zealand on the 19th inst from Albert Docks.

One can almost hear Harold proudly relaying the tonnage of the ship to his uncle, since these details were always of great interest to him and assiduously reproduced in the *Reminiscences*. Two days later, Henry Herron's son Ralph (who was always close to Harold and had spent several weeks in Karori in early 1895 when visiting family in New Zealand) went to the railway station to bid them farewell on behalf of the family, alongside '[a] large gathering of their friends'.[135] It was almost a *royal* departure.

While her New Zealand roots were imprinted in her brain, to resurface time and again in her fiction, KM's three years in London had effectively cut the ties between herself and her parents' stuffy, middle-class, colonial world. She wanted none of it. If there was a choice to be made between art nouveau interior décor and purple sofas in Ladbroke Grove, or a grand house in Wellington, with its incumbent dull round of parties and the same old faces, the choice was an overwhelmingly easy one. In a parting shot to Eileen Palliser, KM announced her battle plan: 'When I get to New Zealand, I'll make myself so objectionable that they'll *have* to send me away.'[136] And, true to her word, that was exactly what she did.

Chapter 7   Thorndon: 1906–1908

VOYAGE HOME

The Beauchamp family, minus Aunt Belle, who had successfully bagged her English husband, once more regrouped for the long voyage home, boarding the passenger ship, the S.S. *Corinthic*, at Gravesend on 18 October, just four days after KM's eighteenth birthday. On board the ship was an English cricket team,

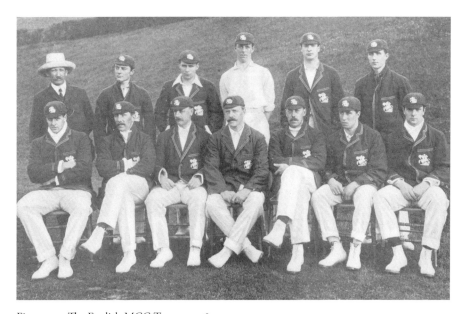

Figure 7.1 The English MCC Team, 1906.

put together by the Marylebone Cricket Club (the 'MCC', the home of English cricket) and composed of 'little known amateurs',[1] on their way to a financially disastrous tour of New Zealand; the players were, however, the only silver lining to KM's dark cloud. As far as Harold was concerned, the only sensation of the voyage was 'the discovery of a case of smallpox, which was landed at Capetown'.[2]

When KM left Queen's College, Miss Wood had given her a leaving present. She clearly knew her student well after three years. The gift was a thick black notebook, inscribed as follows:

To Kathleen Beauchamp
from
Clara F. Wood
In very affectionate remembrance of 41 Harley Street
July 14th 1906

With so many weeks at sea and little else to do, KM now took the opportunity to make entries in several different notebooks, including Miss Wood's, revealing a growing frustration with her family, and especially her parents, as well as an increasing introspection as she tried to analyse herself and her emotional world. Most of the latter was fictionalised in *Juliet*, which she carried on writing as the ship made its long journey to the other side of the world.

KM's escalating sexual impulses were still uppermost, however, and she quickly developed a crush on one particular member of the cricket team, who she called 'Adonis' because of his devastating good looks; elsewhere she also referred to him as 'R'. Possibly this was R. H. (Ronny) Fox, who had actually been born in Dunedin in New Zealand but had moved to England as a young boy.[3] This New Zealand connection would certainly have been one reason for KM to have made some sort of initial overture to him. The ship's captain, himself a cricket enthusiast, gave free rein to the glamorous young cricketers aboard his vessel. Every afternoon, one portion of the deck was allotted to them for games of one sort or another, including five-a-side hockey. According to the fast bowler, P. R. May, 'Fox, by bringing many of his Rugger tricks into play, gained notoriety as a real rough 'un [. . .] Many were the bruises inflicted.'[4] If there was fun to be had, it seems that Fox was always in the thick of it, even managing to twist his ankle as the boat neared Tasmania. Another reason why Ronny Fox might have initially come to KM's attention was the fact that almost every day he won either first or second prize in the ship's daily sweepstake. At the on-board fancy-dress ball, Fox once more brought attention to himself when he appeared dressed as a Maori chief. Other possible suspects for 'Adonis' could have been P. R. (Percy) May and Johnny Douglas, who were highly proficient fast-bowlers:

Figure 7.2 Ronny H. Fox.

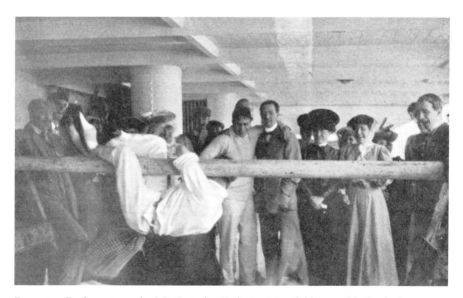

Figure 7.3 Deck sports on the S.S. *Corinthic*. Katherine Mansfield is possibly the shadowy
female figure to the right of the man with the white dog collar.

Each might have been a candidate for the 'Adonis' description in his own way – May was boyishly handsome, Douglas more rugged (he later went on to claim an Olympic Gold medal as a middleweight boxer). Douglas was known to be a man who lived life to the full; little is known of May's personal life.[5]

In an early photograph album belonging to KM there exist two photos of Fox on board the *Corinthic*, one with Johnny Douglas, and one with both Douglas and May. Whoever 'Adonis' / 'R' was, by the time the *Corinthic* reached the tropics, KM could barely contain her sexual desires. In a piece entitled 'At Sea', she gave vent to her passion in very creative prose, the fin-de-siècle / Decadent literary influence still flowing freely through her pen, the air heady with the scent of gardenias:

Figure 7.4 Percy R. May, Johnny Douglas and Ronny H. Fox.

Swiftly the Night came. Like a great white bird the ship sped onward – onward into the unknown. Through the darkness the stars shone, yet the sky was a garden of golden flowers, heavy with colour. I lay on the deck of the vessel, my hands clasped behind my head, and, watching them, I felt a curious complex emotion, a swift mysterious realisation that they were shining steadily & ever more powerfully into the very soul of my soul. I felt their still light permeating the very depths, and fear & ecstasy held me still, shuddering.

There is some fearful magic in their shining, I thought. As the power of the sunlight causes the firelight to become pale & wasted so is the flame of my life becoming quenched by this star shining. I saw the flame of my life as a little little candle flickering fearfully & fancifully, and I thought before long it will go out and then. Even as I thought I saw there where it had shone – darkness remained.

Then I was drifting, drifting – where – whence – whither. I was drifting in a great boundless purple sea. I was being tossed to and fro by the power of the waves, and the confused sound of many voices floated to me. A sense of unutterable loneliness pervaded my spirit. I knew this sea was eternal – I was eternal – this agony was eternal.

So, smiling at myself, I sit down to analyse this new influence, this complex emotion. I am never anywhere for long without a like experience. It is not one man or woman that a musician desires – it is the whole octave of the sex, & R. is my latest. The first time I saw him I was lying back in my chair & he walked past. I watched the complete rhythmic movement, the absolute self confidence, the beauty of his body, & that Quelque which is the everlasting & eternal in youth & creation stirred in me. I heard him speaking – he has a low full, strangely exciting voice, a habit of mimicking others, a keen sense of humour. His face is clean cut like the face of a statue, his mouth absolutely grecian. Also, he has seen much & lived much and his hand is perfectly strong and cool. He is certainly tall, & his clothes drape the lines of his figure. When I am with him a preposterous desire seizes me. I want to be badly hurt by him. I should like to be strangled by his firm hands. He smokes cigarettes frequently & exquisitely fastidiously.

Last night we sat on deck. He taught me picquet. It was intensely hot. He wore a loose silk shirt under his dress coat. He was curiously excitable, almost a little violent at times. There was a suppressed agitation in every look, every movement. He spoke French for the greater part of the time with exquisite fluency, and a certain extreme affectation – he has spent years in Paris. The more hearts you have the better, he said, leaning over my hand.

I felt his coat sleeve against my bare arm. O one heart is a very pinched affair, I answered – in these days one must possess many. We exchanged a long look and his glance inflamed me like the scent of a gardenia.

Yesterday afternoon a game of cricket was in progress on the deck. R began bowling – I stood & watched. He took a few slow steps & then flung the ball at the wicket with the most marvellous force. Time & again he did it – each ball seemed to be aimed at my heart. I panted for breath – – –[6]

It must have been hard for her to escape her parents' eagle eyes for long enough to lie flat out on the deck of the ship and stare up at the stars, allowing them to quench 'the flame of her life'. In the repetition and alliteration of 'little little candle flickering fearfully & fancifully' and 'drifting, drifting – where – whence – whither', there is deliberate – almost forced – artistry, as the writer–artist practises her craft. In this mode of writing, the sea could only possibly be one colour – purple – the colour of Rippmann's sofas. In the full grip of an adolescent emotional maelstrom and, at this point in her life, never knowingly under-egging her pudding, she declares: 'I knew this sea was eternal – I was eternal – this agony was eternal.'

The mood then changes and she turns to an analysis of the reason for her agony (and at this point still thinking of herself as a 'musician': 'It is not one man or woman that a musician desires – it is the whole octave of the sex, & R. is my latest'), openly declaring her bisexuality as well as her desire for 'R', the cricketer. It was a good thing Harold could not see what she wrote next: 'When I am with him a preposterous desire seizes me. I want to be badly hurt by him. I should like to be strangled by his firm hands,' in language similar to that being employed in *Juliet*, still being written at this time. KM's Greek god, mature and experienced, must surely have known what he was doing, but perhaps was not aware of how eager and willing – 'panting', in fact – the young New Zealand girl was to experience many 'hearts'.

In the second half of the diary entry, KM discusses her attraction for 'R' a little more, and then moves on to an excoriating put-down of her parents:

We deny our minds to the extent that we castrate our bodies. I am won-dering if that is true? & thinking that it most certainly is. Oh, I want to push it as far as it will go. Tomorrow night there is to be a ball. Thank Dieu I know that my dancing is really beautiful. I shall fight for what I want yet I don't [know] definitely what that is. I want to upset him, stir in him strange depths. He has seen so much, it would be such a conquest. At present he is – – I do not know – I think intensely curious & a little baffled. Am I to become eventually une jeune fille entretenue. It points to it. O God, that is better far than the daughter of my parents. What tedious old

bores they seem. They are worse than I had even expected. They are prying
& curious, they are watchful & cat-like, they discuss only the food. They
quarrel between themselves in a hopelessly vulgar fashion. My Father spoke
of my returning as damned rot, said look here he wouldn't have me fooling
around in dark corners with fellows. His hands, covered with long sandy
hair, are absolutely evil hands. A physically revolted feeling seizes me. He
wants me to sit near, he watches me at meals, eats in the most abjectly bla-
tantly vulgar manner that is describable. It is like a constant long offense,
but I cannot escape from it. And it wraps me in its atmosphere. When I
pass him the dishes at table, or a book, or give him a cushion, he refrains
from thanking me. He is constantly suspicious, constantly overbearingly
tyrannous. I watch him walking all the deck, his pale hideous speckled
trousers, his absurdly antediluvian cap. He is like a cat sometimes I think,
except that his eyes are not like a cat's eyes – they are so pale, so frightfully
offensive. When he is astonished or when he eats anything that pleases him
I think they must start from his head. He watches the dishes go round,
anxious to see that he shall have a good share. I cannot be alone or in the
company of women for five minutes – he is there, eager, fearful, attempting
to appear unconcerned, pulling at his long drooping red-grey moustache
with his hairy hands. Ugh!

   She is completely under his influence, suggestible & easily upset. Tells
him what he must & must not do, looks constantly uneasy. They are both
so absolutely idealistic – they are a constant offense to me. The sight of
them causes me to feel utterly changed – I hesitate in my manner, appear
constrained. They have no idea of the fitness of things. I shall never be able
to live at home – I can plainly see that. There would be constant friction.
For more than a quarter of an hour they are quite unbearable, & so absolutely my mental inferiors. What is going to happen in the future. I am full
of a restless wonder, but I have none of that glorious vitality that I used to
have so much. They are draining it out of me – – –[7]

Most adolescents like to push things 'as far as they will go', and KM's burgeoning
sexual feelings seem completely normal one hundred years on; however, putting
them down on paper, examining them, questioning them, as she does in this
passage, points to an unusual frankness – certainly unusual for the time in which
it was written. Her distaste for her parents is another normal adolescent reaction, but it is the *detail* of her descriptions that give them so much vitality. And
curiously, it was when she was in the company of *women* that Harold appeared
worried: 'he is there, eager, fearful, attempting to appear unconcerned,' pointing
perhaps to an early recognition by her parents that KM was perhaps not quite
'normal' when it came to affairs of the heart. There is speculation that she even

believed herself to be engaged to 'R' for about three weeks, but if so, no record survives, and the family were quick to hide it.[8]

As well as writing these frank diary entries and continuing with *Juliet*, KM was, of course, still writing poems, though the ones written on this trip have little of the intensity of her other on-board writing. 'The Child of the Sea', however, is quite different. It was never completed, but is yet another example of KM's figure of the child poised between the worlds of real life and mythical otherness – both vibrantly alert and human, yet also wistful and spirit-like, with an enchanted, changeling-like presence:

Here in the sunlight wild I lie
Wrapt up warm with my pillow and coat
Sometimes I look at the big blue sky

The wide grey sky, the wide grey sky
And ever the clouds move slowly by
The fierce shrill note of the sea-birds' cry
Here in my strange bed.

The endless sea, the endless sea
And the song that is sung repeatedly
In every rhythm and time and theme
Till I shriek aloud . . . but it deafens me.

The changing light, the changing light
Purple and gold change to the night
A wide strong blue when the sun is bright
A riot of colour – a wonder sight.

Valley and hill, valley and hill
I am swept along – I never am still
I have cried, I have cursed, I have prayed my fill.

It carries me near the loved one.

Here we
And the shivering song of the poplars
And away in the distance the sea.[9]

The use of repetition, seen in the notebook entries above, is now used to poetic effect, offering a rhythmic quality to her vision, as once more she lies on the deck of the ship and watches her watery world pass by. Immediately underneath the poem, she wrote:

Edgar Allan – Atmosphere – untidiness of landscape – Height, river, small boat, Italy, colour purple – the result of fire – manuka – Ai. Hotel man with daughter – willows the yellow transparent effect.

When N Z is more artificial she will give birth to an artist who can treat her natural beauties adequately. This sounds paradoxical but is true.[10]

The influence of Edgar Allan Poe in the impressionistic first three lines is evident, and the poem is followed by an Oscar Wilde-inspired aphorism. There would be plenty more of those to come.

The *Corinthic* continued on her journey, beyond Cape Town, where the unfortunate case of smallpox was landed, past various Australian ports, across the Tasman Sea and eventually on to New Zealand, landing on 6 December 1906, at the height of an antipodean summer. Harold must have believed that once his wayward daughter was home, he would have her more firmly under his control but in this he was mistaken.

The arrival of the *Corinthic* in Wellington was the subject of a news report, as was its most illustrious passenger, that stalwart of Wellington commerce, Harold Beauchamp, in a piece entitled 'A Merchant Abroad': '"Yes", as our friend of pantomimic fame has so frequently observed, "here I am again", after having been absent from "the brightest gem that adorns the Imperial diadem" just nine months.' More information is gleaned about his trip: 'The last English summer, he said, was something to be remembered: nearly five months' of uninterruptedly brilliant weather – genial warmth, bright sunshine, clear skies, and,

Figure 7.5 Wellington, 1906.

what was most pleasing to a New Zealander, a complete absence of high winds!' His thoughts on British social and immigration policies are then given, followed by a description of the East End of London, which contrasts so sharply with the lives of his well-to-do family:

> 'Why are the arms of England still open to receive the paupers an unde-sirables of every country', he said in reply to a question. 'Visit the East End of London – that district lying between Shoreditch and High-street, Whitechapel – and I think you will agree that the time has arrived when the cry of "England for the English," or "Britain for the British" should be raised with no uncertain sound. I walked through one street, Brick Lane, where I failed to see one English name, and where all the names over the shops were painted in Yiddish. Even newspaper posters, giving the contents of the Daily Mail, Daily News, and other London dailies, were displayed in that tongue. It goes without saying that the aliens residing in the quarter I have mentioned have squeezed out the original occupants (British), many of whom, have passed on to swell the ranks of the unemployed. These unemployed were just preparing for the winter campaign before I sailed. At that season of the year men, women, and children, beating tins and other musical (?) instruments to attract attention, march about in hundreds and make a house to house canvass, with a view to collecting sufficient to keep body and soul together.'[11]

Harold's racist views on immigration in 1906, however unsavoury, certainly represented the majority view at that time. In addition, his description of the immense poverty in the East End of London tells us much about the city to which KM was so desperate to return. It was one thing to have money and live in Harley Street, W1, but quite another to live in abject poverty in Whitechapel, E1, and to have to beg in order to survive. The cushion of her father's wealth had kept KM immune from such misery.

75 TINAKORI ROAD

Family life returned to some sense of normality, back at no. 75, that house which KM conjured up so memorably in her notebooks in 1916, when, follow-ing the death of her brother, she wrote:

> Oh, I want for one moment to make our undiscovered country leap into the eyes of the old world. It must be mysterious, as though floating – it must take the breath. It must be 'one of those islands'. . . . I shall tell everything, even of how the laundry basket squeaked at '75'.[12]

Figure 7.6 Katherine Mansfield, 75 Tinakori Rd.

Several family members were missing from the home, however: young Leslie was away at boarding school – Waitaki Boys' High – in the South Island; Aunt Belle, now Mrs Harry Trinder, was *finally* enjoying all the comforts of married life and her own home, back in England; and Grandma Dyer was now living with her eldest daughter elsewhere in Wellington. KM's moodiness and self-absorption in her misery at being back in New Zealand meant that she did not visit her Grandma during the whole of December. Grandma Dyer remarked on this fact but showed no resentment. When the old lady died on New Year's Eve, just three weeks after the family's return, KM's guilt was palpable. She wrote to Sylvia Payne on 8 January 1907, 'I have been living too – in the atmosphere of Death. My Grandmother died on New Year's Eve – my first experience of a personal loss – it horrified me – the whole thing.'[13] In later life, KM would immortalise her grandmother in the New Zealand Burnell stories, as well as in numerous poems and notebook entries, assuaging her guilt, perhaps, from that December in 1906, when she had failed to do the right thing.

In the same letter, however, KM turns her grief on its head, and blames Wellington – and possibly New Zealand itself – for her grief: 'Death never seemed revolting before – This place – steals your Youth – that is just what it does – I feel years and years older and sadder.'[14] She had been home for exactly a month and life was already unbearable:

> I feel absolutely *ill* with grief and sadness – here – it is a nightmare – I feel that sooner or later I must wake up – & find myself in the heart of it all again – and look back upon the past months as – – – – cobwebs – a hideous dream. Life here's impossible – I can't see how it can drag on – I have not one friend – and no prospect of one. My dear – I know nobody – and nobody cares to know me – there is nothing on earth to do – nothing to see – and my heart keeps flying off – Oxford Circus – Westminster Bridge at the Whistler hour – London by hansom – my old room – the meeting of the Swans – and a corner in the library. It haunts me all so much – and I feel it must come back soon – How people ever wish to live here I cannot think –
>
> Dear – I can't write anything – Tonight I feel too utterly hopelessly full of heimweh.[15] If you knew how I hunger for it all – and for my friends – this absence of companionship – this starvation – that's what it is –[16]

There were so many memories of her three years in London to attach her misery to: the beauty of London itself – that beating heart of Empire – but even life at Queen's College, her old room and those Swanswick literary society meetings. In her despair, everything about her old life was now gilt-edged, without discrimination. She must have been hard to live with, even as she found her family and her surroundings impossible. Guy Scholefield, the friend of Harold's who wrote the chapter on KM in the *Reminiscences*, noted of her aspirations, 'In those days, the intellectual leanings of a young girl were treated very much as if they were mumps. They were inevitable but would pass away.'[17] There was no question of KM attending Wellington's recently founded university college, where she might have found more congenial company than her immediate family, as well as an outlet for her creativity.

Without the freedom of her London life and the absence of parents, now, if KM wanted anything she had to ask her father. Harold, for whom the keeping of strict weekly family accounts was a matter of principle (and a duty foisted on his wife Annie from the early days of their marriage), liked to know every detail of where his hard-earned money was going. Ruth Herrick claimed that 'Annie Beauchamp was a pleasant and kindly woman who had a difficult time with Harold, especially about money.'[18] Ida Baker went further, noting that 'Katherine told me of the family trials each time the weekly accounts had to be submitted to him.'[19] An early autobiographical story, 'New Dresses' (1912), uses German names for what is, nevertheless, a tale clearly based on the Beauchamp family in Thorndon and those dreaded weekly accounts, even down to the mother's name, 'Anna':

'By the way, have you got this month's draper's bill?'

She had been waiting for that – had known it was coming. [. . .]

She stared at Andreas, vacantly. 'Bill – Bill did you say, dear? O, I'll look it out in the morning.'

'No, Anna, hold on.' Andreas got up and went over to the cupboard where the bill file was kept. 'To-morrow's no good – because it's Sunday. I want to get that account off my chest before I turn in. Sit down there – in the rocking-chair – you needn't stand!'

She dropped into the chair, and began humming, all the while her thoughts coldly busy, and her eyes fixed on her husband's broad back as he bent over the cupboard door. [. . .]

'He's keeping me in suspense on purpose,' she thought. '[. . .] I know our income and our expenditure. I'm not a fool. They're a hell upon earth every month, these bills.'[20]

For KM, there were few solaces to this new life back home, even though schoolfriends back in England were not exactly leading exciting lives. Ida was stuck in Montagu Mansions, in the family's flat just off Baker Street, at the mercy of her irascible father. Vere, having taken a job as a theatre usherette, expected excitement but found nothing but drudgery; she was now situated in the country, living with her mother and working in a local bank. KM did not care. She was convinced that life in London would be *very* different for her, if she could only persuade her parents to let her return. In the meantime there was music – her cello – and there was the Trowell family, minus Tom and Garnet. Ida was sending her cuttings about Tom, which fed her passion; KM, of course, was still writing to him, though he only very occasionally replied to her. She was undaunted by such setbacks, and the Trowells would now become KM's spiritual family – musical, bohemian and artistic – with no whiff of the commerce to be found at no. 75, until they too would leave to make a new home for themselves in London with their twin sons. Until such time, KM took as many music lessons as she could, and relished the time spent at 18 Buller Street, where the talk was always of the boys' triumphs. With the Trowells she could be herself; at home she was the problem daughter, whom no one quite knew how to handle. As she went to and fro from Buller Street to no. 75, neighbours remembered her 'passing swiftly down Tinakori Road – the cumbersome 'cello apparently no burden – and singing as she sped down the hill'.[21]

Harold, using his connections in parliament, and as a friend of the then Chief Librarian, Charles Wilson, as well as the Chairman of the Library Committee, William Fraser, managed to obtain for Vera and KM reading rights at the well-stocked parliamentary library, which was another consolation. Records show that KM was a regular borrower, reading an eclectic mix of classic and modern

Figure 7.7 Mr Thomas Trowell.

Figure 7.8 The Houses of Parliament, Wellington, with the General Assembly Library to the
        right.

fiction, as well as books on social reform. Her reading card has sadly now disappeared, but thanks to Scholefield (who himself would later become the Chief Librarian), we still have a record of what interested her at this time:

> Kathleen studied in philosophy such works as Heine's *Ideas*, Nietzsche's *Dawn of Day*, and *Bushido*, by a Japanese author (Dr. Inazo Nitobe) [. . .] She revelled in the poets: Henley, Browning, Yeats amongst them; and in the literary critics, like James, Thompson (*French Portraits*) and Shaw; dramatists like Ibsen and Maeterlinck; and the lives of innumerable artists and poets. Her philosophical reading culminated in Marholm's *Psychology of Women* [. . .][22]

Aside from music and reading, another solace for KM was the holiday cottage Harold had had built while the girls had been in England, on land he had bought near the rocky promontory called Downe's Point, at the opposite end of Day's Bay to their former rented holiday home, The Glen. It was a very small, simple cottage, on the edge of the seashore, with an adjoining woodshed and washhouse. When there were storms, the waves would splash the front windows. When KM needed to escape, here was her refuge. Otherwise, there were dances, new clothes, parties and concerts, which certainly appealed to Vera and Chaddie but left KM unsatisfied. All the sisters agreed, however, that the boys they had known prior to their London trip were now impossibly provincial and completely unsuitable as suitors. The English cricket team that had accompanied them on their voyage home became a regular fixture at the best social gatherings but eventually even they returned to England, leaving the young Wellington girls mourning their absence. According to their relatives, the girls were now '"frightfully English. Nothing in NZ was good enough for them."'[23] Harold's meteoric rise in the business world provoked some jealousy, as did their large house, plus the fact that the girls had been sent to London for part of their education. It meant that old friends now felt uncomfortable in their company, and the three sisters spent a good deal of time together.

Early in 1907, when it was still summer and the weather could be relied on, Annie Beauchamp gave one of her celebrated garden parties, possibly the first after their return from England. During the party, an accident took place in Little George Street, that mean little lane just below no. 75: a young workman had been run over and killed. News of the death reached the family in the big house above, but it was decided to continue with the festivities. Later in the afternoon, Vera went down to the dead man's family with a basket of food. In 1921, fourteen years after the incident took place, KM would fictionalise the events of that fateful afternoon in one of her most celebrated stories, 'The Garden Party'. In her version, the person who takes a basket of food down to the grieving widow and five children is the protagonist, 'Laura': clearly, KM herself and not 'Meg' (Vera Margaret). Many years later, Vera would remark 'how absurd she had felt "in one of those enormous hats we used to wear in those days", and how she had had to tilt it sideways to get through the cottage door'.[24] Whether KM herself cared about the accident is not recorded, but fourteen years on, she certainly felt compelled to send herself back in time to that fateful day and to fictionalise the events in her story:

> Now the broad road was crossed. The lane began, smoky and dark. Women in shawls and men's tweed caps hurried by. Men hung over the palings; the children played in the doorways. A low hum came from the mean little cottages. In some of them there was a flicker of light, and a shadow, crab-like, moved across the window. Laura bent her head and hurried on. She wished now she had put on a coat. How her frock shone! And the big hat with the velvet streamer – if only it was another hat! Were the people looking at her? They must be. It was a mistake to have come; she knew all along it was a mistake.[25]

'The Garden Party' is one of KM's longer New Zealand stories and part of the 'Sheridan' cycle. Here is the 'Burnell' family under a different name and slightly older; gone are the young children, the ubiquitous Stanley Burnell and the sensual Beryl. Instead, KM presents us with the development of the adolescent mind and its gradual succumbing to adult values and morals. On the surface, the story reads as a homely vision of youthful femininity and middle-class values, set within the picturesque New Zealand landscape. Yet these values, these notions, are the backdrop for a discourse on the plight of the working classes, the presentation of staid, middle-class reaction to social inferiors, and a child's last attempt to understand the world naturally and simplistically, without the need for a social mask, though this mask becomes more stiflingly present each time Laura, the protagonist, at the onset of adulthood, tries to shy away from it. In addition, and most importantly, it is a war story, another hymn to KM's beloved dead brother, Leslie, killed by a faulty hand grenade on 6 October 1915, before he ever got to the front itself. Here, she recreates him as Laurie, the brother of the protagonist Laura, their twin names reinforcing their attachment, similarity of outlook, and even appearance. J. Laurence Mitchell affirms that 'the key to understanding the special bond between KM and her brother is surely to be found in what they alone in the family shared – an androgynous nature.'[26] At a fancy-dress ball in Wellington in 1915, Leslie would even be mistaken for KM, such was the physical resemblance, and family friends later confirmed that he was '"what would nowadays be called a pansy"'.[27] The two characters – and especially Laura – do not belong to the snobbish, vulgar and materialistic Sheridans / Beauchamps. They are a world apart.

But the writing of this landmark story was many years into her future. Meanwhile, KM's moods grew blacker and people noticed. Vera and Chaddie were invited to spend a little holiday on a relative's sheep station – their sister was not invited. Chaddie, who was also writing to Sylvia at this time, noted, 'I wish dear old Kass was here too, but sad to relate she was not asked.'[28] Instead, as the antipodean summer faded and autumn approached, KM started using her notebooks to find a creative outlet for her misery, as well as her sexual feelings. In an entry for 26 February 1907, she now tried another nom de plume, one with a more Germanic ring: Kathie Shonfeld (literally a German translation of the French *beau – champ*: fair – field). Soon the 'a' in Kathie would become 'ä' and the metamorphosis would be complete. Now many of the notebook entries were written in the third person and referred to 'Käthie'. She even sent Ida a photograph, taken on the wooden balcony of no. 75, signed 'Käthie' at the bottom, emphasising her new persona.

Her notebooks for March 1907 contain pages of quotations from books she was reading at this time, reading being one means of escape from her situation and her family. There were quotations from George Eliot, John Stuart Mill, Marie Corelli and Marie Bashkirtseff, but by far the greatest number were taken from Oscar Wilde's works, and particularly *The Picture of Dorian Gray*:

No life is spoiled but one whose growth is arrested.

O.W.

We are not sent into the world to air our moral prejudices.

O.W.

If you want to mar a nature you have merely to reform it.

O.W.

The only way to get rid of a temptation is to yield to it.

O.W.[29]

All the above are words spoken by the novel's hedonistic dandy, Lord Henry Wotton, whose libertine principles fascinate the protagonist, Dorian Gray. For KM at this time, these aphorisms became almost a mantra for how she wanted to live her life – untrammelled by convention – and indeed, using the acronym 'A.W' (A Woman), she even attempted her own versions:

Ambition is a curse if you are not armour-proof against everything else, unless you are willing to sacrifice yourself to your ambition.

A Woman.

It cannot be possible to go through all the abandonment of Music – and care humanly for anything human afterwards.

A Woman.

All Musicians, no matter how insignificant, come to life emasculated of their power to take life seriously. It is not one man or woman but the complete octave of sex that they desire . . .

A.W.

You feel helpless under the yoke of creation. A.W.

To have the courage of your excess – to find the limit of yourself!

A.W.[30]

Letters to Ida at this time – at least one a week – became the vehicle for outpourings of her frustration, misery and occasional periods of elation. Frustratingly, KM forced her to destroy them many years later so we only have Ida's memories of what they contained:

> I read of Katherine and her beloved brother struggling down an embankment along the sea's edge to where rows of palm trees stood with tousled, wind-torn heads of bunched leaves, rattling in the wild air . . . Katherine clasping her 'cello on her way to a music lesson with old Mr Trowell . . . returning to her room, wildly elated by all she had seen and heard, only to find a bundle of stockings on her bed, put there by her mother to be mended! . . . refusing to join in all the social activities of the family.[31]

Music, of course, was a solace. Letters to Tom were sent, and the proximity of the Trowell parents and young Dolly brought her news of the twins' life in London, which, though welcome, could only have reinforced the misery of her own life in the colonial backwater of Wellington. Millie Parker, the daughter of a Wellington pharmacist and niece of Robert Parker, KM's former piano teacher, became a good friend at this time through her connection with Mr Trowell (her family lived next door to the Trowells in Buller Street). Millie (piano), KM (cello) and Mr Trowell (violin) made up a little trio and played together every week. Even after the Trowells moved to London in September 1907 to be with the twins, the two young women continued to play together. Millie always remembered KM 'dressed in brown, for she had a fancy to play in a frock that "toned" with the 'cello, as though with a desire to merge herself with the instrument and that indeed was an understanding characteristic of her clever playing'.[32] A love of flowers also bonded the two girls; they would bring flowers to their practice sessions and enjoyed giving them names such as 'Dignity' and 'Impudence'. After a day spent together in the Botanic Gardens, they came across a five-bar fence with a line of cabbage trees in front, which KM instantly read as a stave of music. Together, they 'hummed the melody through first as treble, then as bass but found no tune either way, so it was put down as "a strange native pattering melody'". KM's considerable accomplishment on the cello at this time was also noted by Millie:

> At the time I knew her Kass Beauchamp was a remarkable 'cellist for the short period which she had then been studying the instrument, and she was a person of unexpected replies, too, I recall. To a party of friends one afternoon she played the Boellmann Variation Symphonique very beautifully. At the conclusion of the piece someone exclaimed, 'I do wish I could play the 'cello.' 'So do I!' was the quick response.[33]

Meanwhile, as his daughter's emotional life spiralled downwards into misery and frustration, Harold Beauchamp's career continued on its upward trajectory. On 13 April, the *Free Lance*, in its front-page column titled 'All Sorts of People', printed the following chirpy report on its front page:

> Mr. Harold Beauchamp, the popular head of the go-ahead firm of W. M. Bannatyne & Co., has been cheerfully elected chairman of the Board of the Bank of New Zealand. [. . .] All people that on earth do dwell know Harold Beauchamp. He is the beau ideal of a dapper, suave, acute commercial man who has always known what to do at the right time and has done it. He has been a member of the Board for eight years, having been appointed to the position by the government, and no other member of the Board could carry out the duties better.[34]

Harold could not have painted a more flattering portrait had he dictated the article himself.

47 FITZHERBERT TERRACE

The Beauchamp family could now count themselves within the top echelons of Wellington society, and Harold decided this called for an even bigger house to reflect his newfound importance better. Accordingly, in May 1907, the family moved a stone's throw away to the much grander 47 Fitzherbert Terrace (originally numbered '4'); this house had its own ballroom, croquet lawn, extensive gardens and grand pillared entrance, but without the encroaching slum areas that had dogged the views from no. 75. It even had its own smoking room, which KM used frequently, developing that strong habit that would remain with her till her death. 'Nice' girls, of course, never smoked; it was another way in which Wellington society considered KM bohemian. Musical evenings in the new ballroom offered a diversion and dancing frequently followed. In a story

Figure 7.9 47 Fitzherbert Terrace, Thorndon, Wellington.

fragment written in May 1922 and called 'A Family Dance', KM's memory of dances at no. 47 and the grand ballroom are brought vividly to life:

The excitement began first thing that morning by their father suddenly deciding that, after all, they could have champagne. What! Impossible! Mother was joking! A fierce discussion had raged on this subject ever since the invitations were sent out, Father pooh-poohing and refusing to listen, and Mother, as usual, siding with him when she was with him ('Of course, darling: I quite agree') and siding with them when she was with them ('Most unreasonable. I more than see the point'). So that by [this] time they had definitely given up all hope of champagne, and had focussed all their attention on the hock cup instead. And now, for no reason whatever, with nobody saying a word to him – so like Father! – he had given in.

'It was just after Zaidee had brought in our morning tea. He was lying on his back, you know, staring at the ceiling, and suddenly he said: "I don't want the children to think I am a wet blanket about this dance affair. If it's going to make all that difference to them; if it's a question of the thing going with a swing or not going with a swing, then I'm inclined to let them have champagne. I'll call in and order it on my way to the Bank."'

'My dear! What did you say!'

'What could I say? I was overcome. I said: "That's very generous of you, Daddy dear," and I placed the entire plate of cut bread and butter on his chest. As a kind of sacrifice to the darling. I felt he deserved it and he does so love those thin shaves of bread and butter.'

'Can't you see the plate,' cried Laurie, 'gently rising and falling on his pyjama jacket.'

They began to laugh, but it really was most thrilling. Champagne did make all the difference – didn't it? Just the feeling it was there gave such a different . . . Oh, absolutely![35]

Even here, one can detect a slight note of one-upmanship on the part of the father, knowing that the champagne will reflect very well on himself and demonstrate to the wider community his ability to provide such luxuries for his family.

In KM's new bedroom, right at the top of the house and overlooking the road, which she discouraged all other members of the family from entering, she tried to recreate the fin-de-siècle style of aesthetics she had encountered at Walter Rippmann's house. She kept the curtains permanently closed, which she felt produced 'a fascinating twilight', and filled the room with the heady scent of cut flowers, the ambiance enhanced by a reproduction of Velázquez's sensual *Rokeby Venus* on one of the walls, which she had picked up on one of her visits to the National Gallery in London, accompanied by half a dozen smaller nude studies. Her writing desk she placed underneath the curtained windows. Her polished chestnut-brown cello leant against a wall, a permanent reminder of London, Tom Trowell and freedom. Books, books and more books lined the walls. However perturbed her mind, her fastidious nature meant that her room was always tidy, with everything in its place – another trait that remained with her all her life and one she shared with her mother, Annie: 'Mrs. Beauchamp would refuse a cup of tea having a drop of milk spilt in the saucer: "That's for *servants*!" she would say.'[36] In a notebook entry, KM's closeted, isolated world is brought to life within the setting of a dull, grey, rain-swept Wellington autumn:

Oh, this monotonous, terrible rain. The dull, steady, hopeless sound of it. I have drawn the curtains across the windows to shut out the weeping face of the world – the trees swaying softly in their grief and dropping silver tears upon the brown earth – the narrow, sodden, mean, draggled wooden houses, colourless save for the dull coarse red of the roof–and the long line of grey hills, impassable, spectral-like.

So I have drawn the curtains across my windows, and the light is intensely fascinating. A perpetual twilight broods here. The atmosphere is heavy

with morbid charm. Strange, as I sit here, quiet, alone, how each posses-
sion of mine – the calendar gleaming whitely on the wall, each picture,
each book, my 'cello case, the very furniture – seems to stir into life. The
Velasquez Venus moves on her couch ever so slightly; across the face of
Manon a strange smile flickers for an instant and is gone, my rocking chair
is full of patient resignation, my 'cello case is wrapt in profound thought.
Beside me a little bowl of mignonette is piercingly sweet, and a cluster of
scarlet geraniums is hot with colour.

Sometimes, through the measured sound of the rain comes the long,
hopeless note of a foghorn far out at sea. And then all life seems but a
crying out drearily, and a groping to and fro in a foolish, aimless darkness.
Sometimes – it seems like miles away – I hear the sound of a door opening
and shutting.

And I listen and think and dream until my life seems not one life, but a
thousand million lives, and my soul is weighed down with the burden of
past existence, with the vague, uneasy consciousness of future strivings.

And the grey thoughts fall on my soul like the grey rain upon the world,
but I cannot draw the curtain and shut them out.[37]

Locked away in her room, KM could write, and transport herself back to
London, her spiritual home. In the following notebook entry she projected
herself into the future, envisaging her life as a professional writer, in emotive
language that replicated her inner turmoil at this time:

I groped my way up the dark stairs and down the stone passage into my
little room. Lights from the street outside streamed across the floor and
showed the great piles of books in common dull bindings on the table,
and a small pile of letters, and a tray with tea and bread. Outside the wind
called, shrieked. The rain flung itself over everything, furiously, passionately. I looked out of the window. Below me in the shining street was mir-
rored another London – a drowned city – and I shuddered and drew the
curtains. There was much work to be done – proof sheets to be corrected,
letters to look over and answer. I lit my candle and sat down at the table.[38]

In a little précis for a sketch entitled 'The Growing of Wings', she again saw
herself returning to London. As her main obstacle was her father, he was killed
off: 'Yvonne is born in New Zealand. At the death of her Father she is sent to
London to Miss Pitts who keeps a boarding house for young girls who wish to
study at the various Colleges.'[39] At this time she was reading John Davidson's
The Rosary, a collection of eighty musings and anecdotes on subjects as varied as
'At Cross-Purposes with Life', quotations from which pepper the notebooks at

this time: 'Is Hope only the subtlest form of cowardice?'; 'The first stage of the passionate pilgrimage to intelligence is ennui.'[40] Clearly, KM felt they reflected her own miserable position.

KM – barricaded into her twilight world upstairs – notwithstanding, the rest of the family delighted in life at Fitzherbert Terrace. Chaddie wrote to Sylvia,

> We have a lovely ballroom, which we of course use for music, and it is splendid for sound. Kass has been playing her 'cello so well tonight. I do wish you could have heard the dear old thing. I hate to feel she is so unhappy here isn't it a horrid state to be in so early in life?[41]

It would seem that nothing could lift KM out of her depression, not even Annie Beauchamp's first 'At Home' in her luxurious new residence. Harold was having his moment in the Wellington business spotlight, but so was Annie, in the social whirl of the small colonial capital. Her party – and the new house – were described in great detail in the 'Ladies' Column' of the *Evening Post* by its resident social reporter, 'Priscilla', who always began each column 'My dear Kezia', as if writing a letter:

> It would not be easier to imagine a pleasanter At Home than that given by Mrs. Beauchamp on the Friday of last week. The tea was daintily set out – among tall vases of golden chrysanthemums that looked charming in the yellow-hung dining-room – and the beautiful rooms afforded plenty of room for the many guests. But it was the delightful music – literally home-made, not ordered with the refreshments – that was the feature of the afternoon. Mrs. Beauchamp has reserved a large room for a music-room, and left it, wisely, unfinished, save for seats, a piano, and vivid rugs on the polished floor. Here a most delightful programme by the daughters of the house and Mr. Trowell was listened to with much appreciation. Miss Beauchamp plays the piano most sympathetically, Miss Kathleen is an accomplished 'cellist, and Miss Chad has a charming voice, and chose the most piquant of songs. Add to this Mr. Trowell's fine violin playing, and the result was a musical treat. The three Miss Beauchamps ought to be immense acquisitions to the musical society of Wellington. The hostess, who received her guests in the pretty drawing-room – hung with rose moire curtains against the pale yellow walls – wore a graceful pale green silk voile, with lace insertions, and a black velvet feathered hat. Miss Beauchamp's pretty frock was of white net and lace, Miss Kathleen wore tussore silk, with effective touches of crimson, and Miss Chad, a pinafore gown of pale blue and white foulard, over a lace blouse.[42]

There were many more such parties to be got through for KM, before she could turn her back on the life her parents and her sisters delighted in so much but which she despised. Many years later, of course, older, wiser and with a nostalgic pen, she would write to Murry in 1920:

> Even if one does not acquire any 'fresh meat' – one's vision of what one possesses is constantly changing into something rich and strange – isn't it? I feel mine is: 47 Fitzherbert Terrace, p.e.[43] is colouring beautifully with the years & I polish it and examine it and only now is it ready to come out of the storeroom into the uncommon light of day.[44]

And two years later, in 1922, she wrote to Chaddie, 'Well darling I have to finish a story for the good old Sketch before tea. They have asked me to write them a series. The Sketch always reminds me of the morning room at "47" . . . .'[45] Humour and affection would ultimately replace bitterness and resentment.

AFFAIRS

There was an old friend that KM sought out after her return from England: Maata. On 10 April she sent her a birthday telegram: 'Birthday greetings to my sweetest Carlotta.'[46] The two friends, having exchanged diaries in London, were now in close contact. The diary KM gave to Maata, along with the many letters she sent, has never been recovered, but KM kept Maata's and eventually a typescript was made by Ruth Mantz in 1933. (The original has since disappeared.) On the same day that KM sent the above telegram, Maata wrote in her diary,

> I am 17 today, It is extraordinary how young I am in years and how old in body – ugh! I *am* miserable and oh! so bored . . . . I had a letter from . . . K this morning . . . . dearest K. writes 'ducky' letters. I like this bit. 'What did you mean by being so superlatively beautiful just as you went away? You witch; you are beauty incarnate'. It's conceited of me to like it, but I do.[47]

KM was making as much use as she could of the Day's Bay cottage. It offered an escape from her family and, under the pretext of needing peace and quiet to write, she was able to see Maata, alone. From the evidence which still exists by way of diaries and notebook entries, it is clear that an affair of a sexual nature had been going on for a while between KM and Maata (Carlotta). On 9 February 1907, KM had written the following vignette, 'Summer in Winter', in her notebook:

Figure 7.10 Day's Bay cottage.

Through the wild Winter afternoon Carlotta at the piano sang of love. Standing by the window I watched her beautiful passionate profile. The walls were hung with daffodil silk – a faint golden light seemed to linger on her face. She wore a long black frock and a hat with a drooping black feather.

Her gloves, her great ermine coat, her silver purse were flung over the lounge beside her. The air was faintly scented with the perfume she loved that Winter – peau d'Espagne. There was a little fire of juniper wood burning in the grate and the flames cast into the room strange grotesque shadows that leapt upon the walls, the curtains, that lurked under the chairs, behind the lounge, that hid in the corners, and seemed to point long shadow fingers at Carlotta. She sang and sang and the room seemed warm and full of sunshine and happy flowers.

'Come' her voice cried to me 'and we shall wander in a mystic garden filled with beautiful nonexistent flowers. And I alone possess the key, I alone can search out the secret paths. Lo! there is a bower lit with the pale light of gardenia blossom, and the fountains are filled with laughing water.'

I drew back the heavy curtains from the window – the rain was splashing against the glass. The house opposite repelled me – it was like the face of an old old man drowned in tears. In the garden below rotting leaves were heaped upon the lawns in the walls, the skeleton trees rattled together, the wind had torn a rose bush from the ground – it sprawled across the path, ugly and thorn-encrusted. Heavily, drearily fell the winter rain upon the dead garden, upon the skeleton trees. I turned from the window and in the warm firelit room, with almost a noble defiance in her voice, Carlotta at the piano sang passionately of love.[48]

With its heady scents and colours and its sexual undertone, it is a piece wholly inspired by Symons / Wilde and the fin-de-siècle / Decadent movements, even down to Maata's specific perfume: 'peau d'Espagne'. In his *Studies in the Psychology of Sex* (1905), Havelock Ellis had noted:

Peau d'Espagne may be mentioned as a highly complex and luxurious perfume, often the favorite scent of sensuous persons, which really owes a large part of its potency to the presence of the crude animal sexual odors of musk and civet.[49]

Was this, in fact, the perfume KM was wearing on the night of 11 October 1917, when Virginia Woolf met her for the first time (and not her normal perfume of choice, the much lighter 'Genêt Fleuri'), which caused Woolf to write: 'We could both wish that ones [*sic*] first impression of K.M. was not that she stinks like a – well – civet cat that had taken to street walking.'[50] The vignette's dichotomous title of 'Summer in Winter' reflects the fact that KM, recently arrived back in New Zealand, was experiencing a summer climate, when, after three years in London, she felt that February should, in fact, have been a winter month, which was how it is portrayed here: outside the world is dark and ugly, reflecting her depression, whilst inside, Carlotta exudes warmth and passion.

Another piece written in April 1907, called 'Summer Idyll', takes as its subject the relationship between two women: a Maori and a Pakeha. The names, however, are inverted, so that the Maori is given the English name Marina and the Englishwoman is called Hinemoa (in Maori legend the name of a female lover). The sexuality of the relationship is evident here as well:

In Marina's room the scent of the manuka was heavy and soothing. The floor was strewn with blossoms. Great sprays stood in every corner and in the fireplace and even over the bed. Marina lay straight and still in her bed, her hands clasped over her head, her lips slightly parted. A faint thin colour like the petal of a dull rose leaf shone in the dusk of her skin. Hinemoa bent over her with a curious feeling of pleasure, intermingled with a sensation which she did not analyse. It came upon her if she had used too much perfume, if she had drunk wine that was too heavy and sweet, laid her hand on velvet that was too soft and smooth.[51]

KM seems to have been sexually attracted to both women and men during this period of her life. She was clearly still passionately devoted to Tom Trowell, but given that he was several thousand miles away in London, and the fact that it was difficult at that time for a single young lady to be alone with a man without attracting attention (which KM was wont to do at dances and parties, to the annoyance and embarrassment of her parents), she was now able to explore other, more covert, sexual feelings. Maata's good looks made it easy for KM to find her more than attractive, and she was not discouraged in her approaches.[52]

Meanwhile, still in April 1907, just a few days after she wrote 'Summer Idyll', KM wrote another short piece called 'Night Came Swiftly'; the story reflects a million daydreams she must have had, desperate for Tom to return her passion. In the story, Tom (here called Max), having returned to New Zealand, becomes the lover she has been dreaming of, as desperate to be with her as she is to be with him. The language and tone are suited to cheap penny romances bought at train stations:

> For one moment every pulse in her body seemed to have stopped beating then a wave of scarlet rushed over her.
>
> 'Is it you' she whispered.
>
> 'It is I.' He suddenly came forward and caught her two cold hands in his. 'I'll [. . .] for a moment' he said – his voice shook oddly. Pearl suddenly raised her eyes to his face – the same yet not the same – new lines of suffering and strength and courage.
>
> Then their eyes met. He caught hold of her and kissed her mouth, her eyes, her throat, her cold hands. She felt as though a wild sea storm was sweeping over the sandy wastes of her nature. And then, his arms still round her, she heard him saying 'Pearl, Pearl, I have been dead and now I am alive. I cannot exist without you. I need you – you are Life to me. Pearl, Pearl, hear me. I have come to tell you just this – that I must have you – Pearl, answer me'.
>
> The long year was swept away and had become as nothing. Nothing mattered – if she would but listen and feel his strength. 'I am yours' she whispered. Then Silence fell.[53]

This was all wishful thinking on KM's part, dreaming of a romance that clearly was not going to happen, given Tom's reticence even to write to her.

Being KM, however, her life at this time was complicated by the fact that she was also soon conducting an affair with another woman, twenty-seven

Figure 7.11 Edith Bendall at a Wellington Technical College art class (top far right, holding a cast of Michelangelo's 'Dying Slave'), c. 1905.

years old and therefore nine years her senior – Edith (Edie) K. Bendall, whilst all the time harbouring feelings for Tom. It became a complex few months, increased her moodiness, and made her almost impossible to live with at home.

Edie Bendall, the youngest of eight children, was the daughter of acquaintances of the Beauchamps; her father (born in Bristol in the 1830s) was a marine surveyor and before that had been a sea captain. She was an artist and had recently been studying at art school in Sydney; a photograph of the time shows her in an art class at Wellington Technical College, c. 1905, holding a cast of Michelangelo's 'Dying Slave'. (She had even had a handful of lessons with Frances Hodgkins, who was to become one of New Zealand's most iconic artists.) Edie was attractive and talented, and had recently acquired a small studio in Fitzherbert Terrace. Never one for shyness, KM now renewed her former acquaintance with Edie, and a friendship quickly developed:

I was a worker and that's why she liked me. I was working all day in my studio and at 5 o'clock I went for a walk and she used to come with me. Kathleen asked if she could walk with me every night. I said, 'I'd love you to, Kathleen . . .' I was her real friend in Wellington . . . I was completely taken with her . . . She liked me and she let me know it.[54]

According to Edie, '[KM] wrote me these lovely little letters every night – perfect letters, absolutely beautiful,'[55] none of which survived.

Edie was particularly accomplished at stylised drawings of little children, and indeed, whilst studying in Sydney, she had been given several commissions for such drawings in various magazines. Now back in Wellington as a result of her mother's ill health, she was earning a living producing illustrations for publications in both Australia and New Zealand. KM thought her work would

Figure 7.12 Edith Bendall, pencil drawing of a little girl with a fringe.

make perfect illustrations for the children's verse she had been writing, a typical example of which is 'The Clock':

The clock is always going round,
It never stops, it always goes –
And makes a funny little sound
What does it say – do you suppose?

I stand upon my 'special' chair
When Nurse has cleared away the tea
And see its big white face quite near –
With little marks like 'A.B.C.'

You're half-past-six – I'm half-past-five,
O dear, how very old we are
I wonder if we'll stay alive
Like Santa Claus and Grandmamma?

Before I go to bed at night
Or say my 'Lead me into Heaven'
I kiss the clock with all my might
And whisper – 'Make us eight and seven'.[56]

In her writing of these child verses, KM may well have been emulating her cousin, Elizabeth von Arnim, who in 1900 had written a little book called *The April Baby's Book of Tunes*, with delightful colour illustrations by the well-known Victorian illustrator Kate Greenaway, and which almost certainly was acquired by the Beauchamp family when published.[57] Some of the verses in the book were well known, such as 'Gentle Jesus Meek and Mild', a child's prayer, which KM would use in 'Prelude'.[58] It was exactly this sort of publication that she and Edie had a mind to publish.

The poems and Edie's illustrations were eventually sent off to a publisher in America. Nothing came of the project; the poems were returned but sadly not the illustrations. In addition to her cousin's little book, there were many other influences for these poems, from Robert Louis Stevenson's *A Child's Garden of Verses*, to the Hans Christian Andersen fairy tales of KM's childhood, as well as Walter de la Mare's *Songs of Childhood*, especially his delight in mixing innocent sweetness, wry humour and bathos. Also gaining in popularity in the late nineteenth century, as children's literature developed, were nonsense rhymes and gently irreverent cautionary verses (Lewis Carroll, Edward Lear and Hilaire Belloc being the best known), and it is very likely that KM had encountered examples of these double-edged humorous poems for children alongside the more conventional exalted sentimentality of writing for children in some of the many anthologies then in circulation. Her verses certainly suggest the same pleasure in comic patter and unexpected slips in register and tone. Indeed, the shift in tones in the following two poems is a fine illustration of KM's ability to pastiche and subvert poetic styles, and slip effortlessly from lyricism to parody, even as a schoolgirl. 'A Fine Day' starts with the classic tone of children's nature verse, and ends with a playful echo of a child's prayer ('Thank you God for Everything'); 'A New Hymn' appears to promise a religious note, only to play with nursery rhymes ('Sing a Song of Sixpence' and 'Ring a Ring of Roses', which ends on the lines 'Attishoo, attishoo, / We all fall down') and nonsense verse. The rest of the child verse collection pursues this constant shift between the lyricism of conventional children's verse and the comic patter of late Victorian nonsense verse:

'A Fine Day'

After all the rain, the sun
Shines on hill and grassy mead
Fly into the garden, child,
You are very glad indeed.

For the days have been so dull,
Oh, so special dark and drear,
What you told me, 'Mr. Sun
Has forgotten we live here.'

Dew upon the lily lawn
Dew upon the garden beds
Daintily from all the leaves
Pop the little primrose heads.

And the violets in the copse
With their parasols of green
Take a little 'peek' at you
They're the bluest you have seen.

On the lilac tree a bird
Singing first a little note
Then a burst of happy song
Bubbles in his lifted throat.

O, the Sun, the comfy Sun!
This the song that you must sing,
'Thank you for the birds, the flowers,
Thank you, Sun, for everything.'[59]

'A New Hymn'

Sing a song of men's pyjamas,
Half-past-six has got a pair,
And he's wearing them this evening,
And he's looking *such* a dear.

Sing a song of frocks with pockets
I have got one, it is so's
I can use my 'nitial hankies
Every time I blow my nose.[60]

As well as sharing those evening walks, Edie and KM would meet on Saturday afternoons, mostly at the cottage at Day's Bay, where, according to Edie, 'Kassie poured her heart out on the subject of "Caesar" or her dreadful family, and [she] did her best to be a "good influence".'[61] This was how KM described the little two-room cottage at Day's Bay on 1 June 1907:

I sit in the small poverty stricken sitting room – the one and only room which the cottage contains with the exception of a cabin like bedroom fitted with bunks, and an outhouse with a bath, and wood cellar, coal cellar, complete. On one hand is the sea stretching right up the yard, on the other the bush growing close down almost to my front door.[62]

The trips to Day's Bay were the catalyst for the relationship developing into a physical one. KM's notebooks at this time are a record of her emotional – and sexual – experiences, both past and present; whether embellished for her notebooks or not, they clearly indicate something beyond basic friendship.

A long passage (written in the notebook Miss Wood had given her as a parting gift), with its heading of 'Sunday night', was probably written on 2 June 1907 – winter in New Zealand – just after the description above.[63] Anyone wanting to understand the turmoil of KM's inner life at this time could do no better than to examine this strange, almost hallucinatory passage of writing. Both she and Edie are clearly at Day's Bay, spending the night together. It is still the middle of the night when she begins writing; Edie is asleep as KM records her feelings in her notebook. Some sort of powerful sexual episode has occurred, much anticipated by KM, which makes her reject any previous heterosexual feelings for Tom Trowell (Caesar) and the English cricketer (Adonis): 'I feel more powerfully all those so termed sexual impulses with her than I have with any men.' But there is a sense that these unleashed sexual feelings may not be able to be contained: 'but now I feel that if she is denied me I must – the soul of me goes into the streets and craves love of the casual stranger, begs & prays for a little of the precious poison. I am half mad with love.' There is more than a hint that these feelings – and their physical manifestation – are not new, and have happened on numerous previous occasions:

> And this is really my last experience of the kind – my last – I cannot bear it any longer. It really kills my soul, each time I feel it more deeply, because each time the wound is stabbed afresh and the knife probes new flesh and reawakens tortures in the old.

A passage of striking prose then follows, highly stylised, and redolent with fin-de-siècle and Decadent motifs: 'And so is Life, and so, above all, is Love – a vague transitory fleeting thing, & Pessimism gaunt & terrible stares me in the face, & I cling to old illusions.' She believes that what she is experiencing is real love and that any concept of heterosexual love which she may have had in the past – for Caesar, for Adonis – was never reciprocated: 'Never pure spontaneous affectionate impulse'. In her passion for Edie, however, 'I am child, woman, and more than half man.' This understanding leads her to reflect on the tragedy of such feelings, which, by their nature, can come to nothing (in the formal world in which she lives), and as a result of which she perceives nothing but tragedy ahead: 'my life is a Rosary of Fierce Combats for Two, each bound together with the powerful magnetic chain of Sex.' In addition, she can no longer continually love, with never any reciprocated feelings in the loved one: 'I cannot continue my hard course of loving and being unloved – of giving loves only to find them flung back at me, faded, worm eaten,' and then defiantly, she proclaims: 'I snap my fingers at Fate. I will not dance to the Music of the Marionettes. Damn it all!' A dream-like, hallucinatory passage then follows, in which fence posts outside turn into 'hideous forms of Chinamen', before she is once again enfolded in the embrace of her lover. In the closing lines she invokes Oscar Wilde (who else?), whom she believes was a fellow traveller on her chosen path: 'O Oscar! Am I peculiarly susceptible to sexual impulse? I must be I suppose, but I rejoice.'[64] The passage closes with her expectation of more nights such as these to come. For KM, who lived in a world where only heterosexuality was considered acceptable, Wilde's example offered her some sort of validation for her lesbian tendencies at this time, as well as helping to alleviate the guilt and anxiety brought on by such feelings. In later life, when she no longer had need of this validation, Wilde's importance to her diminished accordingly. In the restricted moral environment of colonial Wellington at the turn of the twentieth century, homosexuality was considered a deviation so horrendous that, as Guy Scholefield would later tell Mantz, the word 'mental' was used to describe such behaviour, even by the courts.

In this confused state, during the same weekend, and presumably before she left with Edie for Day's Bay, she wrote:

> This afternoon a man is coming to see me, to bring his 'cello, to hear me play, and now that the moment est arrivé I do not want to see him. He is bloated, lover of a thousand actresses, roamer of every city under the sun, wealthy, bachelor, and yesterday when I met him I behaved like a fool – simply – for no reason. He hinted by asking to call today – now he comes. Kathie you are a hideous lunatic. He has such a miserably unintellectual head. No – I'm glad about the whole affair. I shall pervert it – – – make it fascinating.[65]

It is clear to even the most novice of psychologists that, at this time, KM was a sexually experimental, hormone-driven, boundary-challenging adolescent, moody and quixotic, to the frustration of her immediate family; she must have been a constant source of anxiety (to her parents) and annoyance (to Vera and Chaddie).

A little over three weeks after the long passage above was written, KM's life seemed to reach some sort of crisis point. Even as she declared her love for Caesar, she had become engaged (again) to an Englishman (unnamed), apparently because of his good looks, and possibly the same man she describes above with his cello:

> June 25th. I hate everybody, loathe myself, loathe my Life and love Caesar. Each week – sometimes every day, tout depends – when I think of that fascinating cult which I wish to absorb me I come to the conclusion that all this shall truly end. Liberty – no matter what the cost, no matter what the trial. I begin hideously unhappy, make God knows how many resolves – and then break them! One day I shall not do so – – – I shall 'strike while the iron is white hot' – and praise Myself and my unconquerable soul. From the amethyst outlook my situation is devilishly fascinating, but it cannot be permanent – the charm consists mainly in its instability. It has existed long enough – I must wander. I cannot – will not – build a house upon any damned rock. But money – money – money is what I need and do not possess. I find a resemblance in myself to John Addington Symonds.
>
> The day is white with frost – a low blue mist lingers daintily among the pine avenue. It is very cold, and there is a sharp sound of carts passing. Quite early, too. A train whistle sounds, a tram passes at the end of the street, the maids are putting away crockery. Downstairs in the Music Room the 'cello is dreaming. I wonder if it shall be under the hand of its Maestro. I think not.

Well a year has passed. What has happened. London behind me, Mimi behind me, Caesar gone. My music has gained, become a thing of 10000 times more beauty & strength. I myself have changed – rather curiously. I am colossally interesting to myself. One fascinating Day has been mine. My friend sent me Dorian.

And I have written a book of child verse – how <u>absurd</u>. But I am very glad – it is too exquisitely unreal. And while my thoughts are redolent of Purple Fancies and the white sweetness of gardenias, I present the world 'with this elegant thimble' – – I have been engaged to a young Englishman for three weeks because his figure was so beautiful. I have been tediously foolish many times – especially with Oscar Fox and Siegfried Eichelbaum – but that is past. This year coming will be memorable. It will celebrate the culmination of the cult – the full flowering of the Gardenia. This time next year I shall have been [with?] Mimi again.[66]

Her sexual feelings for women, which she here calls a ' fascinating cult' and the 'amethyst outlook', she recognises can only blossom once she is rid of her confined life in New Zealand, though she realises it must be tamed if she is to make anything of her life: 'it cannot be permanent – the charm consists mainly in its instability.' ('The Amethyst Outlook' was, in fact, the title of an unfinished novel written at around this time and which she called 'her first book', though it no longer survives.) Independence is what she needs – and therefore, by extension, money. She relates herself to John Addington Symonds, an English poet and literary critic. Although today he is viewed as an acknowledged advocate of male homosexuality in the latter part of the nineteenth century, as attested in his poetry, memoirs and literary criticism, his unexpurgated works were not in public circulation in the 1900s, and he was therefore possibly another 'forbidden' author she was introduced to by Walter Rippmann. 'Mimi' (Vere Bartrick-Baker), her schoolfriend from Queen's, is remembered, and she notes that a 'friend', probably Vere herself since it was she who first introduced KM to Wilde, has sent her a copy of 'Dorian'. She thus offers a view of her divided life. On the one hand, she has written a book of child verse: 'how <u>absurd</u>. But I am very glad – it is too exquisitely unreal', and which she presents to the world as an 'elegant thimble', referencing one of her favourite childhood books, *Alice in Wonderland*, where the Dodo says to Alice, 'We beg your acceptance of this elegant thimble.'[67] On the other hand, her 'thoughts are redolent of Purple Fancies and the white sweetness of gardenias': that is to say, with everything that the Decadent Dorian Gray stands for. In the meantime, she has clearly been involved in heterosexual flirting – aside from her alleged 'fiancé' – with other eligible Wellington men, though she claims this is not where her heart lies. By this time next year, she will be back in London, with Vere, when she can finally 'celebrate the culmination of the cult – the full flowering of the Gardenia'. Overall, this is a heady mix and not one guaranteed to bring long-term happiness.

Nevertheless, a few days later, all her thoughts were turned once more towards Tom Trowell. Mr Trowell, KM's cello teacher, his wife and their daughter Dolly were invited to Fitzherbert Terrace for an evening of music, where undoubtedly the talk would have been of the twins' – and especially Tom's – successes in London. KM plied the family with bunches of camellias when they left:

> I became terribly unhappy, almost wept in the street, and yet Music enveloped me – again – caught me, held me, thank Heaven. I could have died. I should be dead but for that, I know. I sent Mr T. a beautiful book – something that I truly treasure.[68]

All her thoughts and emotions were now turned once more to Tom – her first love:

> Everything about him seems to be made plain – now. I think of him in any every situation, and feel that I understand him too. He must always be everything to me – the one man whom I can call Master and Lover too, and though I know I shall have many fascinating connections in my Life none will be like this – so lasting, so deep, so everything – because he poured into my virgin soul the Life essence of Music – – Never an hour passes free from his influence.[69]

All the while, however, her bisexuality was troubling her: 'I love him – but I wonder, with all my soul – And here is the kernel of the whole matter – the Oscar-like thread.'[70] Now her thoughts were turning towards a literary, rather than a musical career:

> I want to practically celebrate this day by beginning to write a book. In my brain, as I walk each day, as I dress, as I speak, or even before playing my 'cello, a thousand delicate images float and are gone. I want to write a book – that is unreal yet wholly possible because out of the question – that raises in the hearts of the readers' emotions, sensations too vivid not to take effect, which causes a thousand delicate tears, a thousand sweet chimes of laughter. I shall never attempt anything approaching the histrionic, and it must be ultra modern. I am sitting right over the fire as I write, dreaming, my face hot with the coals. Far away a steamer is calling, calling, and – God God – my restless soul.[71]

This early literary manifesto reveals how, even at age eighteen, KM was interested in writing *modern* fiction – what she calls here 'ultra modern' – where effect is the key, not the excesses of plot. But nothing like this could be written until that steamer could take her away from colonial New Zealand, and middle-class sterility and strictures.

A few days later, on 29 June, there was *another* change of heart:

> I do not think that I shall ever be able to write any Child Verse again. The faculty has gone – I <u>think</u>. What a charming morning I have passed! with the Violinist & the Singer. She has a curious resemblance to Mark Hambourg – the completely musical face – We sat in the Violinist's room – the curtains blew in and out the window, & the violets in a little glass, blue & white, were beautiful. And I am sure they both loved me. But this afternoon has been horrible. E.K.B. bored me. I bored her. I felt unhappy, and I think so did she – but she never took the initiative.
>
> And now E.K.B. is a thing of the Past, absolutely, irrevocably. Thank Heaven! It was, I consider retrospectively, a frantically maudlin relationship, & one better ended – also she will not achieve a great deal of greatness. She has not the necessary impetus of character.
>
> Do other people of my own age feel as I do I wonder so absolutely powerful licentious, so almost physically ill. I alone in this silent clock filled room have become powerfully – – – I want Maata. I want her as I have had her – terribly. This is unclean I know but true. What an extraordinary thing – I feel savagely crude, and almost powerfully enamoured of the child. I had thought that a thing of the Past. Heigh Ho!!!!!!!!!!! My mind is like a Russian novel.[72]

Her feelings for Edie had suddenly evaporated and now it was Maata – *again* – that she felt attracted to sexually. As noted previously, it is clear that KM at this time was going through a period of some considerable confusion, as manifested by these rather brutal, wholly self-centred diary entries, in which her sexual feelings seem to be in control of her more rational thought processes. Her disaffection with Edie might also have had a more mundane provenance – annoyance – since the latter had recently fallen in love with a Wellington schoolmaster, Gerald Robison. Yet there must have been something in all those letters which KM used to send her – something to disapprove of; during Edie's honeymoon in 1910, they were allegedly all destroyed by 'a maid' (more probably her parents) going through a chest of drawers. Following a brief meeting in Napier in December 1907, KM and Edie never made contact again.[73]

In these early relationships – whether with men or women – a pattern was emerging that would continue for the remainder of her life. As seen in her earliest passion for Tom Trowell, the instigator of almost every single one of her affairs was KM. She would write most of the letters, and – apart from both Trowell twins, who each, independently, broke her heart – it would be KM who ended the relationship, normally quite suddenly and quite heartlessly. George Bowden and Floryan Sobieniowski would certainly bear witness to this scenario, the latter ruthlessly dumped by KM while he waited vainly for her to come back to him in Paris in the winter of 1909. The relationship with Murry would be trickier. They were hopelessly unsuited to each other emotionally, and she did, in effect, leave him on more than one occasion; nevertheless, as KM grew ever more ill as a result of her tuberculosis, her desire for independence became harder to countenance and, once married in 1918, even though they spent long periods apart, she and Murry were still nominally together at the end of her life.

As 1907 wore on, KM was to be found still flirting with men at parties (*five men have asked me to marry them*),[74] still writing letters to Tom and still desiring women – this time, Vere. Still desperately trying to make something of the relationship with Tom, KM was writing him letters full of sexual innuendo, such as this draft found in a notebook, dated 11 August:

> I belong to you, we belong to each other. And whenever you want me, with both my hands I say – unashamed, fiercely proud, exultant, triumphant, satisfied at last – 'take me'. Each night I go to sleep with your letters under my pillow & in the darkness I stretch out my hands & clasp the thin envelope close to my body so that it lies there warmly, & I smile in the darkness and sometimes my body aches as though with fatigue – but I understand.[75]

But Vere – desirable, petite, dark – was also on KM's mind. She wrote a vignette called 'Leves Amores' ('Casual Loves') and posted it to her in London. This rather morbid story, set in a downtrodden hotel of the same name in Wellington, is written in a wholly Decadent style, and influenced by that great master of fin-de-siècle writing, Arthur Symons, the title copied directly from one of his own erotic poems from the collection *London Nights* (1895). The copy sent to her was found in Vere's belongings after her death. Vere – who had introduced KM to Oscar Wilde and the Decadence of *Dorian Gray* – would have recognised instantly the symbolism of 'beautiful golden lilies', that 'amethyst shadowed staircase' and the green vine with its 'thousand clinging tendrils'.

PROFESSIONAL WRITER

The two younger Beauchamp siblings were not as affected by KM's moodiness and troublesome ways as the rest of the family. Leslie was away at boarding school for much of the year, though when he was at home she clearly delighted in his company and he in hers: 'Chummie became a true friend, and the tie between brother and sister, who felt and thought alike, was strong in those years.'[76] Little Jeanne understood nothing of what was going on in the head of her older sister. Nevertheless, two contrasting reports reveal different facets of KM's personality at this time. On the one hand, a schoolfriend of Leslie's called John Parker remembered KM as 'surly, moody, unpopular and bad-tempered', someone who had poked her tongue out at him as he walked past Fitzherbert Terrace; on the other hand, Jeanne remembered KM as 'child among the children', who used to give a young cousin piggy-back rides around the tennis court.[77] Given the written evidence which remains from this time, it was probably the surly, egotistical KM who had the upper hand, and whose complex diary entries and fiction reflect something of the turmoil of her adolescent self.

Figure 7.13 Leslie and Jeanne Beauchamp with spaniel.

Figure 7.14 Katherine Mansfield with her brother Leslie and her sister Jeanne.

One writer KM particularly identified with at this time was Marie Bashkirtseff (1858–84). In KM's early 1907 list of quotations and aphorisms from favourite authors, there was this: 'Me marier et avoir des enfants! Mais quelle blanchisseuse – je veux la gloire. Marie Bashkirtseff. Russian' ('Get married and have children! But what a washerwoman – I want fame').[78] Marie Bashkirtseff was a Russian-speaking Ukrainian writer, artist and diarist who lived mostly in France, where she was a respected intellectual figure. Her outspoken artistic ambitions and defiant lifestyle were admired by KM, and her premature death from tuberculosis at the age of just twenty-five would later encourage analogies between the two. KM too wanted 'la gloire' (fame), and in her egotistical outpourings, may well have been imitating the writer she so admired. Towards the end of the year, her mood as bitter – if not even more bitter than ever – towards her family, she wrote: 'this morning I do not wish to write but to read Marie Bashkirtseff. But if they enter the room & find me merely with a book their tragic complaining looks upset me altogether.'[79]

KM's diaries however, in August 1907, were full of the Trowell family, for when she was not thinking of Tom and writing to him and about him, she was having cello lessons with his father, which only made her feel closer to the object of her devotion. On 20 August, whilst the wind and rain beat down outside on a miserable winter's night in New Zealand, she wrote in a notebook:

> I came up into my room to go to bed and suddenly, half undressed, I began thinking & looking at Caesar's portrait, and wondering. And I felt that I could have written: Beloved, I could bury my face in the pillow & weep & weep & weep. Here it is night & winter rain. You are in a glory of Summer and daylight, the thunder of traffic, the call of life. I must possess it too. I must suffer & conquer. I must leave here – I cannot look ahead into the long unutterable grey vastnesses of Misty Future years.[80]

A week later, her spirits were raised following a lesson with Mr Trowell, where the subject of marriage was discussed:

> August 27th. A happy day. I have spent a perfect day. [. . .] O joyous time – it was almost inhuman, and to hear that 'Bravely done – you've a real good grip of it all – very good.' I would not have exchanged those words for all the laurel wreaths in existence. [. . .] And discussed – Marriage and Music – the mistake that a woman makes ever to think that she is first in a musician's estimation – it must inevitably be first His Art. I know I understand. And also – talk of sympathy. If I marry Caesar – and I thought of him all the time – I think I could prove a great many things. Mr Trowell said she must share his glories and always keep him on the heights.[81]

To KM, it felt as if Tom's father was offering tacit approval for a future relationship between herself and his son. At least, that was how she read the situation. It was therefore all the more shocking when, the very next day, Ida wrote to her with news that crushed her: apparently, Tom Trowell had started seeing her close friend from Queen's College, Gwen Rouse. KM's initial response was shock, but then this was tempered to a very modern way of seeing the affair as Tom, the artist, seeking 'Experience':

> First, so sorrowful, so hurt, so pained, that I contemplated the most outrageous things; now only old and angry and lonely, & as though everything except my 'cello had lost its interest for me. Now which is it to be. Shall I applaud him in his manner of living. Shall I say – do as you please, live as you like, see Life, gain Experience, increase your outlook. Or shall I condemn it. This is how I think – it's a great pity that Artists do live so, but as they do – well – but I shall not.[82]

Her diary at this time is still painful to read today, so great was her desire to leave for London, and so fearful that there would never be a means to get there. On 6 September she wrote a long entry trying to make sense of her position – and her approach to her father:

> I am frightened and trying to be brave. This is the greatest and most terrible torture that I have ever thought of enduring, but I can have courage, face him bravely with my head high, and <u>fight</u> – for Life, absolutely. O what can happen. Help, support. Here at least I am standing terribly absolutely alone. What can I do. O what can happen. Shall it be Heaven or shall it be Hell. I <u>must</u> win – but I first must face the guns resolutely. It is no good shrinking behind these hedges and great stones, remaining in the shadow. In the full glare I must go to Death or life. [. . .]
>
> [. . .] You must be a woman now & bear the agony of creating. Prove yourself. Be strong, be kind, be wise, and it is yours. Do not at the last moment lose courage – argue wisely & quietly.
>
> Be more man than woman. Keep your brain perfectly clear. Keep your balance!!!! Convince your Father that it is 'la seule chose'. Think of the Heaven that might be yours, that [is] before you after this fight. They stand & wait for you with outstretched hands, & with a glad cry you fall into their arms – the Future Years. Good luck my precious one – I love you.[83]

Clearly, there had been some shouting matches and KM had not argued wisely or quietly. A new strategy was needed.

To make matters worse, Thomas and Kate Trowell and their daughter Dolly were packing up for an imminent move to London, now that the twins were established there. KM wrote on 2 September,

> They leave N.Z., all of them <u>my</u> people, <u>my</u> Father – it has come of course. I used to think – as long as they are here I can bear it – & now? I shall somehow or other go too. You just see![84]

She wrote a heartfelt letter to Thomas Trowell on 26 September, just as they were leaving:

> My dear Mr. Trowell
>
> I cannot let you leave without telling you how grateful I am – and must be all my life – for all that you have done for me – and given me. You have shown me that there is something so immeasurably higher and deeper in Music – than I had ever realised before –
>
> And, do you know, so many times when we have been together I have

felt that I must tell you, how when I came from London friendless – and disheartened – you changed everything for me – – –
Looking back – <u>I</u> have been so stupid and <u>you</u> so patient – <u>I</u> think of that little Canon of Cherubini's as a gate, opened with such great difficulty, and leading to so wide a road! And Music, which meant much before in a vague desultory fashion – is now full of inner meaning.

I wish you everything in the future – Don't you feel – that your Golden Age is coming now – and what I look forward to as the greatest joy I can imagine is to share a programme with you at a London concert –

Thank you for all – and happily <u>not</u> goodbye

Your loving, grateful pupil
Kass.[85]

The date that the letter was sent – 26 September 1907 – was a momentous one in the history of New Zealand, for it was the day the little colony became a Dominion, following in the footsteps of Canada and Australia, for whom the word 'colony' was now deemed more appropriate for other 'less important' parts of the Empire. Practically, the change of name had no real effect: New Zealand was no more independent from Great Britain than it had been before. Harold, Annie and the three older girls were all invited to the magnificent garden party

Figure 7.15 Annie Burnell Beauchamp, 1908.

Figure 7.16 Arthur, Harold and Leslie Beauchamp.

held by the Governor and his wife, Lord and Lady Plunkett, for 2,500 guests, 'where there were some beautiful frocks worn', the ladies of the Beauchamp family included.[86]

The excitement of Dominion Day aside, KM continued to pour her heart into her stories, her novel, *Juliet*, now consigned to a drawer. She befriended her father's secretary, Martha ('Matty') Putnam, who was happy to type up the finished pieces so that KM could start sending them out to publications. (She had also typed up the child poems which had gone to America, accompanied by Edie's illustrations.) According to Scholefield, 'it was [KM's] mother who first realised that [her yearnings] were something deeper than a passing fancy. With her more intimate instinct Mrs. Beauchamp was the first really to believe in Kathleen's literary future.'[87] Harold was more sceptical. Nevertheless, keen to find a way to placate his middle daughter – for the benefit of the entire family – he asked the opinion of a journalist on the New Zealand *Evening Post*, Tom L. Mills. KM soon got wind of this, and brazenly rang up Mills herself and asked him quite bluntly if he would read some of her stories and poems and provide her with his honest opinion. They met at one of KM's favourite Wellington haunts, the fashionable D.I.C. (Drapery and General Importing

Figure 7.17 The D.I.C. Store, Wellington.

Company) department store tearooms off Lambton Quay. Mills, who read the material 'with astonished delight', knew instantly that he 'had discovered a genius right there in Wellington'.[88] He did, however, note that her stories were more of the 'sex-problem' type, which shocked him since he did not believe that puritanical New Zealand could possibly be interested in such material: 'in those days precocity and depravity were almost synonymous.'[89] KM was not in the mood to be rebuked: 'What she wrote about was her own business; the question was: Could she write?'[90] Mills knew KM was a special case. He suggested markets for her work and seems to have converted Harold to the idea that KM had real talent.

Now it was to an Australian periodical, the *Native Companion*, suggested by Mills, that KM started sending her more polished stories. Its editor from August to December 1907 was Edwin James Brady (1869–1952), who was immediately taken with KM's work and published four stories: 'Vignettes' (October issue), 'Silhouettes' (November issue), and 'In a Café' and 'In the Botanical Gardens' (December issue). The first three were signed 'K. Mansfield' and the last one 'Julian Mark' (to disguise the fact that two of the stories in that issue were by the same author). Years later, Brady noted that KM was the literary find of his entire career.[91] There were apparently two other 'sex-complex' stories written by KM at this time. One, called 'In the Garret', was shown to a friend, who was quite shocked by the contents. It was never published and no longer exists. Another,

'From my Bedroom Window', a story of lovers talking on a bench in Fitzherbert Terrace, was apparently published in a New Zealand paper but cannot now be traced. Brady's autobiography recounts his early misgivings that such a young woman could have written the stories:

> When her contributions began to flow in I grew suspicious – the matter and treatment seemed too sophisticated for a girl of seventeen [*sic*]. I thought that perhaps Frank Morton, then in New Zealand, who was also writing for me, might be 'putting one over'. I knew no writer at the time with a more finished literary style than Morton and somehow connected up with him on that line of doubt. So I wrote to Miss Beauchamp and queried her identity. Her father replied assuring me I need have no fear of being imposed on [. . .] I had several stories and sketches of hers in hand and in type when the magazine went out of publication. I regretfully returned accepted manuscripts to contributors. [. . .] I have consoled myself since by reflecting that if the *Native Companion* did no more than open the door of publication to Katherine Mansfield it was worthwhile.[92]

On 23 September 1907, KM's response to a letter from to Brady was brazen, to say the least, but it certainly marked her out as different and attracted Brady to the author and her stories:

> Dear Sir –
>   Thank you for your letter – I liked the peremptory tone –
>   With regard to the 'Vignettes' I am sorry that [they] resemble their illustrious relatives to so marked an extent – and assure you – they feel very much my own – This style of work absorbs me, at present – but – well – it *cannot* be said that anything you have of mine is 'cribbed' – – – Frankly – I hate plagiarism.
>   I send you some more work – practically there is nothing local – except the 'Botanical Garden' Vignette – The reason is that for the last few years London has held me –very tightly indeed – and I've not yet escaped. You ask for some details as to myself. I am poor – obscure –just eighteen years of age – with a rapacious appetite for everything and principles as light as my purse – –
>   If this pleases you – this MSS please know that there is a great deal more where this comes from –
>   I am very grateful to you and very interested in your Magazine.
>   Sincerely
>   K.M. Beauchamp.[93]

Once she had shown her father Brady's letter, Harold, without consulting KM, wrote to Brady himself:

> My daughter, Kathleen, has shown me the letters you have written in respect to her literary contributions, and I desire to thank you sincerely for the practical encouragement you have given her. At the same time, I should like to assure you that you need never have any hesitation in accepting anything from her upon the assumption that it may not be original matter. She, herself, is, I think, a very original character, and writing–whether it be good or bad – comes to her quite naturally. In fact, since she was eight years of age, she has been producing poetry and prose. It may be that she inherits the literary talent of some members of our family, amongst them being my cousin, the authoress of *Elizabeth and her German Garden*, and other well-known books.
>
> As to Kathleen's statement concerning her age, this, I notice, you politely question, but I can assure you that she spoke quite correctly when she told you she was only eighteen years old.
>
> Until the close of 1906 she was a student at a college in London, and left that institution to return to New Zealand with me, and other members of my family, in October of that year. I may add that she has always been an omnivorous reader, and possesses a most retentive memory.
>
> Pardon me for troubling you with these details, but I wished to deal with the two points raised in your kind letter, viz., 'originality' and 'age.'
>
> In concluding, may I ask you to be kind enough to treat this as a private letter and not to mention to Kathleen that I have written you concerning her.[94]

It is to Harold's credit that he wrote to Brady, thereby encouraging the writing career of his daughter. Interesting, too, that Elizabeth, his cousin, was name-dropped into his response; the letter also indicates his change of heart, perhaps, for if his cousin could become a celebrated writer and marry a German aristo-crat, why not *his* daughter? For KM there was now a glimmer of hope that, with publishing success, her dream of returning to London would become a reality. Many years later, on 18 March 1922, in a letter to her father, she wrote: 'I have certainly been most fortunate as a writer. It is strange to remember buying a copy of The Native Companion on Lambton Quay and standing under a lamp with darling Leslie to see if my story had been printed.'[95] It seems that many acquaintances of the Beauchamps were shocked by the content of these early stories, and that this might have impeded for some years a favourable reception for the rest of her work. In conversation with Mantz in the 1930s, Mrs Henry Smith, KM's former headmistress at Miss Swainson's, declared,

It established the attitude of the kind of mind she had. [. . .] Her first stories caused a most unfavourable stir, and people did not seem to read her others until some years afterward. They couldn't get past the local color. People weren't prepared to receive her books.[96]

KM's liminal positioning by a window in 'Vignettes' and 'Silhouettes' is quite marked, perhaps subconsciously revealing her own liminal position in life, since although her physical body was in Wellington, her emotional life (her real life) was bound steadfastly to London. In 'Vignettes', she is back in her old room in Harley Street, before the narrative subconsciously shifts back to New Zealand 'with the hopeless note of a foghorn far out at sea'.[97] The first three quotations are from 'Vignettes':

Away beyond the line of the dark houses there is a sound like the call of the sea after a storm – passionate, solemn, strong. I am leaning far out of my window in the warm, still night air. Down below, in the Mews, the little lamp is singing a silent song.

I lean out of the window. The dark houses stare at me and above them a great sweep of sky. Where it meets the houses there is a strange lightness – a suggestion, a promise.

I lean from my window in the tower. Through the stillness comes the hushed sound of the fountain. I fancy I can hear the rose petals in the garden falling softly.[98]

It is evening, and very cold. From my window the laurestinus bush, in this half light, looks weighted with snow.

And I, leaning out of my window, alone, peering into the gloom, am seized by a passionate desire for everything that is hidden and forbidden. I want the night to come, and kiss me with her hot mouth, and lead me through an amethyst twilight to the place of the white gardenia . . .[99]

The last two quotations are from 'Silhouettes', the story which presumably was one which Mills categorised as the 'sex-problem' type. Clearly present is the influence of Oscar Wilde, with those notions of amethyst twilights and white gardenias. Even the first line of 'In the Botanical Gardens' could have been spoken by Lord Henry Wotton in *The Picture of Dorian Gray*: 'They are such a subtle combination of the artificial and the natural – that is, partly, the secret of their charm.'[100] 'In a Café' offers us a glimpse of the kind of writing KM would develop as a mature artist, with its dialogue form exposing the personalities of the two protagonists, one of them clearly KM herself:

> 'Do you think I should make a good wife?'
> 'That depends.' He stirred his coffee thoughtfully. 'Yes; why not? Interesting, certainly, beyond doubt; and who could do better than marry a problem? Misunderstanding keepeth Love alive.'
> 'I believe that, too,' she said, 'and yet, somehow, it's abominable. Oh! how I want and want things which are out of the question.'
> 'But not a husband, surely?'
> 'I hardly see myself settling down to sentimental domesticity and discussing the price of mutton.'
> 'Ah! now you are being foolish. You know that marriage need not mean that. Mine won't. And I certainly shall marry.'
> 'Oh! oh! oh! – then there are years of bachelorhood ahead of you, extravagant and reckless one.' A sudden tremendous happiness seemed to have sprung to birth in her heart. 'Oh! this adorable life,' she said. 'Oh! the infinite possibilities. Listen; can't you hear London knocking, knocking?'[101]

Sadly for KM, London may have been knocking, but her father still had the key to the locked door firmly in his pocket. Nevertheless, word was getting about the small colonial capital about KM's talent and her desire to go back to London. It seems Harold may finally have had a change of heart. Details of KM's nineteenth birthday on 14 October 1907 were recorded in a letter Chaddie sent to Sylvia, with an important announcement at the end:

> Kathleen has been so lucky in getting such beautiful presents today. Mother gave her green-stone earrings, Father two sweet Liberty broaches [sic], Vera a jewel case, I a back comb, Leslie a writing case, Jeanne a charming bag made and designed by herself, and many others. Oh one was a fascinating old Tiki which I am sure you will love. It is a Maori God to keep away the Evil Spirit and is made of carved bone. [. . .]
> [. . .] Fancy Kathleen going back to London after Christmas I can't bear to think of it, but I know she must go, it is the only thing for her, and I feel her going will bring us all over the sooner. Oh! dear what absolute joy and bliss that would be.[102]

Indeed, on 29 October 1907, the social column of the *Dominion* ran the following short paragraph:

There is some talk of Miss Kathleen Beauchamp's return to London to take up literary work. Miss Beauchamp has been engaged for some little time past on a book of children's stories, for which Miss Bendall has been drawing some of her charming illustrations.[103]

Harold must have said something to indicate that, perhaps after all, something might be done about granting KM's wish to return to London. Certainly, she felt elated enough on 14 November to write to the Trowells, still at sea en route for England, about her plans:

By this time – though I can't yet realise it at all, you are nearly Home – You know I am sure, how very much I have missed you all, and how eagerly I am awaiting news – I pass 18 Buller Street, and just look at it out of the corner of my eye, and cannot feel that I shall not be able just to come in for three minutes – and eat a friendly pea nut with Dolly – over the dining room fire!

Do you know – what I have here, this evening, in my room. Well, the Graphophone!!! and I have had just a musical feast – including speeches from Birmingham – that I am sure it must have been a case of subconscious mind – and I am 11,500 miles nearer you than I feel I am. Miss Watson met me, the other evening at a 'social' (!) and then offered me the use of it – So imagine me today carrying the Graphophone – three packets of records, and the cylinder home in the tram – It was worth the carrying though – when I heard the Beethoven Serenade – [. . .]

[. . .] Today an English Mail came in, and I heard from a man at home that Arnold Trowell is teaching in London. Is that so? And what news is there about the boys? Do tell me a great deal. I get such very second hand information.

[. . .] Kiss London for me – and tell it – that when I come back I shall live in a tent in Trafalgar Square – and only leave it for Bayreuth. I shall be with you soon, and Merry Xmas.

Ever your loving
Kass[104]

The letter demonstrates yet again that there were two strands to KM's life at this time: literature and music, the latter wholly synonymous in her mind with the Trowell family.

Meanwhile, the journalist Tom Mills now became a little fascinated with KM. In his paper, the *Feilding Star*, he started to publicise the *Native Companion* in glowing terms, stating 'already it has won a place amongst admirers of clever original stories and verse' and that 'it should be better known in New Zealand than it is, for it is a magazine of cleverness.' Of the October issue he notes, 'pride of place is given to some clever "Vignettes", by K. Mansfield.'[105] By Christmas he was still plugging both the virtues of the magazine and the talents of KM:

> The Native Companion [. . .] grows more interesting with age. [. . .] There is an evenness of originality running through the whole of the contents that has the effect of making this publication distinct from all others published in Australasia. [. . .] There are two outstanding sketches before us, 'In a Café' (K. Mansfield) and 'In the Botanical Gardens (Julian Mark).[106]

KM, on the other hand, continued to lead her 'suitable appropriate existence', with the Wellington newspapers recording the social life of the distinguished Beauchamp family:

> On Saturday evening the Misses Beauchamp gave a dance for a few of their friends. The rooms were decorated with purple rhododendrons, but the principal attraction was the beautiful garden which the mildness of the night made it possible to enjoy to the full. Mrs. Beauchamp wore grey silk over pink glacé; Miss Vera Beauchamp, black and white; Miss Chad Beauchamp, white net; and Miss Kathleen, black silk voile; Miss Pearce wore a charming frock of blue glacé; Miss McKenzie, pale blue silk with beautiful old lace; Miss Fell, floral silk; Miss Seddon, white glacé; Miss Butts, black dress and quaint Indian jewels; Miss Dean, yellow empire frock.[107]

Life was not, by any means, all bad. When the weather was fair she loved to swim in the baths in Thorndon, where she had learnt to swim all those years ago with little Marion Ruddick. There were trips to the theatre and she even attended a debate at the university college with Tom Seddon, the glamorous son of the former Premier. Her attendance with Tom, however, was met with considerable indignation by some of the female students, since she herself was not actually a student at the college.[108] There were also tennis parties at Fitzherbert Terrace, remembered much later and fictionalised in the story 'An Ideal Family' (1921):

> They were cutting the grass on the tennis court below; he heard the soft churr of the mower. Soon the girls would begin their tennis parties again. And at the thought he seemed to hear Marion's voice ring out, 'Good for you, partner. . . . Oh, *played*, partner. . . . Oh, *very* nice indeed.'[109]

KM and her sisters were also in frequent demand in the small town for their musical talents. At an evening of dramatic sketches held in the Sydney Street

Figure 7.18 Bank of New Zealand Corner, Wellington.

Figure 7.19 Lambton Quay, Wellington.

Figure 7.20 Mackay Booksellers, Lambton Quay, Wellington.

schoolroom, attended by Lady Ward, the wife of the Prime Minister, 'lively music was played by an orchestra of Guild members,' which included one Miss Beauchamp on cello and another Miss Beauchamp on piano.[110] Chaddie also recorded, in a letter to Sylvia Payne, that KM very successfully deputised at a church bazaar for a fortune-teller who had failed to turn up, 'with results that astonished her as much as they pleased the clients'.[111] KM's passion for the cello, however, was now fading, probably because Mr Trowell was no longer there to give her lessons. Certainly, there was no more talk of her becoming a musician.

However, any smiles on KM's face were mostly forced and were part of her strategy to get herself into her father's good books. In private, she was as much in turmoil as ever, as in these turbulent diary entries for 21 and 22 October 1907:

Damn my family – O Heavens, what bores they are. I detest them all heartily. I shall certainly not be here much longer – thank Heaven for that! Even when I am alone in a room they come outside the door and call to each other – discuss the butchers orders or the soiled linen, and, I feel, wreck my life. It is so humiliating. [. . .]

Here in my room I feel as though I was in London. O London – to write the word makes me feel that I could burst into tears. Isn't it terrible to love anything so much. I do not care at all for men – but London – it is Life.

These creatures, May N. & E. K. who try to play with me, they are fools and I despise them both. I am longing to consort with my superiors. What is it with me? Am I absolutely nobody but merely inordinately vain. I do not know – but I am most fearfully unhappy, that is all. I am so unhappy that I wish I was dead – yet I should be mad to die when I have not yet lived at all.

Well, I have sat here for two hours and read – my right hand is quite cold. She is a young fool, and I detest her. As she comes into the room I put down Marie & seize my pen. She leans against the door rattling the handle and says – are you writing a colossal thing or an ordinary thing or anything exciting. How completely inane! I tell her to leave the room at once. Now if this door would open & Mimi walk in – Mimi or Ida or my charming Gwen – how happy I should be – with all three I can be myself. Outside the window there is a lumbering sound of trams and an insipid sound of birds song. Now here comes tea & I yield to the temptation – as usual. [. . .]

22nd. I thank Heaven that at present, though I am damnable, I am in love with nobody – except myself.[112]

Most adolescents go through a phase of hating their families, or at least finding them an embarrassment, and KM was no different. In the resentful mind-set of these diary entries, there were no good points, only bad ones. Her perceived isolation was also brought out here: for KM there was absolutely no one she could confide in within her family, who were all branded as fools. Her desire was to be with her London friends – Vere, Ida, Gwen – with whom she believed she could be herself. The entry also poignantly reveals how much of her life at this time was a pose – in the vein of that master of poses, Oscar Wilde – except that shyness sometimes ruined such posturing and revealed her true self. Even so, the very next day, her ego was back in full force when she wrote: 'I am in love with nobody – except myself.'

UREWERA TRIP

November in New Zealand marks the beginning of summer. Millie Parker announced that she was to take a month-long caravan trip, with six others, through the still mostly wild and spectacularly beautiful volcanic region in the middle of the North Island, sparsely inhabited by Maoris and with a few settler farms. Did KM want to go too? Harold, who, perhaps thinking that a spell of separation between himself and his daughter might cool down the inflamed tempers at no. 47, reluctantly agreed KM could accompany her, though he did not wholly approve of the mix of people with whom she was to travel. The other members of the party were George Ebbett, a lawyer and sheep farmer, and his wife Eliza; another farmer, Hill, who was to be in charge of the horses; another single woman, Annie Leithead; and another couple, Herbert Webber, a Hastings pharmacist, and his wife Elsie. Elsie, who was only three years older than KM (who, in turn, was the youngest member of the party), became close to KM on the trip. KM kept a record of the journey in what is now referred to as 'The Urewera Notebook', mostly written in pencil.[113] The difficulty of the terrain can still be seen in the poor quality of KM's handwriting, who frequently wrote as the carts were being pulled along by the horses, or by weak candlelight in her tent late at night. The notebook's inside cover contains a pencilled quotation from Oscar Wilde, 'A woman never knows when the curtain has fallen,'[114] almost certainly written before she decided to take this particular notebook on her trip.

KM and Millie left Wellington by train on 23 November 1907 for Hastings, a town just under 200 miles from Wellington, on the north-east coast, where they stayed overnight with the Ebbetts, and were joined by the rest of the party the following morning. KM was in high spirits as she left Wellington, her need to lean out of windows undiminished:

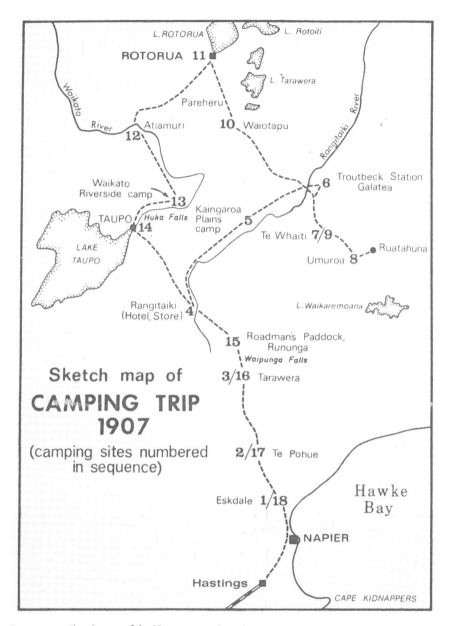

Figure 7.21 Sketch map of the Urewera camping trip, 1907.

There is something inexpressibly charming to me in railway travelling – I lean out of the window – the breeze blows, buffetting and friendly against my face – and the child spirit – hidden away under a thousand and one grey City wrappings bursts its bonds – & exults within me – I watch the

long succession of brown paddocks – beautiful with here, a thick spread-
ing of buttercups – there a white sweetness of arum lilies – And there are
valleys – lit with the swaying light of broom blossom – in the distance –
grey whares – two eyes & a mouth – with a bright petticoat frill of a
garden – creeping round them –[115]

From Hastings, the group made their way by horse-drawn coach (accompanied by a dray, which carried all their provisions and camping equipment) to
Napier and then through the Esk Valley to the small sawmill town of Te Pohue.
According to Elsie Webber's account of the journey, on arrival in Te Pohue,
KM asked to see 'some real N.Z. Bush before leaving for England'. The two
young women went off for several hours, only to return and find the others had
cooked dinner in their absence. Elsie wrote:

> I felt guilty for I should have been doing my share of the chores, but
> the time had flown. K.B. too looked contrite. 'Do you know', she con-
> fessed, 'I am quite hopeless domestically. I have never even made a pot
> of tea. How do you peel potatoes?' 'The same way as you peel apples', I
> replied.[116]

KM, who had only ever known servants and every convenience, initially found
her first experience of camping difficult:

> After brief snatches of terribly unrefreshing sleep – I woke – and found
> the grey dawn slipping into the tent – I was hot & tired and full of
> discomfort – the frightful buzzing of the mosquitos – the slow breathing of
> the others seemed to weigh upon my brain for a moment and then I found
> that the air was alive with birds' song – From far and near they called &
> cried to each other – I got up – & slipped through the little tent opening
> on to the wet grass – All round me the willow still full of gloomy shades –
> the caravan in the glade a ghost of itself – but across the clouded grey sky
> the vivid streak of rose colour – blazoned in the day – The grass was full
> of clover bloom – I caught up my dressing gown with both hands & ran
> down to the river – and the water – flowed in – musically laughing – & the
> green willows – suddenly stirred by the breath of the dawning day – sway
> softly together – Then I forgot the tent – and was happy [. . .][117]

For the first time in her life, she now peeled potatoes and washed dishes. As the
terrain became more difficult, so her writing became more disjointed and note-
like, as she tried to capture her impressions of the people, places and flora on the
journey, in proto-Modernist, proto-imagist prose:

Next day walking and bush – clematis & orchids – meet Mary – by the ploughed field – & at last come to the Waipunga falls – the fierce wind – the flax & manuka – the bad roads – camp by the river – & then up hill – the heat to Rangitaiki – Post letters – came on a peninsula – the purple – the ferns – the clean house – evening – the cream – the wild pigs Woman and daughter – the man – their happiness –[118]

On 26 November the party covered twenty-one miles of difficult and steep mountain terrain, which occasionally necessitated the party dismounting and walking to relieve the horses. That evening, the party visited its first hot spring, at Tarawera. The next day, after more arduous mountainous terrain, the road started to descend until they eventually arrived at the Waipunga Falls and thence on to the Kaingaroa Plains, made up of volcanic pumice sand, eventually arriving at the tiny settlement of Rangitaiki. The following day, 28 November, the party travelled from Rangitaiki, taking a short cut through the Kaingaroa Plains and following an old disused wool-waggon track. In the evenings, the group sang songs around the campfire; according to Elsie Webber, 'K. B. used to sing "Last Sunday morning we missed him from the mat. Puss! Puss! Puss! Puss! Meat! Meat! Meat! Has anybody seen our cat?,"' an old music hall number from 1899. During the trip, it seems that Nietzsche was also a favourite of KM's

Figure 7.22 Rangitaiki Hotel, Taupo district.

Figure 7.23 Group, including Katherine Mansfield, at Galatea.

(possibly to impress her fellow travellers). Elsie remembered, 'She was at that time very keen on Nietzsche's works and often quoted him.'[119]

The next few days were spent travelling into the Urewera hills – densely forested, isolated mountain country – with its small Maori settlements. One of KM's notebook entries describes a visit to a Maori homestead:

> Lunched at a space in the bush cut through a tree – and then by devious routes we came to the pah – It was adorable – Just the collection of huts, the built place, for koumara & potato – We visit first the house – no English then a charming little place roses & pinks in the garden – Through the doorway the kettle & fire – & bright tins – the woman the child in the pink dress & red sleeves in all this black grey How she stands gathering her pleats of dress – she can say just 'Yes' – Then we go into the parlour – photos – a chiming clock – mats – kits – red table cloth – horse hair sofa – The child saying 'nicely thank you' the shy children – the Mother & the poor baby – white & naked – the other bright children her splendid face & regal bearing – Then at the gate of the P.O. a great bright col-

oured crowd – almost threatening looking – a follower of Rua with long Fijian hair & side combs – a most beautiful girl of 15 – she is married to a patriarch, her laughing face, her hands playing with the children's hair – her smiles – across the bad river – the guide the swimming dogs – it flows on he stands in the water a regal figure then his 'alight' & we are out – the absolute ease of his figure – so boneless he speeds our parting journey his voice is so good.[120]

Unbeknown to KM, she actually had Beauchamp relatives living in the Urewera, who were part Maori. One of Arthur Beauchamp's brothers, Frederick George, who had eventually emigrated to Australia in the footsteps of his siblings, also ended up in New Zealand, where he bought land in the Urewera and married a Maori princess from the Tuhoe tribe. All his sons were given Beauchamp family names: George, Sam, John and Arthur. Harold Beauchamp, in his *Reminiscences*, skirted over this state of affairs in the chapter on his forebears, stating, 'what became of Fred I do not know.'[121] It is possible that KM may even have met her relations during her stay in the Urewera, without even realising it.

The party then retraced their steps back on to the Kaingaroa Plains, this time heading westwards towards the Waiotapu Valley, with its geothermal springs, lakes and craters. On 4 December they continued on towards the tourist town

Figure 7.24 Group, including Katherine Mansfield, at Te Whaiti, Whakatane.

Figure 7.25 Hamurama Landing, Rotorua.

Figure 7.26 Panoramic view of Whakarewarewa, Rotorua.

of Rotorua, where they spent four nights, with a stop en route at the spectacular geysers, silica terraces and pools of Whakarewarewa. In an interview many years later, Tom Seddon, the former Prime Minister's son, remembered bumping into KM at Rotorua, where he was also staying at that time:

Sitting on a bench under some willows in the drizzling rain, and looking very despondent, was Kass. She said, 'I'm travelling in a caravan with some people father doesn't approve of and I feel miserable but I've written a marvellous story.'[122]

Rotorua, with its famous lake and geysers, was a well-organised tourist town, with a sanitorium catering for visitors wishing to take the volcanic waters, and with bathhouses, gardens, dinghy rides, tennis courts and gift shops to keep tourists amused. During the party's visit, Elsie Webber recorded:

My birthday fell whilst we were in Rotorua. During the afternoon we were looking in a shop window, I admired a small picture of 2 Maori children. K.B. [Kathleen Beauchamp] went into the shop and purchased it. Later she gave it to me. On the back was written 'Birthday greetings from K. Mansfield'.[123]

KM, though she participated in all the tourist delights, disliked Rotorua intensely. There were far too many tourists; she wrote in her notebook, 'Give me the Maori and the tourist – but nothing between.'[124] There was a nasty sulphurous smell, of course, but mainly she disliked its falseness and pretention after so much natural beauty:

The morning is fine but hot – the nearer they get to the town the more she hates it – perhaps it is smell. It is pretty hot a rise to see the blue lake – They pass Whaka – ugly suburban houses – ugly streets old shaking buses crowds of the veiled tourists – [. . .]
Thursday the loathsome trip –
Friday so tired that she sits in the sanatorium grounds all the morning and that evening –horrid – the people – bowls – [. . .] The wet camp the fear of having to move – She thinks Rotorua is loathsome & likes – only – that little Hell.
Sunday morning the early start, & it seems at each mile post her heart leaps – But as they leave it the town is very beautiful – & Whaka – full of white mist – strangely fanciful – She almost wishes – no – oh, it is too hot where they lunch – she feels so ill – so tired – her headache is most violent – she can hardly open her eyes – but must lean back – each jolt of

the cart pains her – but the further they go – the load begins to lighten –
Then meet a Maori again – walking along – barefooted and strong – she
shouted Tenokoto – and Kathie's heart is warm again – there is no maudlin
affectation –[125]

At this point in the notebook, KM changed her style to reporting events in the
third person for some pages, referring to herself as 'Kathie', a German version of
her name, before this style was discontinued.

Over the next few days the travellers went from Rotorua to Atiamuri, in order
to visit the celebrated Rainbow Falls, and from there to the Aratiatia Rapids
and on to the town of Wairakei and its famous Geyser Valley. From Wairakei,
the party continued on to Taupo, stopping at the Huka Falls en route, finally
arriving at The Terraces Spa Hotel, two miles beyond Taupo, where they spent
the night of 10 December. From 11 to 15 December, the group retraced the
beginning of the trip as they headed southwards towards Hastings, camping
one night in the isolated Runanga Valley, with its solitary roadman's cottage
and paddocks. This spot would be immortalised in one of KM's first stories for
Rhythm, 'The Woman at the Store', whose setting was wholly inspired by the
valley with its remote cottage.[126]

Figure 7.27 Group, including Katherine Mansfield, at Aratiatia Rapids, 1906.

Figure 7.28 Campsite in Runanga.

Before KM and Millie caught the train home to Wellington on 17 December, they spent two nights in Hastings as guests at the home of the Ebbetts:

[On] 16 December, KM paid a visit to Napier, where EKB [Edie Bendall], with whom she had been involved in a passionate relationship earlier in the year, was staying. KM entertained EKB with 'excellent mimicries' of her travelling companions and of fat old Maori women. EKB found KM quite changed. KM had opened the Urewera notebook with a quotation from Oscar Wilde. EKB noted that her 'decadence' (she was thinking particularly of KM's literary poses with 'incense burning in her room') was gone – 'she had come down to earth violently'.[127]

Nevertheless, on the train journey back to Wellington, KM once more reverted to her old persona with its Wildean posing, and started writing in her notebook as if the journey of the past month had barely happened:

In the train – December 17th Has there ever been a hotter day – The land is parched – golden with the heat – The sheep are sheltering in the shadow of the rocks – in the distance the hills are shimmering in the heat – M. and I sitting opposite each other – I look perfectly charming. And I read a little book called The Book of Tea – it is wholly adorable –[128]

The Book of Tea, by Okakura-Kakuzo, published in London in 1906, is a study of the art of the Japanese tea ceremony and, more broadly, of the customs and rituals of traditional Japanese life. An instant best-seller when first published, it is still in print today and would remain one of KM's favourite books. Her posing is also evident in the letters written home during the trip, especially the ones to her mother, where her conversational tone is one of a sophisticated young lady, playing up the humour of her situation to her fastidious mother:

> Grubby, my dear, I felt dreadful – my clothes were white with dust – we had accomplished 8 miles of hill climbing – So after dinner – (broad beans cooked over a camp fire and tongue & cake and tea –) we prowled round and found an 'agèd aged man' who had the key of the mineral baths – I wrapt clean clothes in my towel – & the old man rushed home to seize a candle in a tin – He guided us through the bush track – by the river – & my dear I've never seen such a cure – I don't think he ever had possessed a tooth & he never ceased talking – you know the effect?[129]

Further on in the same letter, KM consciously tries out prose techniques, here replicating a dialogue between herself and a Maori woman, who is holding a baby, and presaging dialogue stories she would write many years later:

> Kathleen – pointing to her own teeth & then to the baby's – 'Ah!'
> Mother – very appreciative 'Ai'!
> Kathleen – pointing to the baby's long curling eyelashes 'Oh!'
> Mother – most delighted 'Aii' –
> And so on – I jumped the baby up & down in the air – and it crowed with laughter – & the Mother & Father – beaming – shook hands with me again – Then we drove off – waving until out of sight – all the Maoris do that –[130]

Two poems were written by KM during the camping trip. The first, 'In the Rangitaiki Valley', was wholly inspired by the beauty of the natural landscape that surrounded her, and that was expressed in a tone of joy and appreciation in the poem itself, as here in the last verse:

Oh, valley of waving broom
Oh, lovely, lovely light
Oh, mystical marriage of Earth
With the passionate Summer sun
To her lover she holds a cup
And the yellow wine o'erflows
He has lighted a little torch
And the whole of the world is ablaze
Prodigal wealth of love
Breast high in the blossom I stand[131]

The second poem, 'Youth', was composed on 15 December, at the end of the trip, whilst KM was staying with the Ebbetts in Hastings before returning to Wellington:

O Flower of Youth!
See in my hand I hold
This blossom flaming yellow and pale gold
And all its petals flutter at my feet
Can Death be sweet?

Look at it now!
Just the pale green is heart
Heart of the flower see is white and bare
The silken wrapping scattered on the ground
What have I found?

If one had come
On a sweet summer day
Breathless, half waking – full of youth I say
If one had come [. . .] from the glen
What happens then?

Sighing it dies
In the dawn flush of life
Never to know the terror and the strife
Which kills all summer blossoms when they blow.
Far better so
Ah! better better so.[132]

Here are all the old themes of fin-de-siècle, Wildean, Decadent poetry: decay and death. It reads as though the trip had barely impacted on KM's consciousness.

Certainly, her mind-set does not seem to have undergone any radical alteration as a result of her experiences; indeed, it could only have highlighted her personal distance from the Old World and everything for which she longed.

FINAL MONTHS

It was a sunburnt, tired but, outwardly at least, still the same KM who returned home a week before Christmas. Later on in her life, images of those weeks spent travelling through the wild heartland of New Zealand would return and inspire several stories; her close proximity to Maori families and their language and customs was another feature of the journey that she appreciated. Maata, the sleek, Westernised princess, was not at all the 'real thing'.

   As ever, the Wellington social columns continued to report the comings and goings of the Beauchamps, welcoming KM back on 18 December: 'Miss Kathleen Beauchamp returned last night from a delightful month's visit to Rotorua.'[133] Nevertheless, Harold, who had been away on business, came back

Figure 7.29 Katherine Mansfield at 47 Fitzherbert Terrace, Wellington.

to find KM as fractious and determined as ever to go back to London. KM wrote to Martha Putnam, to whom she had sent her racy story, 'Leves Amores', to be typed (indicating that she hoped to send it off to a publisher), 'Castles have been tumbling about my ears since Father came home. Do not mention – I pray you – my London prospects to him – he feels very sensitive – but – willy nilly – I GO – I'm determined.'[134] Martha later destroyed dozens of notes from KM, all of which contained an element of resentment against her environment, which she felt was not quite appropriate, given her own position as Harold's secretary. Vera was also away now, the *Dominion*'s social column reporting on 7 December that 'Miss Vera Beauchamp left yesterday for a short visit to Sydney.'[135] In fact, her trip of two to three months would be extended, and she would not return until after KM's eventual departure for London on 6 July 1908.

Whilst KM had been away, Maata's name had frequently been in the social columns. On 23 November, 'Christabel' had announced that 'Miss Martha Grace, the Wairarapa heiress (daughter of the late chief, Tamahau Mahupuka), has recently become engaged to Mr. George McGregor, a half-caste gentleman, belonging to Wanganui.'[136] Maata's marriage, which followed very soon after the news of the engagement, on 5 December, was also reported; Maata was described as 'the well-known and accomplished heiress'.[137] On 21 December, however, it was not KM but Chaddie (as the eldest, in the absence of Vera) who welcomed 'Mrs Macgregor' to no. 47:

> A very pleasant little tea was given by Miss Chad. Beauchamp in honour of Mrs Macgregor, nee Miss Martha Grace. There was music during the afternoon, Mrs Macgregor, Miss Ward, and Miss C Beauchamp singing. The young hostess wore a dark green silk, and the guest of the afternoon was in dark blue taffetas and a hat with feathers.[138]

There was no mention of KM, and no record of the afternoon in her diary. Maata was still only seventeen. The freedom of a married woman must, however, have contrasted starkly with KM's own position, for she could do nothing without the approval of her father. The close friendship was no more but KM never forgot her. An unfinished novel from 1913 would be called *Maata*, with much of KM's own personality transmuted into the protagonist.

On 28 December, KM wrote in her diary, 'I have spent since returning an idle week full of nothingness.' She had spent that day travelling with a musical acquaintance, May Gilmer, since she noted, 'We talk MUSIC. Chiefly Macdowell & Chopin, and I, alas, feel a little superior.' She closed the entry by writing, 'I ought to make a good author. I certainly have the ambition and the ideas but have I the power to carry it all through? Yes – if I get back but not unless I do – but after all why not.'[139]

The New Year – 1908 – dawned with KM's determination more focused than ever: 'The year has dawned. My Year [. . .] Well – I have the brain and also the inventive faculty! What else is needed?'[140] Just that elusive permission from her father. Chaddie, ever placatory, wrote to Sylvia on 10 January, falsifying the situation somewhat, since the mood at home was far from pleasant:

> Kathleen has just returned home from her month away caravanning in the backblocks. She had the most interesting and delightful time, and came home looking so well and awfully brown. Don't be surprised to see her about April, it is quite likely she will be in London by then.[141]

However, something happened which stopped Harold from granting his daughter her request.

Examining the evidence, Ida may perhaps have misremembered the incident occurring at Christmas:

> At Christmas an unfortunate incident occurred which caused the Beauchamps to reconsider their decision about her departure. They were disturbed by a description, which Katherine had written of something that happened at a ball when she had sat out one of the dances with her partner, and which her mother discovered. In her usual fashion, Katherine had embellished the facts when writing them down, and her parents, taking them seriously, not unnaturally thought twice about letting her go to London.[142]

However, given Chaddie's letter above, and the following letter KM sent to the Trowell family, KM's misdemeanour – whatever it might have been – must have occurred later in the New Year. A letter of 10 January reads:

> My dearest Mr. and Mrs. Trowell and Dolly
> It is really as I thought – and I am now hoping to sail for London the month after next – but don't expect me till I send that telegram from Graves End – which I shall most certainly not forget to do. What a magnificent recital Tom must have given on November 23rd. I heard about it from my friend Ida Baker – and she sent me a number of cuttings from the papers –
> Each one seemed finer than the last –
> Do let me tell you my plans. My relations wrote last mail saying that they <u>might</u> take me, as they <u>thought</u> of having a home in London after all – So Father has written and asked them to cable the one word 'Kathleen' if they finally decide to do so – and I shall leave here on receipt of the cable. How

I am going to wait until I hear – I really do not know. Mr Johnson and his fiancée Miss Montague spent an afternoon quite lately with me. He had 'picked up for a song' in <u>Palmerston</u> an <u>old</u> Banks 'cello – so he brought it and played a great deal – Miss Montague is really a very clever pianist – she has such a fine grip of everything she plays, and a particularly full, round tone – He attempted a Klengle Concerto – Poppers Tarantelle – Alla Polacca – Goltermann – and a great deal more – It was not even pleasant to listen to – but Miss Montague enjoyed it. Oh, <u>will</u> that cable to come for me – please Mrs. Trowell, and then I know that it must. I felt I must just let you know how things were shaping. I am so wanting to hear from you – Shall I – soon?

> With much love to you
> from
> Kass[143]

The 'relations' in question refer to Aunt Belle, now Mrs Harry Trinder, of course, married to her stockbroker and living in Surrey. She and her husband had been considering purchasing a house in central London, and it was hoped KM could live there under the watchful eye of relatives. However, they eventually decided against such a move, thus contributing to KM's misfortunes. A telegram was even sent to other Beauchamp relatives in London. Would they have KM to stay and watch over her? There was a one-word response telegrammed back: 'No'.

On 23 January KM wrote a letter to Tom, in German, explaining in a postscript, 'Must write German. There are so many people – who know nothing of this language at all!':

> My dear friend – This last week, Dr Crosby brought me your 'Rêverie du Soir'. I must write you a few lines about it. I find this work so wonderful and lovely – so wistful – and so fervent. Hopefully this year I will hear you play your Rêverie du Soir in a concert! My good friend Ida Baker has given me several pages from the newspapers. What a success merveille it was. Often in my thoughts I have congratulated you. I am coming to England in early March – I hate Wellington – and naturally I am yearning for London. Have you had more Journaux from me? And what do you think of them? Why haven't you spoken about them to me? How is your father? – and your mother too, and also your dear worthy little sister. The house –18 Buller Street – stands so lonely! With greetings for this year 1908.

> Your friend,
> K.[144]

Again, there is no evidence here to suggest her parents' change of heart at this point. Clearly, KM was still in regular correspondence with Tom, sending him clippings of her published stories. It also seems clear that Tom was ever the reluctant correspondent, since news of his achievements was being sent to KM not by himself but by the faithful Ida.

Nevertheless, something shocking clearly happened which made her parents renege on their promise to let her go. Perhaps it was, as Ida remembered, some sort of misbehaviour at a ball. Mantz, in her research notes, talked of a ball at the Savage Club, a men's social club modelled on the original London one. In the 1907 New Zealand club, 'the men wore dress suits, covered in Maori mats and carrying spears, and dancing a haka at the hilarious instigation of Chief Savage, Sir J. Findlay. Eligible young ladies were invited to the balls that followed the new Savages' initiation.'[145] One of KM's musical friends told Mantz:

> She used to meet the bald-headed Chief Savage afterward. [. . .] Kass would leave our practices and say, 'I'm going to the Gardens to meet Sir J.'. I tried to argue with her and tell her that it wasn't 'true, real life'. I told her, 'He is a married man with a reputation!' Finally, I found facts and presented them. Kass said, 'That's a lie!' But she wrote two or three stories in later years that these men appear in.[146]

In the story 'Her First Ball' (1921), the protagonist, Leila (KM), dances with a bald-headed man who unnerves her:

> 'Your first dance, isn't it?' he murmured.
> 'How *did* you know?'
> 'Ah,' said the fat man, 'that's what it is to be old!' He wheezed faintly as he steered her past an awkward couple. 'You see, I've been doing this kind of thing for the last thirty years.'
> 'Thirty years?' cried Leila. Twelve years before she was born!
> 'It hardly bears thinking about, does it?' said the fat man gloomily. Leila looked at his bald head, and she felt quite sorry for him.
> 'I think it's marvellous to be still going on,' she said kindly.
> 'Kind little lady,' said the fat man, and he pressed her a little closer, and hummed a bar of the waltz. 'Of course,' he said, 'you can't hope to last anything like as long as that. No-o,' said the fat man, 'long before that you'll be sitting up there on the stage, looking on, in your nice black velvet. And these pretty arms will have turned into little short fat ones, and you'll beat time with such a different kind of fan – a black bony one.' The fat man seemed to shudder. 'And you'll smile away like the poor old

dears up there, and point to your daughter, and tell the elderly lady next to you how some dreadful man tried to kiss her at the club ball. And your heart will ache, ache' – the fat man squeezed her closer still, as if he really was sorry for that poor heart – 'because no one wants to kiss you now. And you'll say how unpleasant these polished floors are to walk on, how dangerous they are. Eh, Mademoiselle Twinkletoes?' said the fat man softly.

Leila gave a light little laugh, but she did not feel like laughing.[147]

In her diary for 22 October 1907, KM had written, 'I am so eternally thankful that I did not allow J – to kiss me – I am constantly hearing of him, and I feel to meet him would be horrible. But why? It is ridiculous – I used him merely for copy.'[148] There is a curious footnote to the Savage Club ball; a few years later, in 1914, Leslie attended a Savage Club fancy-dress ball dressed as a woman, just before joining up and going to England. He looked so much like KM that someone in surprise said, 'Look, there's Kass.'[149]

If the above ball was not the reason for Harold's change of heart, then perhaps Martha had finally shown her boss, Harold, a typescript of the racy 'Leves Amores', with the action taking place in 'The Thistle', the well-known Wellington inn on Mulgrave Street, a stone's throw from the parliament buildings, making it seem all the more vivid – and lurid.[150] Another contributory factor might have been a strange diary entry, written in between two 1909 entries which could well belong to an earlier date. Indeed, years later, when editing KM's journals, Murry pencilled in a comment on the page where it appears: 'These entries do not belong to the same time.'[151] The entry reads:

> Night. J'attends pour la premiere fois dans ma vie le crise de ma vie.[152] As I wait, a flock of sheep pass down the street in the moonlight. I hear the cracking [of] the whip & behind the dark heavy cart – like a death cart, il me semble. And all in this sacrificial light. I look lovely. I do not fear, I only feel. I pray the dear Lord I have not waited too long for my soul hungers as my body all day has hungered & cried for him. Ah come now – soon. Each moment, il me semble, is a moment of supreme danger, but this man I love with all my heart. The other I do not even care about. It comes. I go to bed.[153]

The flock of sheep indicates that KM might well have been at the little cottage in Day's Bay when she wrote the entry, and not in London. It also appears that she was waiting for a male caller to arrive, someone recently met, and for whom she had developed a strong physical attraction. If the dating of the entry is as suggested here, then Tom Trowell was – temporarily – no longer in her thoughts:

'The other I do not even care about.' Could 'le [*sic*] crise de ma vie' indicate her first sexual experience with a man? It is impossible to be certain, but if this diary entry had been seen by her parents, there would undoubtedly have been some sort of confrontation. In addition, as if matters were not already complex enough, Tom Mills later stated that, at about this time, he had received a letter from KM explaining that she was being blackmailed. Apparently, she had been advised to write to Mills by Harold (who seemed to have an inordinate amount of confidence in this young journalist) because he felt that Mills's connections with the Wellington police from his time as a reporter there might be of use. It seems Harold's confidence was justified. Mills travelled down to Wellington, spoke to the police and '[s]oon after, as a result of some unofficial pressure, a certain "anonymous young man" sailed from Wellington.'[154]

Whatever might have occurred between KM and her dance partner at the ball, or the man at Day's Bay, or the discovery of her racy vignette, or a gentleman blackmailer, it was deemed serious enough to stop her plans in their tracks. Pat Lawlor, who befriended Maata in later years, recorded that she climbed up to KM's room in order to comfort her friend after whatever crisis had occurred, since KM had been locked in her bedroom by Harold.[155]

Reading over the events of these last few months in Wellington, it seems that KM made little effort to help her own cause by leading the sort of life that would have made her parents more compliant. By 10 February, her goal as far away now as ever, her moods had reached a crisis point: 'I shall end of course – by killing myself.'[156] Just over a month later, on 15 March, recognising the strong influence of Wilde and *Dorian Gray* on her outlook in life, and even subconsciously suggesting that, like Wilde, she herself was creating the very conditions for her own exile, she wrote,

> I purchase my brilliance with my life. It were better that I were dead, really. I am unlike others because I have experienced all that there is to experience – but there is no one to help me. Of course Oscar – Dorian Gray has brought this S.S. to pass.[157]

The *Dominion* did not help matters – perhaps it was KM herself who supplied the information to the social columnist, in an attempt to force her father's hand – reporting on 18 March that 'Miss Kathleen Beauchamp is leaving next month for London, where she intends to engage in literary work.'[158]

Outwardly at least, in a show of defiance to the world, KM's life betrayed little of her inner turmoil. Vera, on her extended stay with relatives in Sydney, was a regular recipient of KM's chatty missives during these last few months. Indeed, from the end of January, the only extant letters by KM are those sent to Vera, and one sent to Sylvia Payne in March. On 17 January she wrote to

Vera, telling her that she had just finished writing a 'London' story called 'The Education of Audrey', which would eventually be published in the *Evening Post* on 30 January 1909. It is a displacement tale, where KM imagines herself in London, rich, happy and with the sort of musical and artistic friends she desired. KM is clearly Audrey, a singer, and the male protagonist, Max, an artist, is a make-believe version of Tom Trowell, with a touch of Rippmann thrown in for good measure. Even the Wellington wind makes an appearance, as she fictional-ises Tom's departure for Europe:

> 'Oh, Max! Do you remember our parting? – that terrible place; you had to catch the evening boat. I walked down to the ferry with you along the road. I had no shoes and stockings on – do you remember? And the wind. You had proposed to me that afternoon with unqualified success on the back verandah, and we tried to kiss each other before the boat went, but the wind blew all my hair across my face.' Audrey flung back her head and laughed. 'Oh, what children!' she said. 'I watched that ship put out to sea; you stood by the rail, waving me a little friendly greeting. I was crying, without a handkerchief. I remember going back to my room, kneeling by the window, looking up at the fierce sky, and praying, "Oh, God, keep him, keep him!"'

Max's house is very much a replica of Walter Rippmann's, heady with the colours and smells of Decadence and Symbolism:

> There were prints of beautiful women on the walls, and the graceful figure of a girl holding a green shell in her arms stood on one of the tables. There was a long low couch upholstered in dull purple, and quaint low chairs in the same colour. The air was full of the odour of chrysanthemums, the blossoms arranged in pewter bowls on the mantelshelf, and bookcases and tables.

Audrey herself is poised at a moment in her life when she can realise all her dreams:

> 'Love,' she said, 'is a means to the end. You must have gone through all the abandonment of love. You must have been bruised and scarred by his mighty fetters. You must have been tossed upon the very sea of passion, and if you can escape free in body and soul, there lies before you such a wide wind-swept waste of freedom, such promise of happiness in this freedom that you run forward, your arms outstretched to take the whole world into your embrace.'[159]

KM wrote two further stories in January 1908. 'Juliette Delacour' is a morbid tale of a little girl whose invalid father dies whilst playing with her, and whose life thereafter becomes cloistered and dark. 'The Unexpected Must Happen', written at the same time, has a married couple, Judith and Guy, toy with each other's emotions, as Judith's lover, Cecil, is due to arrive. In a little twist of luck, the two men meet at the door of the house. Cecil is invited in:

> But there came no sound from the sitting room. Then suddenly the door opened, the two men came out – talking excitedly, her husband paused to put on a coat and hat and the next moment the hall door had clicked behind them and she was alone![160]

Neither story offers much by way of artistic merit. However, another story, 'Vignette: By the Sea', is a beautifully poetic piece of creative writing, where KM's talents as a writer are clearly evident. Written in February, it is a fiction-alised version of a long diary entry, where KM describes a visit to Island Bay, near Wellington. Her proto-modernist eye for detail, as a means of expressing so much more, is evident in her description of the Italian sailors, and the fey lines which follow, captivate and enchant:

> And now the Italian fishermen are sailing in, their white sails bellying in the breeze. Several come rowing in a little boat. They spring ashore, the light shines on their crisp black hair, it shines on their faces, so that their skin is the colour of hot amber on their bare legs and strong brown arms. They are dragging towards them the boat, the long black, wet rope running through their fingers and falling in a bold pattern on the foam-blown sand. They call to one another – I cannot hear what they say – but against the long, rhythmic pulsing of the sea their voices sound curiously insignificant, like voices in a dream.
> And there are exquisite golden brown sprays and garlands of sea weed, set about with berries, white and brown. Are they flowers blown from the garden of the Sea King's Daughter? Does she wander through the delicate coral forests, seeking them, playing upon a little silver shell, her long hair floating behind her?[161]

Another innovative story, written in March, was 'The Yellow Chrysanthemum', her first experiment in the use of dialogue, a form she would later return to with great success, especially in 1917, when she wrote several pieces using varia-tions on dramatic forms.[162] As an exercise in mimetic technique, such pieces helped hone her narrative technique; as noted above, she had even experimented slightly with the form in a letter sent to her mother whilst on her camping trip. The symbolism of the title, of course, needs no explanation. Indeed, the whole fragment is imbued with the influence of Oscar Wilde, and in particular his early drama, *The Duchess of Padua*, from 1891:

RADIANA: O, O, the perfume of the dead body . . .
GUIDO: It is the smoke from the candles . . . The night air has blown their light out . . .
RADIANA: O the dead body of the Summer.
GUIDO: (fiercely) Why are you so pale? Why are you so pale? Why are you shuddering? Close your eyes . . . close your eyes . . .
RADIANA: Guido! . . .
GUIDO: Hold me! Hold to me! I shall hold your little hands against my face . . . Feel how hot I am . . . and you so cold . . . Your fingers are damp . . . and there is a strange scent . . . Radiana! Radiana! Horror! Horror! I am holding a dead body . . . It is the perfume of your dead body . . . and I am afraid. Ah! how loathsome!. . . I shall wrap you round in your hair . . . shut out your face . . . hide your hands, cover your pale feet . . .
(Suddenly he rises from the couch where he has been kneeling, and wrenches one of the yellow curtains from the windows. He flings it over her body.)
CURTAIN.[163]

Death, love, decay, extreme emotion: all were expressions of KM's mind-set at this time. A letter to Vera written towards the end of March 1908, hints at the contents of 'The Yellow Chrysanthemum':

The voice of the chrysanthemum is heard in the land. Two blossoms – so full of colour that I feel they are lighting the dead summer on her journey – greet you from my table. Flowers like Tom's music seem to create in me a divine unrest – They revive strangely – dream memories – I know not what – They show me strange mystic paths – where perhaps I shall one day walk – To lean over a flower – as to hear any of his music is to suddenly [have] every veil torn aside – to commune soul with soul – This is like the hysteria of 17 it's the conviction of experience – Sister –[164]

This was all rather dramatic and probably more than Vera wanted to hear, even if she understood the contents.
    Plans for a move to London, both overt and covert, continued unabated. A letter to Sylvia Payne was written from Day's Bay on 4 March. She and Chaddie had gone over to the little cottage for a short stay, accompanied – in

true Beauchamp style – by a maid, to get some fresh sea air following a bout of illness:

> It has only three rooms – two bedrooms fitted with bunks – and a wide living room [. . .] we bathe and row and walk in the bush or by the sea – and read – and I write – while she pursues the gentle art of fashioning camisoles. One could not be lonesome here – I seem to love it more each day – and the sea is a continually new sensation with me.

The letter is fascinating for what it reveals about KM at this time. Her correspondence with Sylvia was evidently prodigious, including the sending of numerous telegrams: 'Have you received one tenth of my wireless messages?' Following a paragraph about her memories of school, she reveals more about herself:

> My life has been so strange – full of either sorrow – or excitement – or disgust or happiness. In a year to have lived so much! And I have not made a friend. It is no good I can have men friends – they persist in asking for something else. Do you know Sylvia *five* men has [*sic*] asked me to marry them. [. . .] but it is the stupid truth – I have been reading – French & English – writing and lately have seen a great many Balls – and loved them – and dinners and receptions. They have such a different meaning for me now – and here. I have finished My First Book. If it never gets published – you shall laugh with me over its absurdities. Also I hope to leave for London next month – It is not unwise of me – it is the only thing to be done. I cannot live with Father – and I must get back because I know I shall be successful – look at the splendid tragic optimism of youth! One day – you must please know my brother. He knows you very well indeed – and he and I mean to live together – later on. I have never dreamed of loving a child as I love this boy. Do not laugh at me when I tell you I feel so maternal towards him. He is intensely affectionate and sensitive – he reads a great deal – draws with the most delicate sympathetic touch – and yet is a thoroughly brave healthy boy. Do not let me write of him – he is away at school – and if I go back next month we may not meet for years –[165]

There is undoubtedly some exaggeration here, possibly concerning the five proposals, and she certainly did have close female friends: Edie Bendall and Millie Parker, to name just two. But it was true that she could not live with her father; possibly the stay at Day's Bay, amongst other reasons, was to give father and daughter another break from each other. The 'First Book' was her collaboration with Edie Bendall, never to see the light of day. Probably the most poignant part of the letter is the description of her attachment to her young brother Leslie, especially given the tragic events which were to ensue in 1915. The bond was real and developed here in these eighteen otherwise miserable months. Years later, Siegfried Eichelbaum remembered accompanying KM and Chaddie on the ferry from Day's Bay to Wellington, in order to take them to a debate at the university college, where the motion was 'that women should not be given the vote'. He could not remember what KM thought of the motion, declaring, 'she was too polite to say.'[166]

A couple of weeks later, KM wrote again to Vera about her plans: 'You see that my Mrs Weston plan has also fallen through.'[167] It really must have seemed that the entire universe was conspiring against her and it is to her credit, in a way, that she maintained such a steadfast resolve to leave New Zealand, given the mounting obstacles. Captain T. S. Weston was a naval friend of Harold's. It is not clear what the plan with his wife actually involved but, like all the others, it was still-born. Then there was another potential avenue of hope. She wrote to Vera:

> Mother has the plan of sending us to London to live together – we three in a flat on £300 a year which is amply sufficient – of course knowing that the separation from her & from Father is purely temporary. Now what do you think. Do you think that your duty lies with them now – but if you married you would have to leave home – living here you certainly will not marry – You with music & painting – Chaddie singing etc – I literature – This plan refuses to be discussed on paper – so I shall give it up – I know you can argue it all out – & I waste words & state deep feelings so superficially. But to tell you the absolute truth – I can't stand this life much longer –[168]

More plans, more false hopes. The letters to Vera continued unabated. In a rather grandiose moment of self-importance she condemned New Zealand entirely:

> I am ashamed of young New Zealand, but what is to be done. All the firm fat framework of their brains must be demolished before they can begin to learn. They want a purifying influence – a mad wave of pre-Raphaelitism, of super-aestheticism, should intoxicate the country. They must go to excess in the direction of culture, become almost decadent in their tendencies for a year or two and then find balance and proportion. We want two or three persons gathered together to discuss line and form and atmosphere and sit at the street corners, in the shops, in the houses, at the Teas. People who would quote William Morris and Catulle Mendes, George Meredith and Maurice Maeterlinck, Ruskin and Rodenbach, Le Gallienne and Symons,

D'Annunzio and Shaw, Granville Barker and Sebastian Melmouth, Whitman, Tolstoi, Carpenter, Lamb, Hazlitt, Hawthorne, and the Brontës. These people have not learned their alphabet yet.[169]

The list of authors here replicates a similar list found in that little vignette 'In a Café', published by Brady in Australia a few months before. New Zealand was certainly not the backwater KM made it out to be, but neither was it England or – more specifically – London. However, KM had now reached the point where desperation clouded her judgement. She liked to shock; it made her feel powerful and different to the run-of-the-mill Wellington girls she was forced to mix with at society functions. But this sophisticated pose was merely topsoil. The bedrock underneath that comprised the real KM was composed of misery and despair. Apparently, the journalist Tom Mills was now 'writing me too many letters';[170] his delight in her writing had now started to manifest itself as something more personal. KM was having none of it:

It is a little ridiculous. I cannot keep the men I know *friends*. They persist in drifting into some other ridiculous attitude – I let them drift, and then suddenly see what a big big log we have both bumped against – so I say to myself 'dear me, how inadvisable, but it is certainly copy.'[171]

Harold Beauchamp's reputation in Wellington continued on its upward trajectory, in spite of all the annoyances at home. On 11 April, the *New Zealand Herald* reported that the previous day he had been re-elected as Chairman of the Bank of New Zealand for a further year.[172] Whilst she waited for her father's permission to leave, on 8 May KM enrolled at Wellington Technical School, taking classes in 'commercial subjects' – typing and bookkeeping. Perhaps this was done at her father's request – Harold, with his sensible business head on, thinking that these were skills that might stand her in good stead if she were to move to the other side of the world to try her hand as a writer. Her little Corona portable typewriter would be a constant travel companion later in life.

KM's haven during these long eighteen months in New Zealand was the General Assembly Library, where she spent many hours reading an eclectic range of books. Early in the morning of 11 December 1907, whilst she had been away on her camping trip, the left-hand end of the building, containing the parliamentary debating chamber, had burnt down in a spectacular fire, caused by faulty electrical wiring. The beautiful neo-gothic building, built of wood, burnt quickly. Luckily, a firewall saved the non-wooden General Assembly Library wing that had been recently added.[173] In March – autumn in New Zealand – KM was to be found nestled in the library, from where she wrote a strange diary

Figure 7.30 Reading room of the General Assembly Library, Wellington.

entry, where the proliferation of pine trees echoes yet again that favourite book from childhood, Mrs Molesworth's *Christmas-Tree Land*, now woven into a more heady, fin-de-siècle prose style:

> A wet afternoon in the Library – in March. I have read most strange books here – one on the Path to Rome, one of Maori Art – – – Through the long avenue of pine trees, where the shadow of Night crept from tree to tree. The Autumn afternoon it really would be better to call it so. This is what I want – the little asphalt path like a mauve ribbon, the great fragrant warm sweetness of the pine needles massed & heaped together, ruddy with perfume. Then the trees – hundreds there seem in the dull light, a vast procession of gloomy forms. Now here, now there, the shades of night are trooping softly, the air is heavy with a faint uneasy sound, a restless beating to & fro, a long unceasing sigh, & far away in the distance there is a dreary waste of grey sea – a desert of heaving water.
>
> Grey, grey – there is no light in it at all, & the autumn air is cold with the coldness of drowned men. And Night is rising out of the sea – a ghastly broken form, & the autumn world sinks into that broken embrace, pillows its tired head upon that pulseless heart.

There is a little asphalt path like a mauve ribbon, and it is fringed with a vast procession of pine trees. In this dull light there seem to be hundreds of them. They are huddled together and muffled in their gloomy shadows.

On the earth a fragrant sweetness & pine needles, massed & heaped up, ruddy with perfume. And through the black lace-like tracery of trees a pale sky full of hurrying clouds. Far away in the distance a dreary waste of grey sea, a desert of heaving water.

Grey, grey . . . there is no light at all, and the autumn air is cold with the coldness of traceless spaces. Out of the grey sea creeps the ghastly, drowned body of Night. Her long dark hair swam among the branches of the pine trees, her dead body walks along the little mauve ribbon of an asphalt path. She stretches out her arms and the autumn world sinks into that frozen embrace, pillows its tired head upon that pulseless heart.

And the long procession of pine trees, huddled together, are ghostly fearful snowmen at the wedding with Death.[174]

The predominant words here are grey, pine, trees, cold; ghostly, lifeless forms are everywhere. The only colour present is to be found in the little mauve asphalt path that winds like a ribbon through the narrative, a motif for KM's diminishing hopes of leaving Wellington for the decadent delights of London.

The library had become a real retreat in the last few months of her time in Wellington – somewhere she could read and write in private, away from the inquisitive and prying eyes of the rest of the family. The story 'Taking the Veil' (1922), one of the last complete stories she wrote, looks back to this time in Wellington, and in it, through the character of Edna, she produces yet another portrayal of her youthful self. The Botanical Gardens are there and so too are the gardens of the Convent of the Sacred Heart in Thorndon, which KM would pass on her way to the library: 'Edna made going to the Library an excuse for getting out of the house to think, to realise what had happened, to decide somehow what was to be done now.'[175] In a diary entry for 24 January 1922, she noted:

Wrote and finished Taking the Veil. It took me about 3 hours to write finally. But I had been thinking over the decor and so on for weeks – nay – months, I believe. I can't say how thankful I am to have been born in N.Z., to know Wellington as I do and to have it to range about in. Writing about the convent seemed so natural. I suppose I have not been in the grounds more than twice. But it is one of the places that remain as vivid as ever.[176]

In later years, it appears that trophy hunters may have gone after KM's signature in the large General Assembly Library registers, where the title of every book taken out was recorded and signed for. KM's signature can still be seen for 27 July 1907, when she took out Walt Whitman's *Leaves of Grass*, but, for example, on 22 November 1907, the signature of the person who took out Arthur Symons's *Studies in Seven Arts* has been carefully removed with a razor blade.

On 1 May, KM wrote, in despair: 'I am now much worse than ever. Madness must Be this way. Pull yourself Up.'[177] Back in the General Assembly Library, her favourite place for working undisturbed, she made some observations about her situation:

> I have just finished reading a book by Elizabeth Robins 'Come & Find Me'. Really a clever, splendid book; it creates in me such a sense of power. I feel that I do now realise, dimly, what women in the future will be capable of achieving. They truly, as yet, have never had their chance. Talk of our enlightened days and our emancipated country – pure nonsense. We are firmly held in the self fashioned chains of slavery. Yes – now I see that they are self fashioned and must be self removed. Eh bien – now where is my ideal and ideas of life? Does Oscar – and there is a gardenia yet alive beside my bed – does Oscar still keep so firm a stronghold in my soul? No! Because now I am growing capable of seeing a wider vision – a little Oscar, a little Symons, a little Dolf Wyllarde, Ibsen, Tolstoi, Elizabeth Robins, Shaw, D'Annunzio, Meredith. To weave the intricate tapestry of one's own life it is well to take a thread from many harmonious skeins, and to realise that there must be harmony. Not necessary to grow the sheep, comb the wool, colour and brand it, but joyfully take all that is ready and with that saved time go a great way further. Independence, resolve, firm purpose and the gift of discrimination, mental clearness – here are the inevitables. Again, Will – the realisation that Art is absolutely self development. The knowledge that genius is dormant in every soul, that that very individuality which is at the root of our being is what matters so poignantly.[178]

KM would never take on the mantle of a suffragette – she was always too self-absorbed to spend much energy on concerns exterior to her own. However, it did seem that reading Robins's book helped her gain some sort of perspective on her situation at this time. Oscar Wilde's was clearly not the *only* pathway. A small crumb of comfort came by way of another small publication on 11 June, when the *Dominion* published one of her 'child poems', 'A Little Boy's Dream', whose subject matter of a voyage at sea was clearly uppermost in her mind:

> To and fro, to and fro,
> In my little boat I go,

Sailing far across the sea,
All alone – just little me.
And the sea is big and strong,
And the journey very long,
To and fro, to and fro,
In my little boat I go.[179]

It was also in June that KM wrote the story 'The Tiredness of Rosabel', an early story which utilises the technique of free indirect discourse, where the character of Rosabel, the impoverished young shop worker, is revealed via the narration. This particular technique is neither indirect speech nor directly transcribed interior monologue, but something in between. One of KM's greatest narrative strengths, experimented with here, is her ability to 'become' her fictional characters and to depict with acute psychological insight the workings of their minds, as well as delineating their physical attributes. For each character she develops a distinctive voice and an appropriate narrative strategy:

> She was more than glad to reach Richmond Road, but from the corner of the street until she came to No. 26 she thought of those four flights of stairs. Oh, why four flights! It was really criminal to expect people to live so high up. [. . .] When she stood in the hall and saw the first flight ahead of her and the stuffed albatross head on the landing, glimmering ghostlike in the light of the little gas jet, she almost cried. Well, they had to be faced; it was very like bicycling up a steep hill, but there was not the satisfaction of flying down the other side. . . .[180]

For KM, with her mind always in London though her physical body was in Wellington, the pathos of this story only served to underscore the bleakness of her own position.

In KM's last diary entry (that survives) before she left New Zealand, it seems that some sort of crisis point had been reached. The penny had finally dropped in KM's mind and she realised that in order to achieve her ambition of moving to London, she had to act the part of the dutiful, well-behaved daughter. Had she come to this conclusion earlier, she could have saved herself and her family a good deal of torment. She wrote:

> Now to plan it. O, Kathleen, do not weave any more of these fearful meshes. You have been so loathsomely unwise. Do take wisdom from all that you have and must still suffer. I really know that you can't stay as you are now. Be good – for the love of God – be good, & brave and do tell the truth more & live a better life. I am tired of all this deceit – and the moon

still shines, and the stars are still there. You'd better go & see the Doctor tomorrow about your heart, and then try & solve all the silly drivelling problems. Go anywhere – don't stay here – accept work – fight against people. As it is, with a rapidity unimaginable, you are going to the Devil. PULL UP NOW YOURSELF. It is really most extraordinary that I should feel so confident of dying of heart failure – and entirely Arthur's fault.[181]

'Arthur' refers to her grandfather, Arthur Beauchamp, who was afflicted with a weak heart. All her adult life, KM had concerns about her heart and believed it would be the cause of her early death.

Now it seemed that Harold too had had enough and was finding the whole situation too tiring to prolong any further. He must have called a meeting, at which KM was expected to put her case for leaving, rationally and with composure. She wrote to Vera on 12 June:

July – you can imagine how I wait for the news – my dear – surely the Fates have given me a very just share of anticipation – and Beauchamp Lodge (which, dear, like most of the pleasant things in my life – I owe to you) sounds quite ideal.[182]

It was Vera who had suggested Beauchamp Lodge to the family as suitable lodgings for KM in London (the name itself was propitious) and which cousin Henry Beauchamp in London had confirmed was entirely appropriate; it was a well-run hostel for young women, most of whom were music students. All KM needed now was confirmation of the details of her passage. She told Martha Putnam she was so happy that when she got to London 'I shall sit on the curb of Piccadilly Circus and weep for pure joy.' Martha told Harold, who replied curtly, 'She'll get a policeman to move her on.'[183]

The rest of the letter was written in a more happy and positive frame of mind:

Have you lately read Hans Andersen's Fairy Tales? If you have a copy in the house do look up the Fir Tree. The last sentence is so astonishingly Chopin I read it over & over – and the simple unearthly words flood your soul like the dying phrase of a Majorca nocturne.[184]

As KM read her copy of Andersen's tales, she must have been struck by the similarity between her own position and that of the anthropomorphised protagonist. In the fairy tale, a fir tree is so anxious to grow up and experience greater things that he simply cannot appreciate living in the moment. Cut down and decorated on Christmas Eve and topped with a beautiful gold star, the fir tree expects to be admired over the whole of Christmas. Instead, after one day of glory, when his beautifully decorated branches are plundered for their toys and treats, he is placed in the attic and left to rot. In the spring, now brown and withered, he is taken outside; a little boy removes the gold star – the only decoration remaining – and he is chopped into bits and burnt.

Psychologically, of course, KM could relate to the fir tree's anxious and futile longing for an idealised future which would never come, and she was now wise enough to recognise it. Jackie Wullschlager suggests the tale portrays a certain psychological type – an individual who cannot be happy in the moment because they always expect something even greater to happen to them in the future; continually disappointed, their life becomes one constant feeling of regret. Thus, the fir tree is 'a fantasist, vain, fearful, restless, afflicted with the trembling sensitivity of the neurotic, manically swinging from hope to misery'.[185] Andersen's tale, originally published in 1844 together with 'The Snow Queen', was written very much with the adult reader in mind. Its bourgeois, non-threatening setting enabled its fatalistic tone to be more readily accepted and allowed the reader to identify with the tragic fir tree's demise. Andersen had written tales with unhappy endings before (for example, 'The Little Mermaid' and 'The Steadfast Tin Soldier'), but in 'The Fir-Tree', the note of 'deeply ingrained pessimism, suggesting not only the mercilessness of fate but the pointlessness of life itself, that only the moment is worthwhile',[186] was an innovative departure for the author. The final lines of the story, which KM likened to a 'dying phrase of a [Chopin] Majorca nocturne', are as follows:

> The boys played in the garden, and the youngest had on his breast a golden star, which the Tree had worn on its happiest evening. Now that was past, and the Tree's life was past, and the story is past too: past! past! – that's the way with all stories.[187]

The tale would also, of course, have brought back memories of Mrs Molesworth's *Christmas-Tree Land*. Fir trees and pine trees seemed to litter KM's adolescent consciousness in a quite remarkable way.

The letter to Vera then continued:

> It is sweet of you to come home before I leave – but don't unless you wish – to – you know – dear – I'd love to see you – but I would not like you to leave for that reason – Don't, at any rate – dream of it – until my passage is literally booked – And more I think than any two other people in the world – we don't need to see each other.
>
> Here is a little news – don't call me conceited – I think I am [more] popular than almost any girl here at dances – Isn't it funny – It makes me glad – in a way – but it's a little trying – Shall I tell you the men who like

me – too much – Well Bert Rawson – Arthur Duncan – Mr [?] Chafery –
Ken Duncan – etc. – this is all very much by the way – but I tell you for
this reason – It's so unwise not to *desire* to *please* – & it is so amusing to
find these men talking quite brilliantly about Amiel's Journal –[188]

Judging from the above information, it would appear that KM had not quite
lost *all* her old ways.

By 19 June, all had been decided. As Harold so calmly noted in his
Reminiscences, completely overlooking the turmoil that had led up to his pro-
nouncement, 'There could be no question of standing in her light.'[189] KM wrote
to Vera, 'So, after all, the cable came, and I sail today fortnight – incredibly
delightful Thought! The Papanui leaves from Lyttelton on July 4th. I leave
here by the Maori July 2nd — the cable came on Wednesday morning.'[190]
These dates were, in fact, both out by two days. Her journey would start in
Wellington, from where the *Maori* would take her to Lyttelton on 4 July, to
board the New Zealand Shipping Company's steamer, *Papanui*, sailing for
England on 6 July. The *Papanui*, coincidentally, was captained by Harold's
friend, Captain T. S. Weston, whose wife, Mrs Weston, had somehow become
involved in one of KM's earlier plans to get to London. KM's long letter to Vera
was full of plans, and discussions about what she was taking with her: 'there is
a vast amount of sorting to be done – steamer clothes & otherwise [. . .] I'm
taking only half a dozen books and my photographs.'[191]

There was indeed much to be done and many social events to attend, as
Wellington society bid farewell to 'Miss K. Beauchamp'. On 19 June, there
was an entirely 'violet' tea given by Mrs Rankin-Brown, the wife of a professor of
Classics, 'when violets were introduced in every way that ingenious and artistic
fancy could devise'.[192] A competition was devised whereby all the ladies present
were asked to compose a poem 'on a violet'. This was won by 'Miss Kathleen
Beauchamp', with her offering entitled 'Why Love is Blind':

> The Cupid child, tired of the winter day,
> Wept and lamented for the skies of blue.
> Till, foolish child! he cried his eyes away –
> And violets grew.[193]

Beyond an Edwardian cult for violets, KM was also playing with the rich mytho-
logical resonances of the flower, since in many Greek myths violets spring up
where the blood of the gods or heroes has been shed. The poem itself was published in the *Free Lance* on 27 June 1908.[194] There is no record as to whether
her prize – a pink satin opera bag – made it on to the ship bound for England.
As KM noted on 26 June, in her last letter to Vera before leaving, 'So much

is taking place – farewell teas – & Bridges, and parties – that there is almost a glamour – But seeing the people now so much I realise even more fully – is that possible? – how glad I am to go –.[195]

On 1 July, the Prime Minister's daughter, Eileen Ward, gave a farewell tea for KM at the Prime Minister's residence, Awarua House, a wooden mansion on the Tinakori Road:

> Various entertainments were afforded the guests. A lady with a tea-cup told fortunes, a fine gramophone sang with the voices of Melba and Tettrazzini, and in the drawing room, under the direction of an artistic lady, the guests, blindfolded, drew autograph pictures of pigs in an album which Miss Beauchamp is to bear with her afar.[196]

KM, according to the *Evening Post*, 'wore a dark tweed tailor-made, furs, and a picturesque hat wreathed with large purple asters',[197] though sadly no posthumous image of this intriguing outfit exists.

Also on 1 July, another of KM's vignettes, 'Study: The Death of a Rose', was published in the *Triad*, an avant-garde little arts magazine based in Dunedin, in the South Island. It was one of KM's typical Wilde-inspired, self-consciously Decadent pieces of poetic prose, beginning: 'It is a sensation that can never be forgotten, to sit in solitude, in semi-darkness, and to watch the slow, sweet, shadowful death of a Rose.' The perfect little flower gradually transmutes into something far more corrupt:

> Today it is heavy and languid with the loves of a thousand strange Things, who, lured by the gold of my candlelight, came in the Purple Hours, and kissed it hotly on the mouth, and sucked it into their beautiful lips with tearing, passionate desire.
>
> [. . .] So now it dies . . . And I listen . . . for under each petal fold there lies the ghost of a dead melody, as frail and as full of suggestion as a ray of light upon a shadowed pool. Oh, divine sweet Rose. Oh, exotic and elusive and deliciously vague Death.
>
> From the tedious sobbing and gasping, and hoarse guttural scream-ing, and uncouth repulsive movements of the body of the dying Man, I draw apart, and, smiling, I lean over you and watch your dainty, delicate Death.[198]

The editor of the *Triad* obviously thought New Zealand was ready for such morbid prose, but thankfully for Harold and Annie's precious reputation, its circulation was not large.

Figure 7.31 General view, wharves and shipping, Wellington.

Just a week before her departure, KM attended one social event with Chaddie and her mother, which, for once, must have been a pleasure rather than a chore. An 'at home' was given on 29 June in Wellington by a Mr and Mrs J. Prouse in honour of the celebrated Czech violinist and composer, Jan Kubelík (1880–1940), and his wife. Sadly, there is no extant reference to this event in KM's diaries or letters, nor any evidence that she attended one of his concerts. New Zealand did receive its share of cultural icons in this period; the problem for KM was that none of them stayed. After a few short weeks, there was another ship to transport them thousands of miles away, back to the *real* world.

And so the time had come to set sail, all the details, of course, recorded by New Zealand's eager press. On arrival, KM was to go to Miss Wood at Queen's College for a few days, and then on to Beauchamp Lodge. Uncle Henry Herron, who had died on 6 October 1907, aged eighty-two, could no longer be of assistance, but his wife, KM's Great-Aunt Louey, was charged with keeping an eye on her, as were her sons. In addition, Harold would provide her with an allowance of £100 a year. It was not enough to keep her in the manner to which she was accustomed, but given that the average salary at the time was about £70 a year, it was thought sufficient by her father. The *Reminiscences* record:

Arrangements were made through the London manager of the Bank of New Zealand [. . .] for a yearly allowance of £100, payable monthly in

London. This was ample to make her secure against want, and I know that it did. Mr. Alexander Kay, the London manager [. . .] acted as both father and trusted advisor. [. . .]

Katherine's wants were not great. The life she wished to lead was one not of ostentation or gaiety, but of severe discipline and the self-denial of the artist.[199]

This may have been the line put out by Harold via his trusted friend Guy Scholefield, who wrote the chapter on KM in the *Reminiscences*, but many disagreed. Ida always maintained that one of the reasons KM went off the rails so soon after arriving in England was that she could not live on the money provided for her:

Her father made what I consider to be one fatal mistake; he gave her very little money, only forty shillings a week: thirty shillings for the hostel and ten shillings for everything else — writing paper, music lessons, bus fares, clothes and all the other necessities. This led her into many real difficulties. Katherine had had no financial experience and came from a very comfortable home. Her new poverty infected her with a constant anxiety about money, that dogged her all her life.[200]

Nevertheless, this was all in KM's uncertain future. On 4 July, the *Free Lance* announced, 'Miss Kathleen Beauchamp leaves for England this week by the *Papanui*, to continue her literary studies.'[201] Indeed, on 4 July, with trunks all packed and the endurance test of enough farewell parties to last a lifetime now finally at an end, KM, together with her parents, boarded the *Maori* to sail from Wellington to Lyttelton, from where she finally boarded the *Papanui*, which set sail on 6 July. According to the *Dominion*, there were twenty-five passengers in total on the *Papanui*, of whom only three were women.[202] KM was also one of only three 'saloon class' passengers, and, thanks to the friendship between Captain Weston and Harold, her ticket was complimentary.[203] On board, she would make trouble for herself by composing a small daily paper for the passengers, but with content that was too risqué for the captain, who tried to persuade her to give up this little pastime. Years later, Captain Weston recalled his — by now well-known — former passenger with the terse words, 'Couldn't abide the woman.'[204]

With freedom, of the sort KM had craved for so long, also came responsibility, but somehow, in the heady cocktail of London and liberty, this was overlooked. Even if the 'amethyst outlook', KM's diary codename for her same-sex relationships, was now a thing of the past, for the next three years, at least, KM would make it her business to experience 'life', whatever the consequences. As a result, for many years afterwards, in the town of her birth, society ladies would speak her name in hushed tones. A percipient comment was made by Dr Fyffe (one of her musical acquaintances), a few weeks before she left New Zealand, in discussion with a young Englishman, Ray Willis, who had found KM captivating and remarked on the uniqueness of her personality. Dr Fyffe agreed, but then said, "'She's doomed. [. . .] You know how often pleurisy spells T.B. later on."'[205] He had noticed that KM was prone to chest infections on more than one occasion.

When Mantz interviewed Harold (now 'Sir' Harold) in 1931,

fear lay at the back of his small blue eyes [as he] tried manfully to recall the childhood of his third daughter. 'Her *Journal* hurt many people in New Zealand', he said; then he added, 'But I don't think she meant it that way.'[206]

It would take some time in New Zealand before embarrassment and condemnation would turn to admiration and veneration. Indeed, for many years, a story circulated in Wellington that Harold

had the boats met as they swung at anchor in Wellington Harbor so the early books of his daughter, Kathleen, could be thrown overboard. Others denied the story as 'exaggerated'; in any case, her early published works could not be found in Wellington. Sir Harold had no copy of *Bliss* to leave to New Zealand.[207]

KM left New Zealand a published writer, no longer 'Kathleen Beauchamp' but 'K. Mansfield', still uncertain perhaps of which direction her writing would go, but already with the knowledge that the Victorian style of commonplace analysis and description (and later on, the late Victorian, theatrically opulent prose of Wilde and the Decadents) would not be her literary path. The modernist revelation of character through narrative voice – through suggestion and symbolism – would become her method, where she would offer glimpses into the lives of individuals, families, captured at a certain moment, frozen in time like a painting or snapshot. And though she was not aware of it, as the S.S. *Papanui* steamed away from the shores of New Zealand towards Europe and the glittering lights of London, with KM's eyes resolutely fixed on the horizon ahead and not on the coast left behind, it was New Zealand – mostly Wellington and the streets of Thorndon – that would eventually provide the inspiration for her finest stories.

Notes

The following frequently used texts and libraries are abbreviated thus in the Notes:

ATL
Alexander Turnbull Library, Wellington, New Zealand

CW1, CW2
Gerri Kimber and Vincent O'Sullivan, eds, *The Edinburgh Edition of the Collected Works of Katherine Mansfield: Vols 1 and 2 – The Collected Fiction* (Edinburgh: Edinburgh University Press, 2012)

CW3
Gerri Kimber and Angela Smith, eds, *The Edinburgh Edition of the Collected Works of Katherine Mansfield: Vol. 3 – The Poetry and Critical Writings* (Edinburgh: Edinburgh University Press, 2014)

CW4
Gerri Kimber and Claire Davison, eds, *The Edinburgh Edition of the Collected Works of Katherine Mansfield: Vol. 4 – The Diaries, including Miscellaneous Works* (Edinburgh: Edinburgh University Press, 2016)

HRC
Harry Ransom Center, University of Texas at Austin, USA

L1, L2, L3, L4, L5
Vincent O'Sullivan and Margaret Scott, eds, *The Collected Letters of Katherine Mansfield*, 5 vols (Oxford: Clarendon Press, 1984–2008)

MM
Ruth Elvish Mantz and John Middleton Murry, *The Life of Katherine Mansfield* (London: Constable, 1933)

Introduction
1. Anders Iversen, 'Life and letters: Katherine Mansfield drawing on Kathleen Beauchamp', *English Studies*, 52: 1–6, 1971, pp. 44–54 (p. 44).
2. Regarding the main biographies' attention to her early life, this attention comprises: Kathleen Jones, *Katherine Mansfield: A Writer's Life* (Edinburgh: Edinburgh University Press, 2010), no discussion of her early life; Claire Tomalin, *Katherine Mansfield: A Secret Life* (London: Viking, 1987), 38 pages out of 291; Antony Alpers, *The Life of Katherine Mansfield* (London: Jonathan Cape, 1980), 66 pages out of 466; Jeffrey Meyers, *Katherine Mansfield: A Biography* (London: Hamish Hamilton, 1978), 35 pages out of 296.
3. Ian Gordon, *Katherine Mansfield*, Writers and Their Work, no. 49 (London: Longmans, Green & Co., 1954), p. 7.
4. Gordon, pp. 15–16.
5. HRC: Ruth Elvish Mantz Collection, Box 3. 'Unidentified research notes'.
6. Gordon, p. 19.
7. CW2, p. 59.

Chapter 1. Ancestors
1. See Elizabeth Beauchamp Naylor, *A Colourful Tapestry: Tales of the Beauchamps and Elliots* (privately printed, 2009).
2. Naylor, p. 77.
3. Sir Harold Beauchamp, *Reminiscences and Recollections* (New Plymouth: Thomas Avery & Sons, 1937), p. 4.
4. Beauchamp, p. 4.
5. The full poem was supplied to Mantz by Harold Beauchamp in 1932.
6. Quoted in Gillian Boddy, *Katherine Mansfield: The Woman and the Writer* (Ringwood, Australia: Penguin: 1988).
7. Beauchamp, p. 13.
8. Naylor, p. 86.
9. Ethel Beauchamp Hazelwood, *Life at Anakiwa: The First 100 Years 1863–1963* (privately printed booklet), p. 14.
10. Naylor, p. 241.
11. A. D. McIntosh, ed., *Marlborough: A Provincial History* (Christchurch, NZ: Capper Press, 1977), p. 249.
12. See Julie Kennedy, *Katherine Mansfield in Picton* (Auckland: Cape Catley, 2000), p. 43.

Chapter 2. Harold and Annie Beauchamp
1. HM 77563 Henry Herron Beauchamp, Journal, 1900–1906. Huntington Library, San Marino, California, p. 307.

2. HM77557, Henry Herron Beauchamp, Journal, 1880–1888. Huntington Library, San Marino, California, 17 September 1898, p. 100.
3. HM 77563 Henry Herron Beauchamp, Journal, 1900–1906. Huntington Library, San Marino, California, p. 153.
4. The kakapo, with its yellow–green plumage, is the world's only flightless parrot. Native to New Zealand and revered by the Maori, it is now critically endangered.
5. The tui (also known as koko or parson-bird) is a striking, black-and-white, tufted bird native to New Zealand, highly valued by the Maori, and noted for its unusual call.
6. Beauchamp, p. 30.
7. ATL: MS-Papers-3981-141. Maude Morris, miscellaneous papers.
8. Beauchamp, p. 42.
9. L4, p. 172.
10. Quoted in Kennedy, p. 58.
11. L2, p. 27.
12. Beauchamp, p. 69.
13. CW1, p. 212.
14. CW2, p. 355.
15. *Te Ara Encyclopedia of New Zealand*, <http://www.teara.govt.nz/en/abortion/page-1> (last accessed 10 September 2015).

Chapter 3. 11 Tinakori Road: 1888–1893
1. Terence Hodgson, *Colonial Capital: Wellington 1865–1910* (Auckland: Random Century, 1990), p. 44.
2. Hodgson, p. 44.
3. Hodgson, p. 45.
4. Hodgson, p. 46.
5. Beauchamp, p. 85.
6. Beauchamp, p. 82.
7. Katherine Mansfield Birthplace, 'The House', pamphlet, n.p.
8. Barbara Angus, *A Guide to Katherine Mansfield's Wellington* (Wellington: Katherine Mansfield Birthplace, 1987), p. 3.
9. Job 42: 14.
10. Another theory discusses the possibility that she was born in a hot air balloon, since higher altitudes were supposed to induce birth and Annie was overdue. See Charles Ferrall, 'Mansfield's birth up in the air', *Dominion Post*, 17 February 2007, E 8.
11. CW1, pp. 472–3.
12. CW1, p. 472.
13. CW1, p. 206.
14. HRC: Ruth Elvish Mantz Collection, Box 3. 'Unidentified research papers'.
15. CW4, p. 115.
16. CW4, p. 397, p. 407.
17. MM, p. 65.

18. MM, p. 73.
19. CW1, p. 473.
20. CW4, pp. 226–8.
21. Certain things in this recollection, however, were misplaced, since the cherry trees belonged to Chesney Wold, Karori, as, in fact, did the washerwoman, Mrs Kelvey.
22. The cemetery, as old as Wellington itself (founded in 1840), was the centre of a huge controversy in the 1960s, when part of it was selected as the main route for the new proposed motorway cutting through Wellington. 'The cemetery was closed for three years while about 3700 burials were exhumed and reinterred in a vault under the lower cemetery lawn.' The cemetery is now split in two and linked by a footbridge (Bolton Street Memorial Park brochure). Coincidentally, one of Jane Beauchamp's original land sections adjoined Bolton Street Cemetery.
23. MM, p. 76.

Chapter 4. Chesney Wold, Karori: 1893–1898
1. Beauchamp, p. 85.
2. Francis Braybrooke, '"My Dear Clara" – Karori Eighty Years Ago', *Stockade*, 16: 11, October 1983, p. 9.
3. CW1, pp. 29–31.
4. HRC: Ruth Elvish Mantz Collection, Box 2. 'The Inexplicable Past', p. 8.
5. HRC: Ruth Elvish Mantz Collection, Box 3. 'Unidentified research notes'.
6. CW4, p. 167.
7. CW1, p. 33.
8. CW1, pp. 451–2.
9. MM, p. 77.
10. HRC: Ruth Elvish Mantz Collection, Box 2. 'The Inexplicable Past', p. 8.
11. MM, p. 79.
12. MM, p. 79.
13. CW4, p. 247.
14. See L2, p. 356 (9 September 1919).
15. HRC: Ruth Elvish Mantz Collection, Box 3. 'Unidentified research notes'.
16. Angus, p. 6.
17. HRC: Ruth Elvish Mantz Collection, Box 3. 'Unidentified research notes'.
18. CW1, p. 168.
19. CW1, p. 171.
20. CW1, p. 171.
21. CW2, p. 378.
22. HRC: Ruth Elvish Mantz Collection, Box 3. 'Unidentified research notes'. In KM's 'Summer Idylle' (1907), a story based on the friendship between herself and Maata, one of the characters is called Hinemoa.
23. MM, p. 97. Annie Beauchamp's eldest sister Eliza married William Trapp in 1879, and emigrated to Australia with their son Burney (b. 1880); Eliza and

Burney moved back to New Zealand and Karori in 1899, following the death of her husband.

24. L4, p. 278.
25. MM, p. 99.
26. 'She remained for life and was so appreciated that Mrs Waters left her a section at the end of their property and enough money to build a house [. . .] When she died in 1950 she was buried in the Waters family plot.' Margaret H. Alington, *High Point: St Mary's Church, Karori, Wellington, 1861–1991* (Wellington: Parish of St Mary and the Karori Historical Society, 1998), p. 244.
27. Alington, p. 161.
28. See Alington, p. 99.
29. 'Omana Chimes', 'Katherine Mansfield at School', *N.Z. Dairy Exporter Annual (Inc. Tui's Annual)*, 10 October 1929, p. 38.
30. CW2, p. 416.
31. CW2, pp. 416–17.
32. HRC: Ruth Elvish Mantz Collection, Box 3. 'Unidentified research notes'.
33. A dray is a low, strong cart without fixed sides, mainly used for carrying heavy loads.
34. HRC: Ruth Elvish Mantz Collection, Box 3. 'Unidentified research notes'.
35. MM, p. 2.
36. CW2, pp. 345–6.
37. CW2, p. 365.

Chapter 5. Back to Thorndon: 75 Tinakori Road, 1898–1903

1. L5, p. 61.
2. L5, p. 67.
3. Beauchamp, p. 88.
4. See Ian A. Gordon, ed., *Victorian Voyage, Annie Beauchamp: The Shipboard Diary of Katherine Mansfield's Mother March to May, 1898* (Auckland: Wilson & Horton, 2000).
5. Gordon, *Victorian Voyage*, p. 25.
6. Gordon, *Victorian Voyage*, p. 28.
7. Gordon, *Victorian Voyage*, p. 30.
8. Gordon, *Victorian Voyage*, p. 31.
9. Gordon, *Victorian Voyage*, pp. 50–1.
10. Gordon, *Victorian Voyage*, p. 55.
11. Gordon, *Victorian Voyage*, p. 68.
12. Gordon, *Victorian Voyage*, p. 69.
13. Gordon, *Victorian Voyage*, p. 73.
14. Gordon, *Victorian Voyage*, p. 74.
15. Gordon, *Victorian Voyage*, pp. 81–2.
16. Gordon, *Victorian Voyage*, p. 82.
17. CW4, pp. 176–7.
18. CW2, p. 408.

19. CW1, p. 3.
20. MM, p. 137.
21. ATL: Marion C. Ruddick, 'Incidents in the Childhood of Katherine Mansfield', unpublished typescript MS-Papers-1339, pp. 11–12. Subsequently published in *Chicago Evening Post Literary Review*, 20 April 1928.
22. Ruddick, pp. 5–6.
23. Antony Alpers, *Katherine Mansfield: A Biography* (London: Jonathan Cape, 1954), p. 46.
24. Ruddick, p. 7.
25. Ruddick, p. 9.
26. Ruddick, pp. 9–10.
27. Ruddick, p. 10.
28. Ruddick, p. 16.
29. Ruddick, p. 18.
30. CW4, p. 177.
31. Ruddick, p. 21.
32. Ruddick, pp. 22–3.
33. Ruddick, p. 24.
34. Mrs Molesworth, *Christmas-Tree Land* (London: Macmillan, 1981 [1884]), p. 189.
35. Molesworth, p. 32.
36. Ruddick, pp. 49–50.
37. Ruddick, p. 29.
38. Ruddick, p. 2.
39. Ruddick, p. 33.
40. Ruddick, p. 35.
41. Ruddick, p. 42.
42. Ruddick, p. 59.
43. Ruddick, p. 61.
44. Ruddick, p. 64.
45. Ruddick, p. 68.
46. Ruddick, p. 69.
47. Ruddick, p. 69.
48. CW2, pp. 342–3.
49. L4, p. 261.
50. KM's memories of 'The Glen' may also have been intertwined with another holiday home possibly rented by Harold for the family in 1895 (the year after Lesley's birth), in the same spot but on the seaward side of the Muritai Road, which would then allow for KM's details in the story to be accurate (for example, Stanley leaving by the back door of the cottage to run over the sand dunes and so on). I am grateful to Beverley Randell for offering this tantalising suggestion.
51. Ruddick, p. 72.
52. Ruddick, p. 73.
53. Ruddick, pp. 73–4.

54. L4, p. 258 (30 July 1921).
55. L4, p. 266 (21 August 1921).
56. CW1, p. 6.
57. MM, p. 137.
58. CW4, pp. 169–70.
59. See Tomalin, p. 15.
60. CW2, p. 427.
61. MM, p. 159.
62. HRC, Ruth Elvish Mantz Collection, Box 3. 'Unidentified research notes'.
63. Alpers, *Biography*, p. 50.
64. HRC, Ruth Elvish Mantz Collection, Box 3. 'Unidentified research notes'.
65. See Pat Lawlor, 'Wellington and Katherine Mansfield', *Old Wellington Days* (Wellington: Whitcombe & Tombs, 1959), pp. 167–87 (p. 177).
66. MM, p. 148.
67. CW1, p. 319.
68. MM, p. 153.
69. MM, p. 152.
70. Mrs Jarley and her waxworks feature in Charles Dickens's *The Old Curiosity Shop* (1841).
71. ATL: MSX-5969. Katherine Mansfield's autograph book.
72. CW2, p. 227.
73. CW2, p. 226.
74. Quoted in Tomalin, p. 16.
75. Beauchamp, p. 47.
76. Beauchamp, p. 86.
77. MM, p. 158.
78. CW1, pp. 43–4.
79. Anon., 'Children of the Sun God', *Cremona*, 1: 4, 16 March 1907, p. 37.
80. Martin Griffiths, 'Arnold Trowell – Violoncellist, Composer and Pedagogue' (unpublished thesis, University of Waikato, NZ, 2012), p. 29.
81. 'Christabel', 'Social Gossip', *New Zealand Free Lance*, 3 August 1901, p. 10.
82. Griffiths, p. 49.
83. Anonymous article in the *New Zealand Herald*, quoted in Griffiths, p. 54.
84. CW1, pp. 42–3.

Chapter 6. Queen's College, London: 1903–1906

1. This would lead to confusion in later years, when even the *Encyclopedia Britannica* would give KM's date of birth as 1890.
2. Beauchamp, pp. 87–8.
3. CW3, p. 12.
4. CW3, p. 15.
5. Strangely omitted from the O'Sullivan / Scott edition of the *Letters*. John Middleton Murry, ed., *The Letters of Katherine Mansfield*, 2 vols (London: Constable, 1928), Vol. 2, p. 222.

6. HRC: Ruth Elvish Mantz Collection, Box 3. 'Unidentified research notes'.
7. L1, p. 4.
8. L1, pp. 4–5.
9. HM 77563 Henry Herron Beauchamp, Journal, 1900–1906. Huntington Library, San Marino, California, p. 154.
10. ATL: MSX-5218. Katherine Mansfield, *Buch der Lieder von Heinrich Heine*.
11. L1, p. 9.
12. L1, p. 14.
13. HM 77563 Henry Herron Beauchamp, Journal, 1900–1906. Huntington Library, San Marino, California, p. 163.
14. It is curious to note that on the night of the 1911 national census, both Ida Baker and her sister May were staying at Ridge Cap.
15. Elaine Kaye, *A History of Queen's College, London 1848–1972* (London: Chatto & Windus, 1972), p. 136.
16. CW3, pp. 6–7.
17. ATL: MSX-5969. Katherine Mansfield's autograph book.
18. Ida Baker, *Katherine Mansfield: The Memories of LM* (London: Michael Joseph, 1971), p. 24.
19. The book was unfinished at the time of his death in 1907; it was completed by H. C. Minchin and published by Methuen in 1910.
20. Kaye mistakenly notes in her history of Queen's College that Gregory was made Astronomer Royal, an error subsequently replicated by Alpers in his 1980 biography. See Kaye, p. 128.
21. Baker, p. 25.
22. Alpers, *Life*, p. 31.
23. Kaye, p. 127.
24. CW1, p. 52.
25. Reverend S. A. Tipple, *Sunday Mornings at Norwood, Being Twenty-Two Sermons and Twenty-Two Prayers* (London: Kegan Paul, Trench & Co., 1883), pp. 16–17.
26. ATL: MSX-5969. Katherine Mansfield's autograph book. Maurice Maeterlinck, *La Sagesse et la destinée* (1898), Ch. XVI. 'Whether there is pleasure or misfortune, the happiest man will always be the one in whom the greatest idea lives alongside the greatest enthusiasm' (my translation).
27. HRC: Ruth Elvish Mantz Collection, Box 3. 'Unidentified research notes'.
28. L1, p. 10.
29. The poem, 'Erinnerung – an C. N.' ('Unforgotten – for C. N.') is a love poem by the German poet Eduard Mörike (1804–75). Her memory of these four lines from the much longer poem only loosely follows the original: 'Yes, that was the last time / That, we together, arm in arm / Huddled under a bent umbrella / All was for the last time' (my translation).
30. L1, pp. 191–2.
31. CW1, pp. 201–2.
32. HRC: Ruth Elvish Mantz Collection, Box 2. 'Being natural is simply a pose', p. 23.

33. HRC: Ruth Elvish Mantz Collection, Box 2. 'Being natural is simply a pose', p. 23.
34. CW4, pp. 16–18.
35. CW4, p. 18.
36. CW3, p. 22.
37. L1, p. 5.
38. Baker, p. 24.
39. MM, p. 197.
40. ATL: MS-Papers-6984-47. Ian A. Gordon, Notes re: Katherine Mansfield.
41. CW4, pp. 189–90.
42. Meyers, p. 16.
43. ATL: MSX-5969. Katherine Mansfield's autograph book.
44. Baker, p. 29.
45. CW2, p. 65.
46. CW2, p. 76.
47. Beauchamp, p. 87.
48. CW1, pp. 44–5.
49. Alpers, *Life*, p. 27.
50. CW2, p. 162.
51. Baker, p. 22.
52. MM, p. 178.
53. CW1, p. 79.
54. CW1, p. 134.
55. CW3, pp. 8–9.
56. Alpers, *Life*, p. 27.
57. Baker, p. 19.
58. Baker, p. 29.
59. Boddy, *Woman and Writer*, p. 9.
60. Meyers, p. 18.
61. Baker, p. 22.
62. Baker, p. 26, calls her Evelyn (Eve), perhaps confusing her with KM's cousin, Evelyn Payne.
63. Baker, p. 26.
64. MM, p. 198.
65. MM, p. 182.
66. Baker, p. 26.
67. Baker, p. 26.
68. See Gillian Boddy, *Katherine Mansfield: A 'Do You Remember' Life* (Wellington: Victoria University Press with the Katherine Mansfield Birthplace Society Inc., 1996), p. 22.
69. Ruth Herrick, 'They Were at School Together', *New Zealand Listener*, 7, 25 September 1942, p. 12.
70. Boddy, *Woman and Writer*, p. 9.
71. CW4, p. 15.

72. Alpers, *Life*, p. 34.
73. Meyers, p. 15.
74. Baker, p. 26.
75. L1, p. 11.
76. MM, p. 198.
77. See CW4, p. 152.
78. L1, p. 355.
79. HRC, Ruth Elvish Mantz Collection, Box 3. 'Unidentified research notes'.
80. CW3, p. 23.
81. CW3, p. 15.
82. L1, pp. 7–8.
83. Baker, p. 28.
84. CW2, pp. 271–2.
85. David Daiches, *New Literary Values: Studies in Modern Literature* (London: Oliver & Boyd, 1969), p. 105.
86. *Queen's College Magazine*, 75, March 1904, p. 139.
87. *Queen's College Magazine*, 77, December 1904, p. 226.
88. *Queen's College Magazine*, 77, December 1904, p. 229.
89. *Queen's College Magazine*, 77, December 1904, p. 232.
90. *Queen's College Magazine*, 78, February 1905, pp. 273–4.
91. *Queen's College Magazine*, 78, February 1905, p. 277.
92. *Queen's College Magazine*, 81, April 1906, p. 245.
93. L1, p. 15.
94. L1, p. 17.
95. CW1, p. 15.
96. CW1, p. 16.
97. CW1, p. 10.
98. CW1, p. 12.
99. CW1, p. 17.
100. CW1, pp. 17–18.
101. CW1, pp. 14–15.
102. Ernest Dowson, 'The Visit', in *Decorations* (London: John Lane, 1899):

As though I were still struggling through the meshes of some riotous dream, I heard his knock upon the door. As in a dream, I bade him enter, but with his entry, I awoke. Yet when he entered it seemed to me that I was dreaming, for there was nothing strange in that supreme and sorrowful smile which shone through the mask which I knew. And just as though I had not always been afraid of him I said: 'Welcome.'

And he said very simply, 'I am here.'

Dreaming I had thought myself, but the reproachful sorrow of his smile showed me that I was awake. Then dared I open my eyes and I saw my old body on the bed, and the room in which I had grown so tired, and in the middle of the room the pan of charcoal which still smouldered. And dimly I remembered my great weariness and the lost whiteness of Lalage and last year's snows; and these things had been agonies.

Darkly, as in a dream, I wondered why they gave me no more hurt, as I looked at my old body on the bed; why, they were like old maids' fancies (as I looked at my grey body on the bed of my agonies) – like silly toys of children that fond mothers lay up in lavender (as I looked at the twisted limbs of my old body), for these things had been agonies.

But all my wonder was gone when I looked again into the eyes of my guest, and I said:

'I have wanted you all my life.'

Then said Death (and what reproachful tenderness was shadowed in his obscure smile):

'You had only to call.'

103. Arthur Symons, *Studies in Prose in Verse* (London: J. M. Dent, 1904).
104. CW4, p. 11.
105. CW1, pp. 20–1.
106. CW1, p. 21.
107. L1, p. 15.
108. Alpers, *Life*, p. 34.
109. L1, p. 15.
110. CW1, p. 31.
111. This may be William Charles Hann (1863–1925), who studied with Piatti. See Griffiths, p. 414.
112. CW4, pp. 13–14.
113. CW4, p. 22.
114. CW3, pp. 23–4.
115. Garnet Trowell, 'A Magician of the Cello', *New Zealand Mail*, 4 July 1906, p. 28.
116. Baker, pp. 31–2.
117. L1, p. 18.
118. HM 77563 Henry Herron Beauchamp, Journal, 1900–1906. Huntington Library, San Marino, California, p. 175.
119. MM, p. 218.
120. CW3, pp. 25–6.
121. MM, p. 221.
122. CW4, p. 58.
123. See Tomalin, p. 29.
124. CW1, pp. 50–1.
125. George Bernard Shaw, *Mrs Warren's Profession* (1893), first performed in 1902.
126. ATL: MS-Papers-7798-25.
127. Baker, p. 31.
128. Baker, p. 31.
129. CW1, p. 38.
130. Beauchamp, p. 88.

131. CW1, p. 53.

132. In 1910, the Duke of Argyll would unveil a memorial to Seddon in London, in St Paul's Cathedral.

133. See Anon., 'A Merchant Abroad', *Evening Post*, 72: 136, 6 December 1906, p. 7.

134. HM 77563 Henry Herron Beauchamp, Journal, 1900–1906. Huntington Library, San Marino, California, pp. 179–80.

135. HM 77563 Henry Herron Beauchamp, Journal, 1900–1906. Huntington Library, San Marino, California, p. 180.

136. MM, p. 224.

Chapter 7. Thorndon: 1906–1908

1. Greg Ryan, 'New Zealand', in Brian Stoddart and Keith A. Sandiford, eds, *The Imperial Game: Cricket, Culture and Society* (Manchester: Manchester University Press, 1998), pp. 93–115 (p. 107).

2. Beauchamp, p. 89.

3. For details, see P. R. May, *With the MCC in New Zealand* (London: Eyre & Spottiswoode, 1907).

4. May, p. 4.

5. Information regarding the MCC cricket team kindly supplied by Neil Robinson, Librarian and Research Manager, MCC.

6. CW4, pp. 23–5.

7. CW4, pp. 25–6.

8. HRC: Ruth Elvish Mantz Collection, Box 3. 'Unidentified research notes'.

9. CW3, pp. 27–8.

10. CW3, p. 28.

11. Anon., 'A Merchant Abroad', *Evening Post*, 72: 136, 6 December 1906, p. 7.

12. CW4, p. 191.

13. L1, p. 21.

14. L1, p. 21.

15. (Ger.) 'Homesickness'.

16. L1, p. 21.

17. Beauchamp, p. 193.

18. Meyers, p. 22.

19. Baker, p. 33.

20. CW1, p. 294

21. MM, p. 237.

22. Beauchamp, p. 194.

23. Tomalin, p. 32.

24. Alpers, *Life*, p. 46.

25. CW2, p. 411.

26. J. Lawrence Mitchell, 'Katherine Mansfield's War', in Gerri Kimber, Todd Martin, Delia da Sousa Correa, Isobel Maddison and Alice Kelly, eds, *Katherine Mansfield and World War One* (Edinburgh: Edinburgh University Press, 2014), pp. 27–41 (pp. 30–1).

27. Alpers, *Life*, p. 182.
28. Alpers, *Life*, p. 45.
29. CW4, p. 35.
30. CW4, pp. 36–7.
31. Baker, p. 33.
32. MM, p. 251.
33. MM, p. 251.
34. Anon., 'All Sorts of People', *Free Lance*, 7: 354, 13 April 1907, p. 3.
35. CW2, p. 496.
36. MM, p. 232.
37. CW1, pp. 41–2.
38. CW4, p. 40.
39. CW4, p. 40.
40. CW4, p. 41.
41. Alpers, *Life*, p. 48.
42. 'Priscilla', 'Ladies Column', *Evening Post*, 73: 105, 4 May 1907, p. 15.
43. Probably the French 'par exemple' ('for example').
44. L3, p. 270.
45. L5, p. 67.
46. L1, p. 21.
47. HRC: Katherine Mansfield Collection, 3.6, Maata Mahupuku journal typescript.
48. CW1, pp. 66–7.
49. Havelock Ellis, *Studies in the Psychology of Sex*, vol. 4, *Sexual Selection in Man* (Philadelphia: F. A. Davis, 1905), p. 75.
50. Anne Olivier Bell, ed., *The Diary of Virginia Woolf*, 5 vols (London: Hogarth, 1977–1985), Vol. 1 (1977), p. 58.
51. CW1, p. 68.
52. According to Tomalin, Maata was also at this time, however, making marriage plans: 'Maata married twice. She had two daughters of the second marriage, and spent her fortune lavishly until it was gone: she had "plenty of charm a clever talker and in her adult years a distinct disinclination to sleep by herself" (p. 34).
53. CW1, p. 72.
54. Tomalin, p. 35.
55. Tomalin, p. 35.
56. CW3, p. 41.
57. 'Elizabeth', *The April Baby's Book of Tunes* (London: Macmillan, 1900).
58. See CW2, p. 64.
59. CW3, p. 38.
60. CW3, pp. 38–9.
61. Alpers, *Life*, p. 47.
62. CW4, p. 47.
63. CW4, pp. 47–9.
64. CW4, p. 49.
65. CW4, p. 49.

66. CW4, pp. 49–50.
67. Lewis Carroll, *Alice in Wonderland* (London: Macmillan, 1995 [1866]), p. 35.
68. CW4, p. 51.
69. CW4, p. 51.
70. CW4, p. 51.
71. CW4, pp. 51–2.
72. CW4, p. 52.
73. Tomalin offers a fascinating theory concerning KM's brief relationship with Edie Bendall and a similar relationship between a young girl and an older woman in D. H. Lawrence's *The Rainbow*. See Tomalin, pp. 37–8.
74. L1, p. 40.
75. CW4, p. 53.
76. Baker, p. 34.
77. Boddy, *Woman and Writer*, p. 15.
78. CW4, p. 30. From *Le Journal de Marie Bashkirtseff*, first published in 1887.
79. CW4, p. 57.
80. CW4, p. 53.
81. CW4, p. 54.
82. CW4, p. 54.
83. CW4, pp. 55–6.
84. CW4, p. 55.
85. ATL: MS-Papers-8964. Letters from Kathleen Beauchamp to Mr Thomas Trowell, Esq.
86. Anon., 'Government House "At Home"', *Evening Post*, 27: 77, 27 September 1907, p. 2.
87. Beauchamp, p. 196.
88. Jean E. Stone, *Katherine Mansfield: Publications in Australia 1907–09* (Sydney: Wentworth Books, 1977), p. 13.
89. Beauchamp, p. 197.
90. Beauchamp, p. 197.
91. See Stone, p. 10.
92. Stone, pp. 10–11.
93. L1, p. 26.
94. MM, pp. 225–6.
95. L5, p. 114.
96. HRC: Ruth Elvish Mantz Collection, Box 3. 'Unidentified research notes'.
97. CW1, p. 80.
98. CW1, pp. 78–9.
99. CW1, pp. 83–4.
100. CW1, p. 8.
101. CW1, p. 87.
102. Alpers, *Biography*, pp. 89–90.
103. Anon, 'Social and Personal', *Dominion*, 1: 29, 29 October 1907, p. 3.
104. L1, pp. 28–9.

105. Anon. [Tom L. Mills], 'Australian Magazines', *Feilding Star*, 2: 404, 24 October 1907, p. 2.

106. Anon. [Tom L. Mills], 'Local and General', *Feilding Star*, 2: 456, 28 December 1907, p. 2.

107. Anon, 'Day by Day: A Social Diary', *Dominion*, 1: 27, 19 October 1907, p. 3.

108. See Ian A. Gordon, ed., *The Urewera Notebook by Katherine Mansfield* (Oxford: Oxford University Press, 1978), p. 23.

109. CW2, p. 321.

110. Anon., 'Social and Personal', *Dominion*, 1: 50, 22 November 1907, p. 3.

111. Alpers, *Biography*, p. 80.

112. CW4, pp. 57–8.

113. The most recent edition, fully annotated, is Anna Plumridge's *The Urewera Notebook* (Edinburgh: Edinburgh University Press, 2015).

114. Misremembered by KM, the quotation, from *The Picture of Dorian Gray*, actually says, 'The one charm of the past is that it is the past. But women never know when the curtain has fallen.'

115. CW4, pp. 59–60.

116. ATL: MS-Papers-3981-141. Maude Morris, miscellaneous papers.

117. CW4, pp. 60–1.

118. CW4, p. 62.

119. ATL: MS-Papers-3981-141. Maude Morris, miscellaneous papers.

120. CW4, pp. 64–5.

121. Beauchamp, p. 49. See also Naylor, p. 4.

122. ATL: MS-Papers-6425. Margaret Scott research papers on Katherine Mansfield.

123. ATL: MS-Papers-4010. Henry Graydon Cook. Letters regarding investigations into Katherine Mansfield.

124. CW4, p. 66.

125. CW4, p. 69.

126. First published in *Rhythm*, 11, 1: 4, Spring 1912, pp. 7–21.

127. Gordon, *Urewera Notebook*, pp. 89–90.

128. CW4, p. 78.

129. CW4, p. 81.

130. CW4, p. 81.

131. CW3, p. 34.

132. CW3, p. 36.

133. Anon., 'Social and Personal', *Dominion*, 1: 72, 18 December 1907, p. 3.

134. L1, p. 35.

135. Anon., 'Social and Personal', *Dominion*, 1: 63, 7 December 1907, p. 10.

136. 'Christabel', 'Social Gossip', *Free Lance*, 8: 386, 23 November 1903, p. 8.

137. Anon., 'Social and Personal', *Dominion*, 1: 63, 7 December 1907, p. 10.

138. Anon., 'Ladies Column: Girls' Gossip', *Evening Post*, 74: 150, 21 December 1907, p. 19.

139. CW4, pp. 82–3.

140. CW4, p. 84.

141. Alpers, *Life*, p. 59.

142. Baker, p. 37.

143. ATL: MS-Papers-8964. Letters from Kathleen Beauchamp to Mr Thomas Trowell, Esq.

144. CW4, pp. 85–6 (translation in n. 3, p. 85).

145. HRC: Ruth Elvish Mantz Collection, Box 3. 'Unidentified research notes'.

146. HRC: Ruth Elvish Mantz Collection, Box 3. 'Unidentified research notes'.

147. CW2, p. 329.

148. CW4, p. 58.

149. HRC: Ruth Elvish Mantz Collection, Box 3. 'Unidentified research papers'.

150. The inn has the oldest continuously operated licence in the whole of New Zealand.

151. ATL: qMS-1244. John Middleton Murry Collection. Katherine Mansfield, notebook 2.

152. (Fr.): 'For the first time ever, I await the crisis of my life.'

153. CW4, pp. 106–7.

154. Boddy, *Woman and Writer*, p. 23.

155. Lawlor, p. 177.

156. CW4, p. 87.

157. CW4, p. 89.

158. Anon., 'Social and Personal', *Dominion*, 1: 149, 18 March 1908, p. 3.

159. CW1, pp. 103–5.

160. CW1, p. 110.

161. CW1, p. 111.

162. See 'Two Tuppenny Ones Please', 'Late at Night', 'The Black Cap', 'In Confidence', 'The Common Round' and 'A Pic-nic'.

163. CW1, p. 118.

164. L1, p. 43.

165. L1, pp. 40–1.

166. ATL: MS-Papers-7293-08. Pat Lawlor correspondence relating to Katherine Mansfield.

167. L1, p. 42.

168. L1, p. 42.

169. L1, p. 42.

170. L1, p. 45.

171. L1, p. 45.

172. Anon., 'Personal Items', *New Zealand Herald*, 45: 13722, 11 April 1908, p. 8.

173. Information courtesy of Susan Price.

174. CW4, p. 90.

175. CW2, p. 468.

176. CW4, p. 408.

177. CW4, p. 91.

178. CW4, pp. 91–2.

179. Kathleen Beauchamp, 'A Little Boy's Dream', *Dominion*, 1: 221, 11 June 1908, p. 5.

180. CW1, p.134.
181. CW4, pp.92–3.
182. L1, p.47.
183. HRC: Ruth Elvish Mantz Collection, Box 3. 'Unidentified research notes'.
184. L1, p.48.
185. Jackie Wullschlager, *Hans Christian Andersen: The Life of a Storyteller* (Chicago: University of Chicago Press, 2002), p.248.
186. Wullschlager, p.249.
187. Hans Christian Andersen, *Stories for the Household* (New York: McLoughlin Bros, 1893), p.214. Special thanks to Fiona Oliver, curator at the ATL, for locating this copy, which is, I believe, the version to which KM is referring.
188. L1, pp.47–8.
189. Beauchamp, p.90.
190. L1, p.49.
191. L1, p.52.
192. Anon., 'Social and Personal', *Dominion*, 1: 229, 20 June 1908, p.11.
193. CW3, p.59.
194. 'Christabel', 'Social Gossip', *Free Lance*, VIII: 417, 27 June 1908, p.8.
195. L1, p.53.
196. Anon., 'Social and Personal', *Dominion*, 1: 239, 2 July 1908, p.5.
197. 'Priscilla', 'Ladies Column: Girls' Gossip', *Evening Post*, 76: 4, 4 July 1908, p.15.
198. CW1, pp.138–9.
199. Beauchamp, pp.200–1.
200. Baker, p.37.
201. Anon., 'Social Gossip', *Free Lance*, 8: 417, 4 July 1908, p.8.
202. Anon., 'Shipping News', *Dominion*, 1: 243, 7 July 1908, p.10.
203. See Boddy, *Woman and Writer*, p.24.
204. Alpers, *Life*, p.63.
205. ATL: MS-Papers-11326-051. Letter from M. Ray Willis.
206. Mantz, *KM: An Exhibition*, p.6.
207. HRC: Ruth Elvish Mantz Collection, Box 3. 'Unidentified research notes'.

Further Reading

Alington, Margaret H., *High Point: St Mary's Church, Karori, Wellington, 1861–1991* (Wellington: Parish of St Mary and the Karori Historical Society, 1998).

Alpers, Antony, *Katherine Mansfield: A Biography* (London: Jonathan Cape, 1954).

—— *The Life of Katherine Mansfield* (New York: Viking Press, 1980).

Andersen, Hans Christian, *Stories for the Household* (New York: McLoughlin Bros, 1893).

Angus, Barbara, *A Guide to Katherine Mansfield's Wellington* (Wellington: Katherine Mansfield Birthplace, 1987).

Baker, Ida, *Katherine Mansfield: The Memories of LM* (London: Michael Joseph, 1971).

Beauchamp, Sir Harold, *Reminiscences and Recollections* (New Plymouth: Thomas Avery & Sons, 1937).

Bell, Anne Olivier, ed., *The Diary of Virginia Woolf*, 5 vols (London: Hogarth, 1977–1985), Vol. 1 (1977).

Berkman, Sylvia, *Katherine Mansfield: A Critical Study* (Oxford: Oxford University Press, 1952).

Boddy, Gillian, *Katherine Mansfield: The Woman and the Writer* (Ringwood, Australia: Penguin, 1988).

—— *Katherine Mansfield: A 'Do You Remember' Life* (Wellington: Victoria University Press with the Katherine Mansfield Birthplace Society Inc., 1996).

Braybrooke, Francis, '"My Dear Clara" – Karori Eighty Years Ago', *Stockade*, 16: 11, October 1983, p. 9.

Carroll, Lewis, *Alice in Wonderland* (London: Macmillan, 1995 [1886]).

Chekhov, Anton, *The Bet and Other Stories*, trans. by S. S. Koteliansky and John Middleton Murry (London: Maunsel, 1915).

—— *Selected Stories*, trans. by Richard Pevear and Larissa Volhokonsky (New York: Modern Library, 2000).

'Chimes, Omana', 'Katherine Mansfield at School', *N.Z. Dairy Exporter Annual (Inc. Tui's Annual)*, 10 October 1929, p. 38.

Daiches, David, *New Literary Values: Studies in Modern Literature* (London: Oliver & Boyd, 1969).

Dowson, Ernest, *Decorations* (London: John Lane, 1899).

'Elizabeth', *The April Baby's Book of Tunes* (London: Macmillan, 1900).

Ellis, Havelock, *Studies in the Psychology of Sex*, vol. 4, *Sexual Selection in Man* (Philadelphia: F. A. Davis, 1905).

Gordon, Ian A., *Katherine Mansfield*, Writers and Their Work, no. 49 (London: Longmans, Green & Co., 1954).

—— ed., *The Urewera Notebook by Katherine Mansfield* (Oxford: Oxford University Press, 1978).

—— ed., *Victorian Voyage, Annie Beauchamp: The Shipboard Diary of Katherine Mansfield's Mother March to May, 1898* (Auckland: Wilson & Horton, 2000).

Hazelwood, Ethel Beauchamp, *Life at Anakiwa: The First 100 Years 1863–1963* (privately printed booklet).

Herrick, Ruth, 'They Were at School Together', *New Zealand Listener*, 7, 25 September 1942, p. 12.

Hodgson, Terence, *Colonial Capital: Wellington 1865–1910* (Auckland: Random Century, 1990).

Iversen, Anders, 'Life and letters: Katherine Mansfield drawing on Kathleen Beauchamp', *English Studies*, 52: 1–6, 1971, pp. 44–54.

Jones, Kathleen, *Katherine Mansfield: A Writer's Life* (Edinburgh: Edinburgh University Press, 2010).

Kaye, Elaine, *A History of Queen's College, London 1848–1972* (London: Chatto & Windus, 1972).

Kennedy, Julie, *Katherine Mansfield in Picton* (Auckland: Cape Catley, 2000).

Kimber, Gerri, *Katherine Mansfield: The View from France* (Bern: Peter Lang, 2008).

—— *Katherine Mansfield and the Art of the Short Story* (Basingstoke: Palgrave Macmillan, 2015).

—— and Vincent O'Sullivan, eds, *The Edinburgh Edition of the Collected Works of Katherine Mansfield: Vols 1 and 2 – The Collected Fiction* (Edinburgh: Edinburgh University Press, 2012).

—— and Angela Smith, eds, *The Edinburgh Edition of the Collected Works of Katherine Mansfield: Vol. 3 – The Poetry and Critical Writings* (Edinburgh: Edinburgh University Press, 2014).

—— and Claire Davison, eds, *The Edinburgh Edition of the Collected Works of Katherine Mansfield: Vol. 4 – The Diaries, including Miscellaneous Works* (Edinburgh: Edinburgh University Press, 2016).

—— and Claire Davison, eds, *The Collected Poems of Katherine Mansfield* (Edinburgh: Edinburgh University Press, 2016).

Lawlor, Pat, *Old Wellington Days* (Wellington: Whitcombe & Tombs, 1959).

Lea, Frank, *The Life of John Middleton Murry* (London: Methuen, 1959).

Mantz, Ruth Elvish, ed., *Katherine Mansfield: An Exhibition* (Austin: Humanities Research Center, University of Texas at Austin, 1975).

—— and John Middleton Murry, *The Life of Katherine Mansfield* (London: Constable, 1933).

May, P. R., *With the MCC in New Zealand* (London: Eyre & Spottiswoode, 1907).

McIntosh, A. D., ed., *Marlborough: A Provincial History* (Christchurch, NZ: Capper Press, 1977).

Meyers, Jeffery, *Katherine Mansfield: A Darker View* (New York: Cooper Square Press, 2002).

Mitchell, J. Lawrence, 'Katherine Mansfield's War', in Gerri Kimber, Todd Martin, Delia da Sousa Correa, Isobel Maddison and Alice Kelly, eds, *Katherine Mansfield and World War One* (Edinburgh: Edinburgh University Press, 2014), pp. 27–41.

Molesworth, Mrs, *Christmas-Tree Land* (London: Macmillan & Co., 1981 [1884]).

Murry, John Middleton, ed., *The Letters of Katherine Mansfield*, 2 vols (London: Constable, 1928).

Naylor, Elizabeth Beauchamp, *A Colourful Tapestry: Tales of the Beauchamps and Elliots* (privately printed, 2009).

Norburn, Roger, *A Katherine Mansfield Chronology* (Basingstoke: Palgrave Macmillan, 2008).

O'Sullivan, Vincent, and Margaret Scott, eds, *The Collected Letters of Katherine Mansfield*, 5 vols (Oxford: Clarendon Press, 1984–2008).

Plumridge, Anna, *The Urewera Notebook* (Edinburgh: Edinburgh University Press, 2015).

Ruddick, Marion C., 'Incidents in the Childhood of Katherine Mansfield', unpublished typescript.

Ryan, Greg, 'New Zealand', in Brian Stoddart and Keith A. Sandiford, eds, *The Imperial Game: Cricket, Culture and Society* (Manchester: Manchester University Press, 1998), pp. 93–115.

Stone, Jean E., *Katherine Mansfield: Publications in Australia 1907–09* (Sydney: Wentworth Books, 1977).

Symons, Arthur, *Studies in Prose and Verse* (London: J. M. Dent, 1904).

Tipple, Reverend S. A., *Sunday Mornings at Norwood, Being Twenty-Two Sermons and Twenty-Two Prayers* (London: Kegan Paul, Trench & Co., 1883).

Tomalin, Claire, *Katherine Mansfield: A Secret Life* (London: Viking, 1987).

Wullschlager, Jackie, *Hans Christian Andersen: The Life of a Storyteller* (Chicago: University of Chicago Press, 2002).

Index